The Cambridge English Course

3

Student's Book

CAMBRIDGE
UNIVERSITY PRESS

ISBN 0 521 27879 1 Student's Book 3

Split edition: ISBN 0 521 35737 3 Part A
ISBN 0 521 35738 1 Part B
ISBN 0 521 35739 X Part C

ISBN 0 521 27877 5 Teacher's Book 3
ISBN 0 521 27878 3 Practice Book 3
ISBN 0 521 31627 8 Test Book 3
ISBN 0 521 26245 3 Cassette Set 3
ISBN 0 521 30325 7 Student's Cassette 3

Published by the Press Syndicate of the University of Cambridge
The Pitt Building, Trumpington Street, Cambridge CB2 1RP
40 West 20th Street, New York, NY 10011-4211, USA
10 Stamford Road, Oakleigh, Melbourne 3166, Australia

© Cambridge University Press 1987

First published 1987
Eighth printing 1993

Designed by Banks and Miles, London
Typeset by Text Filmsetters Ltd, London
Origination by C.S. Colour Ltd, London
Printed in Great Britain at the
University Press, Cambridge

Authors' acknowledgements

We are grateful to all the people who have helped us with this book. Our thanks to:
- The many people whose ideas have influenced our work, including all the colleagues and students from whom we have learnt.
- Those institutions and teachers who were kind enough to work with the Pilot Edition of this course, and whose comments have done so much to shape the final version.
- Diann Gruber, Stuart Redman and Martin Dodman for their very useful reports on the Pilot Edition.
- The various organisations who kindly arranged for us to interview members of their staff.
- The people who agreed to talk within range of our microphones: Alwyn Anchors, Philip Berczuk, Barbara Berry, Len Berry, James Bethell, Claire Booker, Penny Buller, Liz Bullock, Kevin Butler, Jeanette Cabeldu, the children of Class 1 at Chilton County Primary School, Frances Crook, Jean-Claude Desbuisson, Roger Elbourne, Debra Freechild, Barbara Gatehouse, Nick Gregor, Susanna Harsanyi, Joanne Haycox, Trevor Hebberd, Vera Hibbert, Michael Hirst, Robert Jackson, Richard Lawson, Louise Lester, Antonio Lopez, Peter Manser, George Melly, Basil Mulford, Marilyn Norvell, Liz Parkin, John Peake, Alan Pearson, Claudia Phillips, Mary Phillips, Nighat Qureshi, Sarah Robbins, Tony Robinson, Fran Searson, Clare Short, Liz Smith, Michael Smith, H.A. Swan, Ian Thompson, Helen Walter, Mark Walter Swan, Tom White, Alison Whyte, Tim Williamson, Jane Woods, Keith Woods, Sumiko Yamagoto, Annemarie Young, and Lindsay Zonderhicks.
- Peter Roach, for his expert and sensible help with the phonetic transcriptions.
- Steve Hall, for doing a wonderful job on the songs.
- Peter Thompson, Dennis Gardner, Andy Taylor, Peter Taylor and the staff at Studio AVP, for making recording sessions seem easy and for creating such a high-quality end product.
- Sue Sheppard, our designer, and her colleagues at Banks and Miles, for their skill, hard work and unfailing perfectionism.
- Linda Radley and her colleagues at Text Filmsetters for their meticulous typesetting.
- Gill Clack, the world's sharpest-eyed proofreader.
- Mark, for all his help and support.
- Adrian du Plessis, Peter Donovan and Peter Ducker of Cambridge University Press; once again we realise how lucky we are in our choice of publishers.
- And finally Desmond O'Sullivan, our editor at CUP, without whose skill, patience and stamina there would simply be no book.

Contents

Map of Book 3

In Unit	GRAMMAR Students will learn or revise these grammar points	PHONOLOGY Students will work on these aspects of pronunciation
1	-ing forms; emphatic structures; *should*; adverbs of degree.	Stress, rhythm.
2	Quantifiers; relatives.	/ɜː/, /eə/ and /ɪə/.
3	*So, nor* with auxiliaries; conditionals; -ing form after prepositions and conjunctions.	Word stress.
4	Modals; verbs with two objects.	
5	Past modals; past conditionals.	*Going to, want to, got to.*
6	Past progressive; reported speech; *say* and *tell*.	Unstressed words; *said, any, many; asked.*
7	Past simple, progressive and perfect; tags.	/ɒ/, /ɔː/ and /əʊ/.
8	Complex sentences; verbs not used in progressive forms; *will*-future.	'Dark' *l*.
9	*Which* and *that*; position of adverbs.	Intonation in relative clauses.
REVISION 10	Revision of tenses; prepositions of place and direction.	Spelling and vowel length.
11	Same word used as noun, verb etc.	Intonation and meaning.
12	Present perfect and simple past.	Contrastive stress; linking words together.
13	Infinitives and -ing forms.	Hearing unstressed words.
14	*Will* used for promising; *they, them, their* with singular reference.	Linking with /r/, /j/ and /w/.
15	Simple past and present perfect progressive; structures with *let* and *make*; negative prefixes.	Stressed and unstressed *e*.
16	Simple past and past perfect.	Hearing unstressed auxiliaries.
17	Passive forms; difficult passive structures; position of adverbs of manner.	Final -ed.
18	Complex sentences with *before*.	/iː/ and /ɪ/; /eɪ/ and /e/.
19	Frequency adverbs; *have* and *have got*.	Hearing unstressed words.
REVISION 20	Reported speech; revision of tenses.	Final clusters; /h/.
21	*Need . . .ing; have something done; should, ought* + passive infinitive.	/eɪ/ and /e/; /w/, /v/ and /b/.
22	Use of *ever*; singular with *anybody, everybody*; structures used in description.	Word stress.
23	Passive structures with modal verbs; negative imperatives.	/θ/ and /ð/.
24	Adverbs of degree; structures used in comparisons.	Contrastive stress; linking.
25	'Unreal' past tenses; conditional structures with *would* and *might*.	Stress-timed rhythm.
26	Prepositions in relative clauses; *keep* + object + adjective; reported speech.	Hearing unstressed syllables; spellings of /ɔː/ and /ɜː/.
27	Future progressive; future perfect.	Weak forms of *have* and *for*; pronunciations of *a* and *o*.
28	Position of prepositions in questions and relative clauses.	
29	*Shall* and *will*; tenses in subordinate clauses; tenses after *I wish* and *if only; should, ought to have . . .*	Weak forms of *have* and *had*.
REVISION 30	*Should have . . .*	Spelling and pronunciation; /ə/.

VOCABULARY: Students will learn about 1,000 common words and expressions during the course.
SKILLS: All units give practice in speaking, understanding speech, reading and writing.

FUNCTIONS, SUB-SKILLS AND SITUATIONS	NOTIONS AND TOPICS
Students will learn to	Students will learn to talk about
Express opinions.	Work: daily routine; aptitudes; preferences.
Describe; define.	The natural world; wildlife.
Compare and contrast.	Interests; activities.
Ask and offer; ask for things without knowing the exact words; describe; define; distinguish formal and informal language; scan text for information.	Advertising; characteristics of objects.
Express opinions; speculate about the past.	Crime and prison.
Narrate; express opinions; evaluate and criticise.	Things happening in sequence; things happening at the same time.
Narrate; structure conversation.	Travel and exploration; things happening in sequence; things happening at the same time.
Warn; announce decisions; persuade.	Beliefs; evidence; knowledge.
Express opinions.	Music; preferences.
Give directions; telephone; use the language of various other situations.	Places; directions; spatial relations.
Take notes; summarise; structure conversation; use formal and informal language.	Aspects of language; attitudes to language.
Link ideas.	News.
Narrate.	Fears.
Promise; predict; summarise; give reasons; give opinions.	Politics and government; personal qualities.
Discuss; evaluate; recommend; use dictionaries efficiently.	Education and upbringing; school subjects; usefulness.
Describe places.	Places; spatial relations; landscape; climate.
Suggest; recommend; explain; give instructions.	Processes: making, repairing etc.; recipes.
Request and offer; borrow.	Need, lack, deprivation; things happening in sequence; international relations and finance.
Advise; suggest; express opinions.	Relationships; love; marriage.
Structure conversation; describe; criticise; use the language of various situations.	Humour.
Express opinions; take notes.	Dealing with materials; physical changes; houses; housing and the homeless; house purchase.
Describe.	People's appearance; personality; proportion.
Scan text for information; take notes; deal with interviews.	Health and illness; medical care.
Describe; scan text for information.	Physical characteristics of things; cars.
Write letters; read for detail; express opinions.	Honesty; truth and falsehood; freedom of information.
Take notes; scan text for information.	Sport; advantages and disadvantages.
Make appointments; make, accept and refuse invitations; make excuses.	Plans; future achievements.
Summarise; express opinions.	Family and roots; living in exile; national culture.
Predict, warn and promise; express regret; express wishes; criticise and evaluate; guess unknown words.	The past and future.
Evaluate; describe and define.	Travel and places; duty and obligation.

Jobs

A I like being on my own

1 You are going to hear twenty children say what they want to be when they grow up. Altogether, they give fourteen different answers. Can you guess what some of the answers will be?

2 Listen to the recording twice. Then work in groups and see if you can remember all the fourteen different answers.

3 Seven people were asked, 'What do you like about your work?' Here are parts of their answers. What do you think the missing words are? Listen to the recording and see if you were right.

1. (*Tony Robinson, writer*) 'I like ....ing on my own; I like organising my own world.'
2. (*John Peake, gardener*) 'What I .... about it is ....ing outdoors.'
3. (*Basil Mulford, pest control officer*) ' ....ing a lot of different people.'
   (*Interviewer*) 'Is there anything about your job that you don't like?'
   (*Basil Mulford*) ' ....s!'
4. (*Vera Hibbert, retired teacher*) 'the relationships with the ....'
5. (*Jeanette Cabeldu, teacher*) ' ....ing with .... all day.'
6. (*Liz Parkin, member of women's working collective*) 'being with women, ...ing together with women.'
7. (*Tom White, worker in car factory and trade union officer*) 'No worker goes to work because he .... it.'

4 Look at the three sentences. They mean the same, but in the second and third sentences 'being outdoors' is emphasised.

I like being outdoors.
What I like is **being outdoors**.
It's **being outdoors** that I like.

Now change these sentences so as to express the ideas in the other two ways.

1. I like working with other people.
2. What I like is organising my own world.
3. It's being alone that I like.
4. I like meeting people.
5. What I like is being able to travel on business.
6. It's having my own office that I like.
7. I like having responsibility.
8. What I like is working in a small personal organisation.

5 What job do you do, or what jobs have you done in your life (including part-time or holiday jobs)? Tell other students, and ask what jobs they do or have done. Ask the teacher for help with vocabulary if necessary.

Now try to guess what other students like(d) about their work, and what they don't/didn't like. Say what you like(d) about your work, and what you don't/didn't like. Use structures from Exercise 4. Examples:

'I imagine what you like is being with other people.'
'I suppose it was the long hours that you didn't like.'
'What I liked best was working with animals.'
'I don't like being in a big organisation.'

6 Look at the 'Job Suitability Questionnaire'. Can you add some more questions in each section?

7 Work with another student. Ask him or her the questions on the questionnaire. Note his or her answers ('Yes' = ✓ 'No' = ✗ 'Don't know' = ?). Useful expressions:

'Sorry, what did you say?'
'What do you mean?'
'Could you speak more slowly?'

8 Try to suggest a suitable job for your partner.

Study the Lesson Summary at the back of the book. Do some of the Practice Book Exercises.

JOB SUITABILITY QUESTIONNAIRE

PERSONALITY

Are you: interested in people?
energetic?
ambitious?
patient?

ABILITIES AND SKILLS

Have you got: a good memory?
a sense of humour?

Are you: artistic?
practical?
logical?
good at organising?

Can you: drive?
speak any foreign languages?

PREFERENCES

Do you like: working on your own?
taking responsibility?

Do you mind: working long hours?
getting up early?
noise?

Would you rather:
work indoors or outdoors?
work in a big organisation or a small one?

How important are these things to you? (extremely/very/quite/not very/not at all)
a good salary
comfortable working conditions
a chance of promotion

B I wander round the kitchen

Listening comprehension; vocabulary; grammar (*should* + infinitive); pronunciation (stress); discussion.

1 Close your books and listen to the recording. What are Tony's two jobs? Can you remember anything about how he spends his day?

2 Read the transcript of Tony's interview, and then see if you can put the pictures in the right order.

INTERVIEWER: How do you organise your work?

TONY: Well, I'm married, so to be alone in the mornings, the first thing is to get rid of my wife, who fortunately has a job, so she gets up in the morning, makes a cup of tea, rouses me, I come downstairs, wander round the kitchen, have my cup of tea, iron her clothes for her that she's put out for me on the first floor landing on top of the ironing board, so I do her ironing – by that stage she's in the bath, so I'm – by that stage it's half past eight, quarter to nine, I'm only half an hour from being on my own – come down and make sure she's got all her lunch in a bag, by that stage I've finished my tea, I've finished the ironing, she's out of the bath, I'm in the bath, she goes upstairs and gets dressed; by the time – if this is all synchronised properly – by the time I get out of the bath and go upstairs she's fully dressed; and then by the time I'm dressed and come

downstairs she's just about to hop on her bicycle and go off to work, which makes it about nine o'clock or nine fifteen.

And then I'm on my own. And I fluffle around for half an hour, putting off sitting down, make myself another cup of tea; but I'm usually working by ten o'clock. Then I work till twelve o'clock, half past twelve, then reward myself with some lunch, have a cup of tea, waste another ten minutes, start working about one o'clock again, and work till two o'clock, half past two.

Thereafter I become a househusband, and get the house organised for the evening when my wife comes home, at anywhere between six and seven o'clock, and the house has got to be tidy or I get into trouble. And doing it all myself involves doing most of the housework, most of the ironing, all the washing, a good part of the cooking . . .

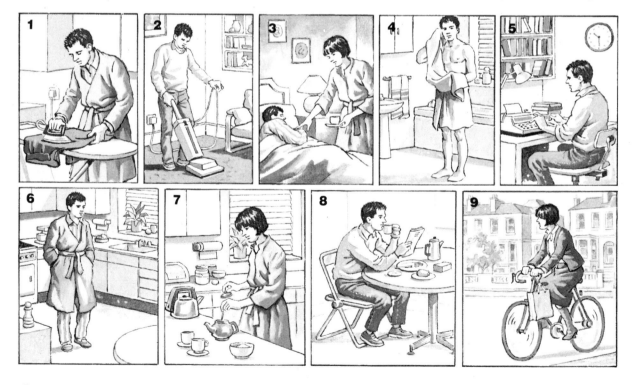

3 Tony is a writer and 'househusband'. He works alone all day. Would you like his kind of life? Why (not)?

4 Complete the text with the words and expressions in the box. You may need to make small changes. You can use a dictionary or ask somebody for help if you like.

able	all day	anywhere between	careful
chance	cooking	extremely	get rid of
grow up	housework	ironing	job
on business	on one's own	organise
outdoors	put off	relationships	salary
shopping	trade union	washing
waste (time or money)			

Bill Radford has a .... in a small factory. He doesn't much like the work, but he enjoys the .... with the other workers, and he gets on well with the boss. He belongs to a ...., and helps to .... the work of the local branch. Sometimes he has a .... to travel ...., which he enjoys very much.

His wife, Ann, has been unemployed for the last two years. She stays at home and looks after the house. After getting their six-year-old daughter Sally ready and driving her to school, she starts on the housework. Although she likes being ...., she finds .... boring, and doesn't like to stay at home .... So she tries to get through the washing up, the ...., the ...., the .... and so on as quickly as possible. This takes her .... two and three hours; after that she usually has lunch. She doesn't like to .... time, so after lunch she goes off to the public library and reads books on politics or history until it's time to fetch Sally from school. In the evenings Bill and Ann share the ....

At weekends they try to spend some time ....: they often go walking in the country, or take Sally on trips to places like the zoo or the seaside.

Money is a big problem. Bill doesn't earn a very good ...., and their income is hardly enough for three people to live on, so they have to be very .... about what they spend. They can't really afford to keep the car, and will have to .... it soon, but they have decided to .... selling it until Sally is old enough to go to school by bus. They are just not .... to save money, and they're .... worried about their old age. Sally wants to be a teacher or a nurse when she ...., but Ann and Bill hope she will do something where she can earn enough money to live a better life than her parents.

5 Choose words and expressions to learn from Exercises 2 and 4. Compare notes with other students. Do you choose words because they are common, because they are important, because they are useful, because you are interested in the subject, because you like the sound of them, because they are easy to learn . . . ?

6 Pronunciation. The first five stressed syllables are marked. Which other syllables do you think are stressed? Listen to the recording and see if you were right.

Well, I'm married, so to be alone in the mornings, the first thing is to get rid of my wife, who fortunately has a job, so she gets up in the morning, makes a cup of tea, rouses me, I come downstairs, wander round the kitchen, have my cup of tea, iron her clothes for her that she's put out for me on the first floor landing on top of the ironing board . . .

7 Complete some of these sentences about work. Then see if other students agree with you.

1. I think people should be able to start work at the age of ....
2. I don't think people should start work before the age of ....
3. I think people should be able to retire when they are ....
4. I (don't) think .... should be paid more.
5. I (don't) think .... should be paid less.
6. I (don't) think .... should earn more than ....
7. I (don't) think housewives should be paid ....
8. I (don't) think men and women who do the same jobs should ....
9. I (don't) think trade unions should ....
10. I (don't) think .... should ....

8 Report to the class.

'We all agreed that nurses should be paid more.'
'Two of us thought that housewives should be paid a salary, but the other two disagreed.'
'Most of us think people should be able to start work at the age of thirteen.'

Study the Lesson Summary at the back of the book. Do some of the Practice Book exercises.

Wildlife

A Every ten minutes

Vocabulary; reading comprehension; discussion.

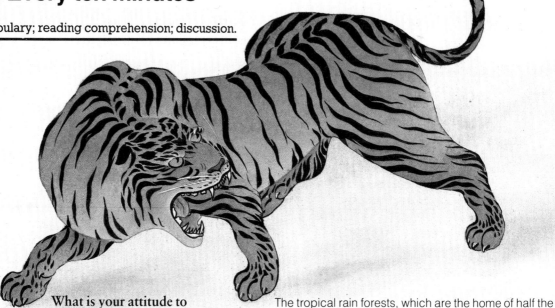

1 What is your attitude to hunting animals 1) for sport 2) for their fur 3) for food?

2 Read the text and answer the questions.

Every ten minutes, one kind of animal, plant or insect dies out for ever. If nothing is done about it, one million species that are alive today will have become extinct twenty years from now.

QUESTION: What is your reaction to this information?
a. You already knew.
b. You're surprised and shocked.
c. You don't believe it.
d. You're not very interested.
e. Other.

The seas are in danger. They are being filled with poison: industrial and nuclear waste, chemical fertilisers and pesticides, sewage. The Mediterranean is already nearly dead; the North Sea is following. If nothing is done about it, one day soon nothing will be able to live in the seas.

QUESTION: Which of these sources of poison is *not* mentioned in the text?
a. factories
b. lavatories
c. atomic power stations
d. oil tankers
e. farms

The tropical rain forests, which are the home of half the earth's living things (including many rare animals and plants), are being destroyed. If nothing is done about it, they will have nearly disappeared in twenty years. The effect on the world's climate – and on our agriculture and food supplies – will be disastrous.

QUESTIONS:
1. Do you know any places where rain forests are being destroyed?
2. Do you know why the world's climate will be affected?

Fortunately, somebody *is* trying to do something about it. In 1961, the World Wildlife Fund was founded – a small group of people who wanted to raise money to save animals and plants from extinction. Today, the World Wildlife Fund is a large international organisation. It has raised over £35 million for conservation projects, and has created or given support to National Parks in five continents. It has helped 30 mammals and birds – including the tiger – to survive. Perhaps this is not much, but it is a start. If more people give more money – and if more governments wake up to what is happening – perhaps the World Wildlife Fund will be able to help us to avoid the disaster that threatens the natural world, and all of us with it.

QUESTION: Does the text say where the WWF gets its money from?

3 Read the texts and put in the words from the boxes. You may have to make some small changes.

OPERATION TIGER

create	left	remain	save

Fifty years ago there were 100,000 tigers in the wild. Today there are not more than 5,000 .... In 1972 the World Wildlife Fund launched 'Operation Tiger' to ....the tigers that .... Nine tiger reserves have been .... in India and three in Nepal.

THE LAST THIRTY ORYX

almost	hunter	rare	survive	zoo

By the 1970s, ... had killed .... all of the Arabian oryx. The WWF helped to capture the last 30 .... oryx and send them to Phoenix .... in Arizona, where a herd of these .... animals has been built up.

THE LAST FIFTY NÉNÉ GEESE

alive	less	live	natural	successfully

A few years ago .... than 50 Néné geese were left .... in the wild. The British Wildfowl Trust raised 700, and the WWF transported 200 to Hawaii, where they are .... and breeding .... again in their .... surroundings.

THE SEAS MUST LIVE

chemical	death	fur	hunt	in danger
international	nuclear	poison	whale	

In 1976 the WWF launched its biggest .... campaign, 'The Seas Must Live'. The seas are polluted by pesticides, ... waste and other .... are being hunted to extinction. Turtles are killed for their meat, shell and oil, crocodiles to make handbags and shoes, walruses for their ivory. Seals are beaten to .... to provide .... coats. Many species of these animals are .... of dying out. The WWF is working to provide sea sanctuaries where whales, dolphins and seals cannot be ....

(Information taken from a WWF advertisement)

4 The texts in Exercise 3 are about four different things that the WWF has done. Which do you think is the most important? Can you arrange them in order of importance? Find out if other students agree with you.

5 Choose some vocabulary to learn from the texts in Exercises 2 and 3. Compare notes with other students, and talk about the reasons for your choices.

6 Work in groups of three or four. Imagine that each group is a wildlife conservation organisation in the year 2500. You have enough money to save several, but not all, of the following from extinction: the lion, the rabbit, the sheep, the cat, the dog, the horse, the golden eagle, the bee, the cobra, the rose. Draw up a list of priorities: three things that you will certainly save, three more that you will save if you have enough money left over, and four that you will not try to save.

Study the Lesson Summary at the back of the book. Do some of the Practice Book exercises.

B Bird, mammal, insect or tree?

Grammar (quantifiers and relatives); vocabulary;
pronunciation; listening comprehension; writing.

1 Listen to the recording and decide what is
being described.

1. birds   mammals   insects   trees
2. birds   mammals   insects   trees
3. birds   mammals   insects   trees
4. mammals   insects   fish   spiders
5. insects   spiders   butterflies
6. mammals   birds   whales   butterflies
7. fish   flowers   pigs   chickens
8. cats   fish   birds   flowers
9. plants   mammals   birds
10. small mammals   small birds   crocodiles
11. butterflies   small mammals   fish   flowers
12. flowers   mammals   birds
13. birds   plants   mammals
14. small mammals   whales   birds   dogs

2 Make some sentences yourself like the ones on
the recording in Exercise 1. See if other students
can say what kind of thing you are describing.

3 Grammar: quantifiers. Put in words from the
box, with or without *of*. (More than one answer
may be possible.)

all	nearly all	most	many	some
several	a few	not many	hardly any	
no/none				

1. .... these plants are good to eat.
2. .... birds can fly.
3. .... other animals have necks as long as
   giraffes.
4. .... insects are useful, but others seem to
   be completely useless.
5. The WWF can only save .... the animals
   that are in danger of extinction.
6. .... my family are afraid of spiders.
7. .... mammals are warm-blooded.
8. Would you like .... these flowers?
9. .... mammals live in the Antarctic.
10. Most snakes are dangerous, but .... them
    have a poisonous bite.
11. .... the British spiders are poisonous.

4 Make sure you know all the words in the box.
Then read the sentences and try to choose the right
animals.

camel	cat	cow	crocodile	deer
dog	elephant	frog	owl	parrot
pig	rabbit	tiger	whale	wolf

1. the only animal in the list that lives in holes in
   the ground
2. a farm animal that will eat anything
3. a farm animal that has four stomachs
4. If you were this bird, you might be able to
   talk.
5. the only land animal in the list that can't jump
6. a mammal that is hunted for its valuable oil
7. a pet animal whose babies are called kittens
8. If you were this animal, you wouldn't need to
   drink very often.
9. a beautiful gentle animal which can run very
   fast
10. an ugly animal with beautiful eyes which is
    very good at jumping
11. a bird that lives on small animals like mice
12. a large fierce animal which belongs to the cat
    family
13. an animal which doesn't normally kill people,
    although everybody thinks it does
14. an animal whose skin is used to make
    handbags
15. If you were this animal, you would chase cats.

5 Grammar. Put in *which/that* or *whose*.

1. a farm animal .... provides milk
2. an animal .... meat is called pork
3. a bird .... eggs people often eat
4. a mammal .... lives in holes in the ground
5. an animal .... neck is longer than its legs
6. an animal .... ears are longer than its tail
7. a bird .... can talk
8. a fish .... lives in fresh water
9. a snake .... bite can kill you

6 Make some definitions like the ones in Exercises 4 and 5. See if other students can decide which animals/birds/plants etc. you are talking about.

7 Can you divide these words into three groups, according to the pronunciation of the vowel?

fur   bear   deer   bird   nearly   earth
rare   world   where   work   fierce

8 Here are three poems about animals. How do you feel about them? (Like/dislike/no reaction/ . . . ?) See if you can find somebody else in the class who shares your reactions.

SOFTLY
Strong and long
The tiger crouches down
Orange and black in
The green grass.
Careful little fawn how
You pass.
(Peter Sandell, aged 8)

MEDITATIO
When I carefully consider the curious habits of
    dogs
I am compelled to conclude
That man is the superior animal.

When I consider the curious habits of man
I confess, my friend, I am puzzled.
(Ezra Pound)

CAGED BIRD
Bars are all she knows.
But every night in her dreams
High and free she flies.
(E. Stabetsi)

9 The last poem in Exercise 8 is a haiku. Haikus have three lines, containing five, seven and five syllables respectively. Can you complete one of these haikus? See if you can write one yourself about a bird, plant or animal.

Outside my window
Snow lies on the high branches.
....

Bears look soft and sweet.
They can run faster than you.
....

Cats live with people.
....
They don't say thank you.

Study the Lesson Summary at the back of the book. Do some of the Practice Book exercises.

"His damned wrist watch keeps me awake all night."

"But you had £5 only last week."

Interests

A Art, bird-watching, cars, dancing,...

Listening comprehension;
pronunciation (stress);
grammar (*so* and *nor*);
discussion.

1 Look at the list in the box. Can you find five things that you are interested in? See if anybody else has noted exactly the same things as you. How many of the things are you not at all interested in?

antiques art babysitting birdwatching cars collecting children's books cooking the countryside dancing dogs drawing driving gardening glass Handel harmoniums history horticulture houses interior design jazz music opera pool reading shooting sign language sport swimming theatre travel walking watching cricket worrying about money

2 You are going to hear short extracts from interviews with nine people. (Their names, in order, are: Liz Bullock, Vera, Basil, 'H-A', Jeanette, Lindsay, Tony, Liz Parkin and Ian.) They are interested in the activities listed in Exercise 1. Write the people's names, and see if you can note down some of their interests as you listen to the recording.

3 Now work in small groups and see how many of the following questions you can answer. When you have answered as many as possible, listen to the recording again and try to complete your answers.

1. Who is interested in sign language?
2. What are Liz Bullock's interests?
3. How many harmoniums has Ian got?
4. Is Vera interested in history?
5. What interest do Basil and Jeanette share?
6. What interest do Vera and H-A share?
7. Is the person who worries about money interested in antiques?
8. How many people say they are interested in reading?
9. Who has the most interests?
10. One of the interests in the list is not mentioned in the interviews. Which?

4 Pronunciation. Some of these words are stressed on the first syllable and some on the second. Can you sort them into two groups? Listen to the recording and check your answers.

antique   collecting   countryside
gardening   harmonium   history
interested   interior   interview
language   pronounce   recording
theatre

5 Grammar. Look at the table and the key. Then add some sentences in each of the four groups.

1. Sarah is interested in money, and **so is** Richard.
   Oliver likes animals, and **so does** Celia.
   ....

2. Sarah can't swim, and **nor can** Mark.
   Celia doesn't collect antiques, and **nor does** Richard.
   ....

3. Mark has got a home computer, but Sarah **hasn't**.
   Sarah plays golf, but Celia **doesn't**.
   ....

4. Oliver **used to** like pop music, and **so did** Mark.
   Sarah **didn't use to** collect stamps, but Richard **did**.
   ....

6 What are your interests? Complete some of these sentences.

1. I'm very interested indeed in ....
2. I'm quite interested in ....
3. I'm not very interested in ....
4. I'm not at all interested in ....
5. I'm bored by ....
6. I think .... is/are very interesting.
7. I think .... is/are quite interesting.
8. I think .... is/are very boring.
9. I used to be interested in ....
10. At the moment I'm doing a lot of ....

Ask for help if necessary.

> *What's the English for...?*

> *How do you spell...?*

7 Exchange lists with another student. Do you have any interests in common? What differences are there?

8 Report to the class. Examples:

'Anna's interested in travel, and so am I.'
'Mary thinks Russian literature is interesting, and so do I.'
'John doesn't like classical music, and nor do I.'
'Alex is interested in economics, but I'm not.'
'Peter used to play a lot of football, and so did I.'

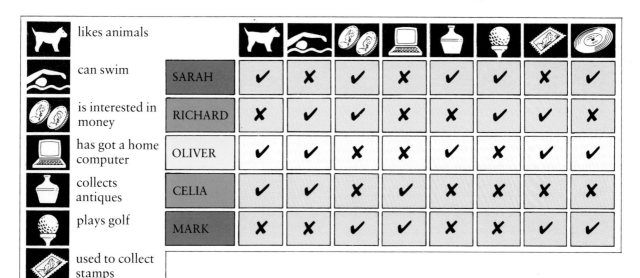

likes animals								
can swim	SARAH	✔	✘	✔	✘	✔	✔	✘	✔
is interested in money	RICHARD	✘	✔	✔	✘	✘	✔	✔	✘
has got a home computer	OLIVER	✔	✔	✘	✘	✔	✘	✔	✔
collects antiques	CELIA	✔	✔	✘	✔	✘	✘	✘	✘
plays golf	MARK	✘	✘	✔	✔	✘	✘	✔	✔
used to collect stamps									
used to like pop music									

Study the Lesson Summary at the back of the book.
Do some of the Practice Book exercises.

B I told you a bit of a lie

Reading comprehension; vocabulary; grammar (conditionals).

1 Read the text. Don't take more than five minutes. You can use a dictionary or ask the teacher for help (but try to guess the meaning of a word first).

clearing up crimes like petty theft and burglary.

Parachutist, 81, wins place of honour at jump

Even experts were a little surprised when a man of 62 turned up at a parachute training school and said he was interested in learning to become a parachutist.

They agreed to put him through the course, but only after giving him a series of tests to prove that he was fit enough. Mr Archie Macfarlane completed the course successfully, surprising everyone with his agility and toughness.

A few weeks later, when he was ready for his first jump, he confessed to the chief instructor: "I told you a bit of a lie. I'm really 75."

That was six years ago and yesterday Archie Macfarlane made his 18th jump. He was given the place of honour – first out of the plane – at a weekend meeting for parachutists over 40 years old.

Archie's interest in parachuting is just one of the hobbies that his wife has to worry about. He also enjoys motorcycling and mountaineering.

Last year he fell while climbing on Snowdon, and had to be rescued by helicopter.

His daughter said: "Sometimes I think he ought to give it all up. But as my mother says, so long as he's happy, it's better than being miserable. He tried hang-gliding once and said he thought it was a bit too easy."

Now Archie is thinking of taking up water-skiing.

(adapted from a press report)

2 Here are three summaries of the text. Which do you think is the best?

1. Archie Macfarlane started parachuting when he was 75, and he has done 18 parachute jumps over the last six years. Recently he was given the place of honour at a parachutists' meeting. When he started parachuting, he told a lie about his age. His wife and daughter are worried about him.

2. Archie Macfarlane is an unusual person. Although he is an old man, he is interested in very tough sporting activities like parachuting, mountaineering and water-skiing. His wife and daughter are worried, but think it's best for him to do things that make him happy.

3. When Archie Macfarlane first learnt parachute jumping, he pretended that he was only 62. In fact, he is much older than that, and he is really becoming too old to take part in outdoor sporting activities. His wife and daughter wish that he would stop motorcycling, mountaineering and hang-gliding.

3 These words and expressions come in the text about Archie Macfarlane. Make sure you know what they mean and how they are used. Then use them to complete the text below.

agreed	become	course	easy	enjoy
expert	fit	interest (in something)		
jump	prove	series	successfully	
surprised	while	worry (about something)		

RUNNING AND CLIMBING

I'm interested in sport, especially athletics, and I run seven or eight kilometres every day.
I particularly .... cross-country running, where you have to run across fields, ... over streams and so on. .... I'm running I think about all sorts of things, and at the end of a run I'm sometimes .... to find that I've managed to solve a problem that was on my mind.

Next year I'm going to try the London Marathon. It's a long, hard race – 26 miles, or 42 kilometres – and you have to be tough to finish, but I very much want to do it. I .... a bit about getting old, and I'd like to .... to myself that I'm still almost as .... as I was twenty years ago.

I'm interested in mountaineering as well as running. I'll never .... an .... climber, but I know what I'm doing in the mountains. I .... completed a .... in snow and ice climbing when I was younger, and I've done a .... of .... climbs in the Alps during the last few years. My wife doesn't share my .... in mountains. She .... to go climbing with me once, but she found that she felt ill as soon as she got above 1,000 metres.

4 Choose some words and expressions to learn from the texts in Exercises 1 and 3. Work with another student and compare your lists. Talk about the reasons for your choices.

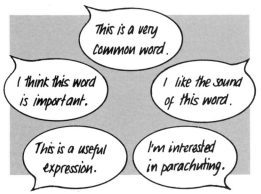

This is a very common word.
I think this word is important.
I like the sound of this word.
This is a useful expression.
I'm interested in parachuting.

5 Grammar. Some people were asked 'What would you do if you had plenty of time and money?' Here are pictures of some of their answers. Try to suggest what they said. Example:

1.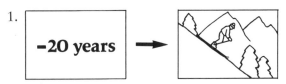

'*If I were twenty years younger, I would spend all my time skiing.*'

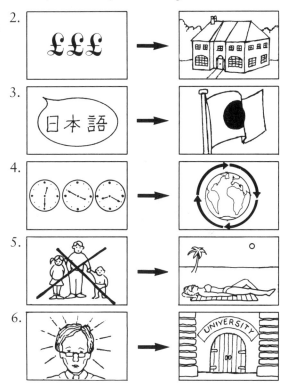

2.

3.

4.

5.

6.

6 What would *you* do if you had plenty of money, or plenty of time, or . . . ? Do a drawing, and see if other students can put it into words.

7 Work with a partner. Write a sentence using the structure If . . . , . . . would . . . Both of you must mime the sentence (act it without words). The rest of the class must try to guess your sentence and write it down.

Study the Lesson Summary at the back of the book. Do some of the Practice Book exercises.

Getting what you want

A Nice woman, 42

Fast reading; listening comprehension; vocabulary; asking for things when you don't know the exact words.

1 Look at the advertisement. Do you believe what it says? Possible answers:

'I'm sure it's true.'   *'It might be true.'*
'It's probably true.'   *'It's probably not true.'*
'It may be true.'   *'It can't be true.'*

2 Fast reading practice. Look at the small ads and see how quickly you can answer the questions.

1. What does the cheapest metal detector cost?
2. A man in South Essex is looking for a friend. How old is he?
3. Will Christine improve your mind or your body?
4. Which costs more – a 400-year-old cottage near Winchester or a 5-bedroom house in Wales?
5. Why is today a special day for Paul?
6. How much will two bottles of Chateau Latour 1964 cost you?
7. What town do you write to for bath, body and face oils?
8. Where can you buy things for a party?
9. How long will it take you to learn to make a guitar?
10. Does the lady who is bored with the cat prefer tall or short men?
11. How much will it cost you to give somebody a pound of smoked salmon and a bottle of champagne (with a message)?
12. You can buy something that was produced on the day you were born. What?
13. Somebody is offering a baby bath for sale. How much for?
14. Does the nice 42-year-old woman smoke?
15. How many nationalities has Olga got?

BILLIARD TABLES bought and sold. Mr Villis. (02805) 66 (Bucks).

GIFT CHAMPAGNE. We post a bottle with your message. From £14.50 incl. Orders or details 0642 45733

CHRISTINE'S beauty treatment and body therapy. 402 6499, 0473 4004

SMOKED SALMON
8oz sliced £5.75, 1lb sliced £11, 2lb 4oz side £16.90, 2lb 8oz side £19.50, 400gms offcuts £5. Prices include UK 1st class postage. Cheques with order. Cornish Smoked Fish Co. Ltd, Charlestown, St. Austell, Cornwall.

400-YEAR-OLD thatched cottage between Winchester/Basingstoke : 3 dble beds, sec gdn & extras. £110,000. (0962) 88109

CHATEAU LATOUR, 1964. 24 bottles, £75 each. Phone (0227) 9848 evenings.

GOING IN TO BUSINESS ? Send £7.45 inc p&p for ' The Beginners Guide to Success in Business.' Comquip Ltd, 189 Highview, Meopham, Gravesend, Kent. (0732) 22315.

C-SCOPE METAL DETECTORS. The ideal family gift to treasure from £39.99 to £449.50. Tel. Ashford (0233) 2918 today for free colour brochure.

BEAUTIFUL farm estate, total 700 acres. Diplomats 4 bed 1832 house. £220,000 ono. 0639 73082

5 BEDROOMED HOUSE in quiet mid-Wales village. 1 acre of land, fishing and shooting available. £42,000. Tel : 059 787 687 (after 6 p.m.).

W. ANGLESEY. 2 dble beds. S/d bung. Lge with patio drs to ½-acre garden, kit/b'fast room, bathroom. Dble glaz/ins. GCH. Garage & util rm, summer hse, grn hse. Scope for extensions. £29,500 o.n.o., quick sale. Tel 040 741031.

MAKE A GUITAR
12 week courses. Details : Totnes School of Guitarmaking, Collins Rd, Totnes, Devon. 0803 65255.

HAVANA CIGARS
And other fine cigars at wholesale prices. Send for list to James Jordan Ltd, Shelley Hall, Shelley, Huddersfield. Tel.: 0484 60227

HAVE A very happy birthday Paul.

NICE WOMAN, 42, seeks close, affectionate friendship with independentish man. Non-smoker, sense of fun, creative. Enjoys walks, talks, sensuality. Photo please. London area. Box (50) 2059.   N50 3

OLGA: RUSSIAN/FRENCHWOMAN from Lille, seeks an Englishman, tall, 50s, open-minded, with whom she can have a close, but stable relationship. Box (50) 2051.   N50 7

OXFORD: lively divorcee, mid forties, bored with solitude and the cat, seeks male, preferably tall, to share local pleasures and pastimes, music, the arts etc. Box (50) 2050.

VERY PERSONABLE, attractive, charming, amusing, considerate graduate, professional – 40 – own lovely coastal home, seeks lady – friendship/marriage – personality more important than age. All nationalities welcome. Box (50) 2052.   N50 6

WARM, ATTRACTIVE, humorous woman, 35 lover of music, literature, cinema, theatre and leftish politics, seeks man of similar inclinations, to share it all with. London. Box (46)1899.   N49 8

SENSITIVE, TALL, caring, unattached man, 55, likes people, music, walking, seeks intelligent, helpful n/s woman, mid forties. South Essex. Box (49)2011.   N49 13

SILVER CROSS detachable coach Pram (navy), shopping tray, excellent clean condition, £30; Carry Cot, £5; Baby Bath, £2.50; Atari system, joystick and paddle sticks, in good working order, needs a new mains adapter, £40; 5 Atari Cassettes, £10 each, very good condition, ideal Xmas presents. — Apply 34 Kynaston Road, Didcot, Oxon. evenings.   415702

THE TIMES (1814-1985). This Xmas give someone an original issue dated the very day they were born. £12.50 or 2 for £21. Tel 01-486 6305 or 0492 3314

PARTYMANIA, everything for your party in one "fun-tastic" store. — 179 Kingston Road, Oxford 513397, own parking.

GIVE HER a luxurious Christmas with a special gift set of soothing bath, body and face oils. Send £9.50 to Claydon Aromatherapy, 107 Marine Parade, Worthing BN11 3QG.

LADIES NARROW SHOES. AA and narrower, sizes 2½-11½. Also wide EE. SAE Muriel Hitchcock Shoes, 3b Castle Mews, Arundel BN18 9DG.

3 Look again at the 'contact ads' (the ones in which people are advertising for friends). Write a contact ad for yourself or a friend.

4 Do you know the pronunciation, meaning and use all of these words? Check them in a dictionary if necessary, or ask your teacher.

advertise   an advertisement   a small ad
a poster   a sale   a bargain   a gift
a catalogue   a price   choice   quality
value   free   cheap   expensive   save

5 Listen to the recording and see how many of the missing words you can fill in.

Hickman's aren't .... you think. A Panasonic VHS video is only £............. If you add up the extras at other ...., it's .... by far .... Hickman's.

McIlroy's .... first for choice, ... and value, so make us first .... Christmas shopping. .... new-look store means an even better choice of gifts for the .... Make shopping part .... pleasure .... Christmas. Experience the new-look McIlroy's.

............, ..., ... on Christmas shopping .... Scat's Cash-and-Carry .... Devizes and Salisbury. There are thousands of .... for .... at cash-and-carry prices all the year round.

6 Do you know how to ask for things when you don't know the exact word? Here are some useful words and expressions.

a thing   a machine   a tool
stuff   liquid   powder   material

square   round   pointed   sharp

a point   an end   a hole   a handle

a thing with a (hole, handle, etc.)

a thing/tool/machine for (making . . . , cutting . . . , etc.)

a thing that you . . . with/in/on/etc.

a thing that goes on top of/under/ . . .

material/liquid/powder/stuff for . . .ing.

How could you ask for these things if you didn't know their names?

a typewriter
'a machine for writing with'

fly-spray
'liquid for killing flies'

a fork	an umbrella	a hat	a bath
a car	beer	soap	glasses tea
string	a hammer	shoe-polish	

7 Now look at the pictures and ask for one of the things illustrated. Don't use its name (if you know it), and don't use your hands. See if the other students can say what you are asking for.

Study the Lesson Summary at the back of the book.
Do some of the Practice Book exercises.

B I've run out of soap

Formal and informal language;
asking, offering and answering;
grammar (verbs with two
objects); speaking practice.

1 Formal and informal language. Read the dialogue and listen
to the recording. Can you write down some of the differences?

(Dance music)

HE: That's really a beautiful
dress.
SHE: Thank you. I'm glad you like
it.
HE: Would you like some more
wine?
SHE: I beg your pardon?
HE: Would you like some more
wine?
SHE: Oh, er, no thank you. But
perhaps you could bring me
a little orange juice?

HE: Yes, of course.

* * *

HE: Here you are.
SHE: Thank you.
HE: Would you like to dance?
SHE: Well, I'd love to, but I'm afraid
I don't know how to tango.
HE: Actually, I think this is a waltz.
SHE: I see. I'm afraid I don't know
how to waltz, either.
HE: Oh, do let me teach you. It's
very easy.

2 Now can you rewrite this dialogue to make it more formal?

ALAN: This is great, Sue.
SUE: Glad you like it. It's dead
easy to make. Have some
more potatoes?
ALAN: Er, no, thanks. But I'd like a
bit more beef.
SUE: Yes, sure. Here you are.

ALAN: Thanks.
SUE: Sauce?
ALAN: Yes, please.
SUE: And have some more wine.
ALAN: Oh, yeah. Great. Thanks.
Say, how's Barry?

3 Here are some words from a dialogue. Can you complete it?

ANDY: going/shops/Mike?
MIKE: Yes/get/something/you?
ANDY: If/mind/haven't/
toothpaste/left/
Could/me/some?
MIKE: OK.
ANDY: like/Mentodent/if/got
MIKE: OK.
ANDY: Oh/run out/soap
MIKE: OK/get/you

ANDY: And/mind/posting/
same/time?
MIKE: Not at all.
ANDY: give/you/money
MIKE: No/wait/come
back/simpler
ANDY: All right.
Thanks/indeed
MIKE: welcome

4 Now practise the dialogue in Exercise 3 with a partner, but
imagine that one of you is hard of hearing, tired, very old or
bad-tempered. Make whatever changes you like.

5 Ways of asking and offering. Match the questions and answers.

1. Excuse me. Could you help me for a minute?
2. Have you got the time?
3. Have you got a light?
4. Shall I give you a hand with the cooking?
5. Can you lend me some stamps?
6. Sprechen Sie Deutsch?
7. Could I borrow your car for half an hour?
8. Have you got change for £5?
9. Would you like to come and have a drink this evening?
10. Could I use your phone?

a. Sorry, I don't smoke.
b. I'm afraid I haven't got any.
c. Sorry, I'm using it.
d. Sorry, I'm not free. My sister's coming round.
e. Just after five.
f. I'll have a look. Just a moment.
g. Sorry, I don't understand.
h. Well, I'm in a bit of a hurry.
i. Of course. It's over there on the table.
j. That's very kind of you.

6 Grammar: verbs with two objects. Look at these sentences from the lesson.

Perhaps you could bring me a little orange juice?
I'll get you some.
Shall I give you a hand?
Can you lend me some stamps?

Bring, get, give and *lend* can be used with two objects – an indirect object (*me* and *you* in the examples), and a direct object (*a little orange juice, some,* etc.).
A lot of other verbs can be used with two objects; for example, *buy, teach, tell, order, send, write, offer, make, do, pass, show*.
See if you can make some examples from the table.

Can you lend Could you bring I've just bought Can you teach She never tells I've ordered I'll send Susan has written May I offer Shall I make Can you do Could you pass Let me show His mother got	me you him her us myself John	something nice Chinese anything some water a telegram two photocopies a new car the house a drink a sandwich steak and chips some new pyjamas a strange letter a spoon the timetable the truth a ballpoint	. ?

7 Now go round the class making and replying to requests.
Use at least four of the following beginnings: *Could you lend/tell/get/make/teach/give/show me . . . ?* See Exercise 5 for possible replies.

8 Work in pairs. Make up and practise a conversation including some or all of the following: a request; an offer; an invitation; a question; a disagreement; a misunderstanding. Possible situations: borrowing a car; borrowing clothes; looking for a room to rent; in a restaurant; trying to buy a computer; looking for somewhere to camp; first day in an English-speaking country. Ask the teacher for help if necessary.

How do you say 'dictionnaire' in English?

How do you pronounce 'c-o-m-b'?

What's this called?

What does ... mean?

Study the Lesson Summary at the back of the book. Do some of the Practice Book exercises.

Crime and punishment

A What are prisons for?

1 Listen to the song.

TAKE THIS HAMMER

Take this hammer, and carry it to the captain
Take this hammer, and carry it to the captain
Take this hammer, and carry it to the captain
You tell him I'm gone, you tell him I'm gone.

If he asks you was I running (*three times*)
You tell him I was flying, tell him I was flying.

If he asks you was I laughing (*three times*)
Tell him I was crying, tell him I was crying.

I don't want no cornbread or tomatoes (*three times*)
They hurts my pride, they hurts my pride.

I'm gonna bust right, bust right past that shooter
  (*three times*)
I'm going home, I'm going home.

(American prison work song)

2 Why does society send people to prison, in
your opinion? Try to think of at least three
reasons. Do you think they are all good reasons?

3 Listen to the recording. How many different
reasons for prison are mentioned?

4 Do you think prison is successful as a
deterrent? Do you think it successfully
rehabilitates criminals? Why (not)? You will hear
recordings of Frances (who works for a prison
reform organisation), Nick (an ex-prisoner), and
Penny (a probation officer). Listen and see if they
agree with your opinions. Try to sum up in your
own words what they said.

5 Now you will hear Frances and Nick talking about what it is like to be in prison.
1. Before you listen, try to predict what they might say.
2. While you listen, take notes.
3. After listening, compare your notes with another student's. Did you both understand the same things?

6 Vocabulary study. Choose the correct words to complete the sentences.

1. Prison may do some good to some kinds of *crime/criminal*.
2. Prison does not usually *succeed/success* in *rehabilitating/rehabilitation* criminals.
3. Long prison sentences may have no more *effect/condition* than short ones.
4. Many people who *commit/make* crimes are social failures. They need help, not *punish/punishment*.
5. Prison is not a very *success/successful deter/deterrent*, because most criminals are never *prevented/caught*.
6. One *reason/condition* for sending people to prison is to protect *social/society*.
7. Some people say that prison life should be hard. They feel that prisons are meant to *punish/rehabilitate* people, not to give them a comfortable life.
8. Other people think that more money should be spent on improving prison *conditions/effects*.
9. One *advantage/disadvantage* of probation is that it is cheaper than prison.

7 Work in groups of three or four. Each group must find answers to the following questions.

1. Should fewer people be sent to prison?
2. Which kinds of criminals should be sent to prison?
3. What should be done with the others, instead of sending them to prison?

Study the Lesson Summary at the back of the book. Do some of the Practice Book exercises.

B Danger – little old ladies!

Reading comprehension; grammar (past conditionals and modals); pronunciation; speaking practice.

1 Work in pairs. One person in each pair should turn to page 153 and study the newspaper report 'LITTLE OLD LADY IN KNIFE RAID'. The other person should prepare questions to find out the information listed below. When both students are ready, they should close their books, and then ask and answer the questions. Finally, both students should look at page 153 and check that the answers were correct.

Find out:
1. the place, day and time of the incident
2. the little old lady's appearance and dress
3. what exactly happened
4. the names of the people involved
5. what the police did
6. how much, if anything, was stolen

2 Do this in the same way as Exercise 1 (but the person who read the text last time should prepare the questions this time, and vice versa). The newspaper report is on page 154, and is entitled 'MUGGER MEETS LITTLE OLD LADY'. The questioner should find out the same information as in Exercise 1.

3 Grammar. Write answers to the following two questions.

1. If you had been the shop assistant in the first report, what would you have done?
   (*If I had been the shop assistant, I would have . . .*)
2. If you had been the lady in the second report, what would you have done?

Now complete these sentences.

3. If the mugger had known what Lady Tucker was like, he would not have . . .
4. If Lady Tucker had not hit the mugger, . . .
5. . . . , the lorry driver might not have come to help.
6. . . . , the mugger would have got back on his bicycle.
7. . . . bicycle, he could have got away.
8. . . . would not . . . if she had not kept yelling.
9. If Lady Tucker had been an ordinary old lady, the mugger might have . . .
10. The mugger should have . . . He should not have . . .

If . . . had (not)	been . . . , hit come etc.	. . . would (not) have might could	attacked . . . been got etc.

4 Now write three or more sentences about yourself, using the following structures.

If I had (not) . . . when I was younger, I would have . . .
If I had . . . , I might have . . .
If I had had more money/time last year, I could have . . .
I should never have . . .

5 Pronunciation. Listen to the following sentence (from the interview with Nick Gregor in Lesson 5A). How are *going to* and *want to* pronounced?

I couldn't just say you know, OK, I'm going to go for a walk now, I'm going to go out and see some friends of mine, or I want to do this – I couldn't do that.

6 Pronunciation. Listen to the recording. How many words are there in each sentence? (Contractions like *I'd* count as two words.)

7 Work with another student (but don't sit with him or her). One of you is beginning a ten-year prison sentence; the other is the prisoner's mother, father, husband, wife, ex-teacher or partner in crime. Each person must write a note blaming the other person for the prisoner's problems, beginning *If I/you had(n't)* . . . When you are ready, exchange notes and write answers, using the same structure.

8 Work in groups of three. Prepare and act out *either* a dramatisation of one of the texts in Exercises 1 and 2, *or* another scene involving a criminal, a victim and a policeman or policewoman.

Study the Lesson Summary at the back of the book. Do some of the Practice Book exercises.

Stories

A A dream

1 You are going to hear the first part of a story. Before you listen, look at the words and expressions in the box. (They come in the story in the same order.) If there are any that you don't know, ask about them or look them up in a dictionary. What do you think happens in this part of the story? Listen to the recording and see if you are right.

by myself	tent	camp-sites	facilities
safer	convenient	I camped rough	hidden
hedge	wood	pleasant	I pitched my tent
moped	plastic	supper	I went to sleep

2 Now listen to the second part of the recording twice. When you have done that, work in small groups and try to remember and write down what you heard as exactly as possible. The words and expressions in the box will help you (but three of them shouldn't be there).

unusual	episodes	hard to tell	1930s
World War 2	on farms	barn	children
didn't last	scenes	laughing	smiling
puzzled	connect		

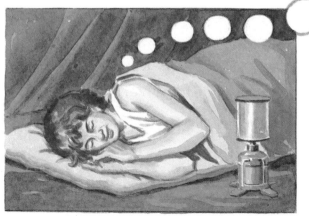

3 Now listen to the end of the story.

4 Pronunciation. Here are the first two sentences of the story.

A few years ago I was travelling in France. I was by myself, and I was travelling on a moped.

Copy the sentences and try to mark the stressed syllables. Listen to the recording and check your answers. Then practise saying the sentences. Note:
1. Unstressed syllables are pronounced more quietly and quickly than stressed syllables.
2. Stressed syllables are pronounced at roughly equal intervals.

5 Pronunciation. How are these words usually pronounced: *was, and, for, of, to, that, were, from*? Listen to the recording and see if you were right. Practise saying the sentences again. Then ask other students what they were doing yesterday at a particular time.

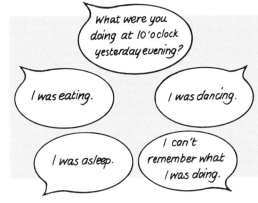

Tell the class what you have found out.

6 Have you ever had an experience of telepathy (knowing or dreaming what is happening to somebody else)? Or have you ever had a dream which told you what was going to happen in the future? Or have you ever experienced a strange coincidence? Work in groups of four or five, and tell your stories to the group.

Study the Lesson Summary at the back of the book. Do some of the Practice Book exercises.

Listening comprehension;
pronunciation; grammar
(reported speech); reading,
writing and telling stories.

B My heart is too full for words

1 Here are the beginnings of three stories. Choose one of them and then listen to the recording. You will hear some more sentences. Write the sentences which continue your story.

A: 'My heart is too full for words' she whispered,
B: Sally pulled out a gun,
C: Mary brought her horse round

2 Pronunciation.

1. Do you know how to pronounce these three common words?

said   any   many

2. Can you say these sentences?

I asked.	I asked for some advice.
I asked what she wanted.	She asked to see the manager.
I asked her name.	He asked them to stay.

3 Grammar: reported speech. What did they say?

1. She said 'I'm tired.'
   She said that she was tired.
2. He said 'We've only just started talking.'
3. She said 'It's getting late.'
4. He said 'It's still early.'
5. She said 'I've got to get up early in the morning.'
6. He said 'Tomorrow is another day.'
7. She said 'Tomorrow is another very busy day.'
8. He said 'You'll feel much better after another drink.'
9. She said 'I'll just have one more before I go.'
10. He said 'What are you going to have?'
    He asked her what she was going to have.
11. She said 'What is there?'
12. He said 'Which do you prefer – white wine, red wine or beer?'
13. She said 'What else is there?'
14. He said 'How do you feel about a small whisky?'
15. She said 'Can you just get me some water?'
    She asked him if he could just get her some water.
16. He said 'Can I get you a gin and tonic?'
17. She said 'Do you know where my coat is?'
18. He said 'Do you really want to go?'
19. She said 'Are you as stupid as you look?'
20. He said 'Have I said something to annoy you?'
21. She said 'How can you possibly think that?'
22. He said 'Oh, do stay.'
    He asked her to stay.
23. She said 'Go and jump in the river.'

4 Look at the pictures. Can you suggest what the questions and answers were? Example:

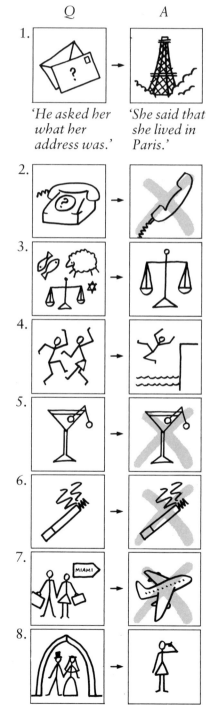

Q   A

1. 'He asked her what her address was.'   'She said that she lived in Paris.'

2.
3.
4.
5.
6.
7.
8.

5 Here are some 'mini-sagas' (50-word stories). Read them and say what you think of them. Examples:

'I think the first one is very good.'
'I don't think much of the second.'
'What do you think of the fourth one?' 'There's nothing in it.'
'I think the fifth is better than the fourth.'

1. THE INNER MAN
Their marriage was a perfect union of trust and understanding. They shared everything – except his desk drawer, which through the years remained locked. One day, curiosity overcame her. Prised open, there was – nothing. 'But why?' she asked, confused and ashamed. 'I needed a space of my own', he replied sadly.

(Christine M. Banks)

2. HOMER'S ODYSSEY IN 50 WORDS
Odysseus was a cunning, resourceful man who fought with the Greeks against Troy. Sailing back from the war, he and his crew met with a number of menaces – such as Circe, the witch who turned men into pigs – and overcame them. But it took him ten years to get home.

(C. C. Shackleton)

3. AN EXILE TRIES TO WRITE A MINI-SAGA
Wolverhampton in the winter. Frost on the railway lines. It's so drab. Sometimes I long for the tropics where I came from. The sun at zenith every day. The pleasures of open-air restaurants every evening. But there's work in Wolverhampton. You expect all my feelings in fifty words?

(V.V. Fisher)

4. LOVE AMONG THE LAUNDRY
When Sally found a man's striped sock curled among her clothes at the launderette she returned it to the tall dark young man with a shy smile. They met there every week for several months, then were seen no more. One of their wedding presents had been a washing machine.

(Molly Burnett)

5. ALIEN ECONOMY
The flying saucer landed in Alf's orchard. Alf's mower had stopped again. The alien pointed to the apples. Alf pointed to the mower. The alien mended the mower. Alf gave him some apples. The alien left. Alf's lawn mower gave no more trouble and never used another drop of petrol.

(Tony Ellis)

CHOOSE ONE OR BOTH OF EXERCISES 6 AND 7

6 Mini-sagas. Work alone or with two or three other students, as you prefer, and write a mini-saga in exactly 50 words. (You can invent a story, or tell a story that you know, or write about something that has happened to you.)

7 Modernising a story. Work with two or three other students. Take a traditional children's story (for instance, *Cinderella*, *The Sleeping Beauty*) and change it to bring it up to date.

Study the Lesson Summary at the back of the book. Do some of the Practice Book exercises.

Travel

A The sun was in the north

Grammar (tenses); vocabulary;
reading and listening comprehension.

1 Read the text and look at the map. If the
Phoenician sailors set off in 600 BC, where do
you think they were (roughly) in: December
600; May 599; July 599; December 598?
If there are any words you don't know, use a
dictionary, ask somebody, or try to guess.

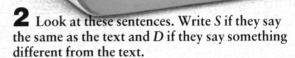

THE SUN WAS IN THE NORTH

The Portuguese discovered the west coast of black Africa
500 years ago. But historians believe that, 2,000 years
earlier, the Phoenicians may have travelled right round
Africa in small boats from Suez to Gibraltar and back to
Egypt.

The journey was planned by the Egyptian pharoah
Necho in 600 BC. He was interested in finding a sea route
from Egypt's eastern coast on the Red Sea to Alexandria
on the Mediterranean. In those days, nobody knew how
big Africa was, and he believed it would be easy to follow
the African coast round to Morocco and back to Egypt.

Necho hired crews of Phoenicians to make the journey.
The Phoenicians lived at the eastern end of the
Mediterranean, where Lebanon and Israel are today.
They were interested in Necho's plan, because their
traders wanted to find a new route to their markets in the
western Mediterranean, avoiding waters which were
controlled by their Greek rivals.

According to an old story reported by the Greek
historian Herodotus, the Phoenicians set off at the
beginning of winter in 50-oared sailing ships, rowed to
the eastern tip of Africa at Cape Gardafui, and then sailed
south-west on the monsoon winds. Month after month
went by, and they sailed further and further south. During
their journey, the weather became steadily colder, and
the seas rougher, and the Phoenicians were amazed to
see that the sun was now in the north at midday. They
must have thought that they would never see their homes
again. But after six months, the coast turned west; they
went round the Cape of Good Hope and at last began to
travel north.

While they were sailing up the west coast of Africa they
ran out of food, and had to land to collect more supplies.
This delayed them, and it was only after fifteen months
that they reached a country they knew – Morocco. From
there they went on to Gibraltar and then sailed east to
Egypt. When they eventually arrived home, they had
been away for over two years, and had travelled
25,000km.

2 Look at these sentences. Write *S* if they say
the same as the text and *D* if they say something
different from the text.

1. Necho had business reasons for finding a sea
   route round Africa.
2. He didn't think it would be such a long
   journey.
3. The Phoenicians traded with countries in the
   western Mediterranean.
4. The Greek historian Herodotus went with the
   Phoenician sailors.
5. They started from the eastern Mediterranean.
6. They got lost on the way south, and sailed in
   the wrong direction.
7. The weather got better after they had gone
   round the Cape of Good Hope.
8. It took them a long time to get from the Cape
   of Good Hope to Morocco.
9. One reason for this was that they stopped in
   West Africa to get more food.
10. Morocco was the first country they recognised
    on the way north.
11. The whole journey took nearly two years.

3 Look at Exercises 1 and 2 again, and choose
some words and expressions to learn. Compare
your list with another student.

4 Work in groups. Your job is to write the story of Marco Polo's journey to China. You can get the information you need:
– from the map
– from the pictures
– from the tape-recording
– from the grammar exercise
– from the teacher (if you ask the questions in correct English).

You don't need to include all the information in your story – just put in what you think is most important.

Marco Polo's route to China

GRAMMAR EXERCISE
Put in the correct tense (simple past, past progressive or past perfect).

1. After the two brothers (*return*) from China, they (*plan*) a new journey.
2. While they (*travel*) to China, Marco (*keep*) a diary.
3. Marco (*become*) ill while they (*cross*) Afghanistan.
4. This (*delay*) them for a year.
5. After Marco (*recover*), they (*go*) on.
6. Several times they (*have*) to change their route to avoid wars and bandits.
7. In China, Marco (*become*) the emperor's friend and adviser.
8. While he (*work*) for the emperor, he (*travel*) all over the Far East on imperial business.
9. The Polo family (*stay*) in China for twenty years.
10. In 1292, when the emperor (*get*) old, they (*decide*) to return home.
11. When they (*arrive*) in Venice, they (*tell*) everyone about their experiences, and Marco (*publish*) his diary.
12. But people (*think*) they (*lie*). Nobody (*believe*) their fantastic stories about the strange countries they (*visit*) and the wonderful things they (*see*).

QUESTIONS
You can get this information from the teacher if you ask questions in correct English:

1. The names of Marco Polo's father and uncle.
2. Their reason for making the first trip to China.
3. Marco's age when he left Venice.
4. The length of the journey.
5. The date when they arrived in China.
6. The countries to which Marco Polo travelled when he was working for the emperor.

They saw some wonderful things unknown in Europe.

a kind of stone that would burn (coal)

a mineral like cloth that wouldn't burn (asbestos)

a liquid mineral that could be used as fuel (petroleum)

enormous nuts with juice inside (coconuts)

Marco was surprised to find that China was more civilised than Italy.

Cities like Hangzhou had good roads

public parks

canals with bridges that ships could go under

underground drainage systems

a police force, a fire brigade and a postal service

B You can say that again

Listening comprehension; conversational expressions; grammar (tags); pronunciation; speaking practice.

1 Listen to the conversation. Where exactly do you think it takes place?

LUCY: So I said, well, I said, if that's what you think, there's nothing much I can do about it, is there? I mean, you can't please everybody, can you?

MARY: No, dear, of course you can't. Well, frankly, I never expect anything from men. I mean, they're all the same, aren't they?

LUCY: You can say that again, Mary. Well, anyway, –

TRAVELLER: Excuse me –

LUCY: – then he wanted to go and see one of his old girlfriends who lives in Birmingham – or rather, Wolverhampton.

TRAVELLER: Excuse me, could I have a timetable for Manchester, please?

MARY: Did he really?

LUCY: So I said, you can go and see her if you like –

MARY: Yes.

TRAVELLER: Hello!

LUCY: – but don't expect me to be here when you get back.

TRAVELLER: Excuse me. You do work here, don't you?

MARY: Work here? Oh, yes, love. Yes, we do. So what did he say to that?

TRAVELLER: I'M SORRY TO INTERRUPT YOUR VERY IMPORTANT DISCUSSION, BUT COULD I HAVE A TIMETABLE, PLEASE, IF IT'S NOT TOO MUCH TROUBLE?

LUCY: Well, really! There's no need to shout, dear. We're not deaf. Here you are. Where was I? Oh, yes. So he said he was going to go anyway – at least, he didn't say he wasn't . . .

TRAVELLER: No, a timetable for Manchester, not Birmingham. I want to go to Manchester, you see.

LUCY: I beg your pardon?

TRAVELLER: Manchester, not Birmingham.

LUCY: Well, make up your mind, dear. Here you are. So then I went to stay with my sister for a week.

MARY: Did you? You said you might.

LUCY: And I met this boy.

MARY: You didn't!

LUCY: Yes I did. A really nice guy. He's the manager of a record shop – at least, he's going to be next year.

TRAVELLER: Excuse me. This is a timetable for Wolverhampton.

LUCY: Just a minute, dear.

ANNOUNCEMENT: The next train to arrive at platform 3 will be the delayed 10.56 service for . . .

2 Here are some words and expressions that come in the conversation. Why are they used? Can you match each one with its meaning or purpose in the conversation?

WORDS AND EXPRESSIONS (1)
Well, anyway, . . .
I mean
frankly
You can say that again.
Excuse me.
. . . if it's not too much trouble.

MEANINGS/PURPOSES (1)
'I want to interrupt politely.'
'I'm giving a reason for what I've said.'
'I strongly agree.'
'To get back to the main point . . . '
'I'm giving my opinion very directly.'
Sarcastic 'polite request', really meaning 'Why aren't you doing your job?'

WORDS AND EXPRESSIONS (2)
Well, really!
Here you are.
Where was I?
at least
or rather
I beg your pardon?
Just a minute.
. . . you see.

MEANINGS/PURPOSES (2)
'I can't remember what I was saying.'
'What did you say?'
'I'm giving you something.'
'I want to correct myself.'
'I don't want to pay attention to you yet.'
'I'm giving an explanation.'
'I think you're behaving badly.'
'What I said was more than the truth.'

3 Grammar. Complete the sentences.

1. There isn't a waiting-room here, ... there?
2. You don't want to travel on Sunday night, ... you?
3. These trains are really dirty, ... they?
4. 'I wasn't trying to travel without a ticket.' 'No, of course you ....'
5. 'You have fastened your safety belt, ... you?' 'Yes, I ....'
6. 'I'd love to go to India.' '............ you really?'
7. 'I flew to Miami last week.' 'You ....!' 'Yes, I ....'
8. 'I'll be in Cardiff next month.' '............ you? How long for?'
9. 'I'm trying to get a job as an air hostess.' '............ you?' 'I certainly ....'
10. 'Excuse me. Can you help me with my luggage?' 'I'm sorry. I'm afraid I .... just at the moment.'
11. 'Don't forget your passport.' 'Don't worry. I ....'

4 Pronunciation revision. Some of these words are pronounced with the vowel /ɒ/ (like *not*); some with /ɔ:/ (like *north*); and some with /əʊ/ (like *note*). Can you write the words in three lists according to their pronunciation? Can you add any more words to the lists?

all   boat   coast   go   gone   got
home   hope   long   lost   more   most
oar   off   on   saw   slow   small
stop   story   those   thought   walk
war   water   wrong

5 Look at Exercise 1 and choose some words and expressions to learn. Show your list to another student, and explain the reasons for your choices.

6 Work in pairs or groups of three. Make up and practise a conversation in a station, in an airport, on a train or on a plane. Include two or more of the following: a delay, a pleasant surprise, an unpleasant surprise, a misunderstanding, an interesting meeting. Use some of the words and expressions from the lesson.

Study the Lesson Summary at the back of the book.
Do some of the Practice Book exercises.

Believing and imagining

A Evidence

Speaking; listening comprehension;
grammar (complex sentences).

1 Make a list of things that children believe in
(for example, ghosts, Father Christmas). Speak
to three other students and find out which of the
things on your list they believed in when they were
children.

2 You are going to hear two six-year-old
children, Sarah and Mark, talking about what they
believe in. Copy the following list; as you listen to
the recording, write ✓ if a child says that he or she
believes in something, ✗ if he or she doesn't
believe, and ? if you can't tell.

spacemen   dinosaurs
superheroes   ghosts
the tooth fairy   dragons
Father Christmas   sea-monsters
the Easter rabbit

IF I CAN PROVE HIS CONNECTION WITH ORGANIZED CRIME, MAYBE ...

3 Here are some sentences from the conversation
with the children. Can you complete them without
listening again?

1. Why do you believe .... spacemen?
2. Because I've .... of lots of people going
   up to the moon.
3. Because you've never .... them outside
   the TV, and none of your friends ....
4. And you're sure that .... the tooth fairy
   .... puts the money there?
5. You don't think it .... possibly be
   anybody else?
6. 'Cause I don't believe that anyone ....
   could bring .... presents at Christmas
   time.
7. I don't think anyone else .... try ....
   jump down the chimney.
8. Because I haven't seen .... dragon bones.
9. Is there anything else you believe .... ?
10. Because they .... be the last descendants
    of the dinosaurs, as it .... in my *First
    Book of Facts*.
11. I've been to the seaside lots of times, and I
    haven't seen a sea-monster ....
12. But maybe they're out farther .... you've
    seen.
13. If they're sea-monsters they're big, ...
    they?
14. So you'd probably see them, ... you?
15. Yes, but if they .... so far away you
    .... think they .... just fish.

34

4 What did you think about the world when you were small? What evidence did you have for your beliefs? Write two or three sentences.

When I was small I thought that . . .
I never believed in . . . , because . . .
It seemed obvious to me that . . .
I had the impression that . . .
It looked as if . . .
I wondered whether . . .
I didn't realise . . .
For some reason or other, I thought . . .
. . . This was because . . .
. . . The reason was that . . .

WORK IN PAIRS OR SMALL GROUPS, AND DO ONE OR MORE OF THE FOLLOWING EXERCISES.

5 Prepare a short talk (to be given by one member of the group). In the talk, you have to explain to the rest of the class why they should believe in ghosts, visitors from space, werewolves, or something else of the same kind.

6 Listen to the recording two or three times, and then look at the pictures. You must make up a story which explains the sounds in the recording, and which includes the people and things in the pictures.

7 You are detectives working for the missing persons office in a big city police headquarters in Scotland. A man has been found wandering in the streets, suffering from loss of memory. Look at the following pieces of evidence and then try to make up a theory about the man – what he does, where he comes from, etc.

1. The man looks European; he has a dark complexion and black hair. He is about 40, tall and athletic, but rather overweight.
2. He is dressed in pink silk pyjamas, made in Bangkok.
3. When questioned, he only says 'I can't remember', in English but with a strong French accent.
4. His hands are covered with engine oil.
5. He has a bag containing the following:
   – $60,000 in US currency
   – photographs of three beautiful women (two European, one oriental)
   – a photograph of the British Minister of Defence
   – a receipt from a car-hire firm
   – two love letters: one in English, beginning 'My darling Freddy' and the other in French, beginning 'Serge, mon amour'
   – a gun with the number removed
   – a screwdriver
   – a silver spoon
   – one more thing (you choose)

Study the Lesson Summary at the back of the book. Do some of the Practice Book exercises.

B Secret thoughts

Listening comprehension; pronunciation; speaking practice; grammar (verbs not used in progressive).

1 Read the text and listen to the recording. The sentences in brackets ( ) are the motorist's secret thoughts.

A motorist comes back to his car. A traffic warden is standing beside it.

TRAFFIC WARDEN: Excuse me, sir.
MOTORIST: Yes?
  (Oh, no, not again.)
TW: Is this your car?
M: Yes, it is.
  (No, it's the Queen's private aeroplane, you fool.)
TW: I'm afraid you're parked on a double yellow line, sir.
M: Good heavens, am I really? I'm so sorry, I didn't notice.
  (She'll never believe that. Let's try flattery.)
  I say, what a pretty uniform.
  (You look like a camel wearing a tent.)
TW: I'm sorry, sir, but I'll have to give you a ticket.
M: I see.
  (If you do, I'll kill you.)
TW: May I have your name, please, sir?
M: James Baxter.
  (My name is Tarzan, terror of the jungle. I am going to tear your uniform into little pieces and stuff them down your throat.)

2 Close your book and listen to the recording. Can you remember any of the secret thoughts?

3 Now read this text. Try to imagine what the shop assistant is thinking. Then listen to the recording: you will hear one possible version of the assistant's secret thoughts.

A customer is trying on shoes in a shoe shop.

CUSTOMER: No, I'm afraid they don't quite fit. Could I try another pair, please?
ASSISTANT: Of course, madam.
C: Yes, these ones fit quite nicely, but I don't think this shade of red really suits me. What do you think?
A: I think the colour suits you very well, madam.
C: I'm afraid I'm giving you a lot of trouble . . .
A: Oh, no, madam, not at all.
C: . . . but I think I'd like to try that pair over there.
A: But you've already tried those ones on, madam.
C: Well, I think I'll try them again just to make sure.
A: Very well, madam.
C: No, I was right the first time. They suit me very well, but they don't quite fit.
A: No, madam.

4 Pronunciation. Listen to the recording, and write the numbers of the sentences that you hear.

1. I see what she wants.
2. I'll see what she wants.

3. They never come to see me.
4. They'll never come to see me.

5. I need your help.
6. I'll need your help.

7. The children probably want something to eat.
8. The children'll probably want something to eat.

9. My parents live with us.
10. My parents'll live with us.

11. How do you get to work?
12. How'll you get to work?

13. How much time do you need?
14. How much time'll you need?

Now say these sentences.

She'll never believe that.
I'll have to give you a ticket.
I think I'll try them again.
I'll kill you!

5 Look at Exercises 1 and 3. Choose some useful words and expressions to learn. Discuss your list with other students.

SCHWADRON

6 Work in groups of three or four. Complete five or more of the following conversations. In each conversation, use the *will* future (*I'll/you'll/he'll* etc.) at least once, and use one of the verbs *think, feel, hope, want, know, believe, like, love, need, remember, understand, seem, look.* (Note that these verbs are not usually used in progressive forms.) When you have completed the conversations, act some of them for the other students.

FATHER: What are you doing this evening, Sylvia?
DAUGHTER: ....
(SECRET THOUGHTS: ....)
FATHER: ....
(SECRET THOUGHTS: ....)

WIFE: How do you like my hair, darling?
HUSBAND: ....
(SECRET THOUGHTS: ....)
WIFE: ....
(SECRET THOUGHTS: ....)

TEACHER: Do you all understand?
STUDENTS: ....
(SECRET THOUGHTS: ....)
TEACHER: ....
(SECRET THOUGHTS: ....)

BOSS: ....
SECRETARY: ....
(SECRET THOUGHTS: ....)
BOSS: ....
(SECRET THOUGHTS: ....)

POLITICAL SPEAKER: ....
(SECRET THOUGHTS: ....)
(AUDIENCE'S SECRET THOUGHTS: ....)

PATIENT: ....
DOCTOR: ....
(SECRET THOUGHTS: ....)
PATIENT: ....
(SECRET THOUGHTS: ....)

OFFICER: ....
SOLDIER: ....
(SECRET THOUGHTS: ....)
OFFICER: ....
(SECRET THOUGHTS: ....)

Study the Lesson Summary at the back of the book.
Do some of the Practice Book exercises.

Music

A I slid into it

Listening comprehension; grammar (*which* and *that*);
intonation; writing practice.

1 Make sure you understand the words in the
box. Then listen to George Melly talking about his
career, and put the pictures in order.

art gallery	band leader	fed up	jazz
journalist	popular	professional	
public house	(a) record	trumpet	

2 Grammar: *which* and *that*. In some sentences,
it does not matter whether you use *which* or *that*.
For example:

I sang a song **which/that** I had learned from Bessie
Smith.

But in some sentences you can only use *which*. In
these sentences from George Melly's interview,
you could not use *that*. Work in groups of three or
four, and try to write rules about each kind of
sentence.

1. And much to the surprise of the editor of
   the newspaper for *which* I was working, I
   resigned . . .
2. . . . there was a movement afoot among young
   people to revive old jazz, the jazz of the
   twenties and early thirties, *which* was exactly
   the period I was interested in.
3. Mick Mulligan, who was a trumpet player and
   band leader, and I, er, decided to go
   professional, *which* we did in the very early
   fifties.

3 Now look at some more sentences from the same interview, and decide how the blanks can be filled:
– only *which*
– *which* or *that*

1. Although we were a band .... was constantly in employment, we weren't particularly well paid.
2. And jazz, ... had been popular, became very unpopular, especially among young people.
3. First I wrote about pop music, funnily enough, a subject of .... I knew very little.
4. We have a comfortable band bus or wagon, with special seats in .... one can relax.
5. There are only five of us, ... is a help.
6. The things .... made me bored with it at the end of the fifties and early sixties, we have changed.
7. It seems to me a subject .... has not yet been covered except in articles.

4 Pronunciation of sentences with *which* and *that*. Repeat these sentences after the recording; pay special attention to pauses and intonation. Then try to pronounce the sentences in Exercise 3 (use *that* and then *which* in sentences 1, 6 and 7), and check with the recording to see if you were right.

a. I sang a song that I had learned from Bessie Smith.
b. I sang a song which I had learned from Bessie Smith.
c. They played the jazz of the twenties and early thirties, which I was especially interested in.
d. We decided to go professional, which we did in the early fifties.
e. I resigned from the newspaper for which I had been working since the early sixties.
f. I resigned from *The Observer*, for which I had been working since the early sixties.

5 Len and Barbara Berry are semi-professional folk singers. Listen to them singing a folk song; then work in groups, using the pictures to write the story of their career. You can use your imagination.

Barbara sang with father at work

Married . . .

Len made auto parts at Unipart

Barbara looked after the children

Both sang with Scouts

Son took them to folk club

Now they earn ¹/₃ of money from singing

. . . ¹/₃ of money from wooden toys

. . . ¹/₃ of money from curtains, covers

They have made a record

39

B Audiences

Expressing opinions; grammar (position of adverbs); reading skills; listening for details; speaking practice.

1 Look at the picture and listen to the recording. For each piece of music, try to write down the name(s) of the instrument(s) you hear. One of the recordings has a 'surprise' instrument which is not in the picture. Try to guess what it is.

2 Now listen to the recording again. After each piece of music, tell someone sitting near you how much you like it.

'I like that very much / a lot.'
'I don't like that very much.'
'I quite like the music, and the person plays the instrument beautifully.'
'I think that person plays the synthesiser very badly.'
'The instrument has a nice sound, but I don't like the melody at all.'
'I haven't got a good ear for music, so I can't judge very well if it's good or not.'

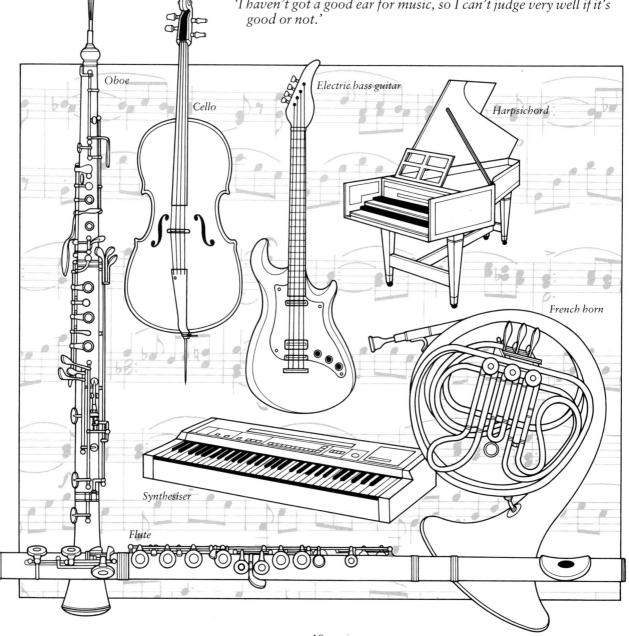

3 Read the story below. There are four sentences missing, which you will find at the end of the story. Try to decide where the sentences go.

THE WORST MUSICAL TRIO
There are few bad musicians who have a chance to give a recital at a famous concert hall while still learning the rudiments of their instrument. This happened about thirty years ago to the son of a Rumanian gentleman who was owed a personal favour by Georges Enesco, the celebrated violinist.

Three years later the boy's father insisted that he gave a public concert. 'His aunt said that nobody plays the violin better than he does. A cousin heard him the other day and screamed with enthusiasm.' However, nobody bought a ticket since the soloist was unknown.

'Then you must accompany him on the piano,' said the boy's father, 'and it will be a sellout.'

Reluctantly, Enesco agreed and it was. Before the concert began Enesco became nervous and asked for someone to turn his pages.

In the audience was Alfred Cortot, the brilliant pianist, who volunteered and made his way to the stage.

The soloist was of uniformly low standard and next morning the music critic of *Le Figaro* wrote: 'The man whom we adore when he plays the violin played the piano. Another whom we adore when he plays the piano turned the pages. But the man who should have turned the pages played the violin.'

(from *The Book of Heroic Failures* by Stephen Pile)

The missing sentences:

On the night an excited audience gathered.
Enesco agreed to give lessons to the son, who was quite unhampered by musical talent.
There was a strange concert at the Salle Gaveau last night.
Although Enesco feared the consequences, he arranged a recital at the Salle Gaveau in Paris.

4 Listen to the recording and answer the questions.

George Melly
1. What kind of audience does he prefer?
2. Write down two sorts of places where he sings, and one sort of place he doesn't like singing.

Len and Barbara Berry
1. Is interest in folk music increasing or decreasing at the moment?
2. Have the places where they sing got more or less comfortable?
3. In their audiences, is there more or less: drinking, smoking, demand for political songs?

Alwyn Anchors
1. Does he think that groups play better music at the beginning of their careers or after they have been successful for a while?
2. (Note that the 'Proms' are concerts of classical music.) Does Al think people's taste in music gets broader or narrower as they get older?

5 Choose a question from this list, or make up a question of your own about people's tastes in music. Ask everyone else in the class your question, and report on what you find out.

1. What is your favourite sort of music?
2. Do the people you live with and your close friends share the same tastes in music as you?
3. Where do you listen to music most – at home, in the car, . . . ?
4. If you could choose one musical instrument to be able to play brilliantly, what instrument would you choose?
5. Do you like having background music while you are working?
6. Where do you tend to listen to music?
7. How often do you go to concerts?
8. Do you buy records, cassettes or compact discs? If so, how often?
9. What usually makes you decide that you want to buy a certain record (or disc or cassette)?
10. Have you got one or two favourite performers (or groups or orchestras) at the moment? If so, who?
11. Have your musical tastes changed since you were younger? If so, in what way?
12. What instrument do you most like the sound of?
13. Do you have an ear for music?
14. Do you ever sing in the bath or while you are working?
15. Would you like a child of yours to be a professional musician?

Study the Lesson Summary at the back of the book. Do some of the Practice Book exercises.

Revision and fluency practice

A Grammar, spelling and listening

Grammar (present and past tenses); pronunciation
and spelling rules; listening practice.

1 Do you know the names of the different
present and past verb tenses? Try to match the
examples with the names (there is more than one
example of some tenses).

1. **I have** often **thought** of changing my job.
2. **It rains** nearly every day in winter.
3. She was tired, because **she had been travelling**
   all day.
4. **I asked** her to come out for a drink, but **she
   was working,** so she couldn't.
5. Do you know that **Phil has written** a novel?
6. 'You look hot.' **'I've been playing** tennis.'
7. **It's raining** again.
8. **I live** in Manchester, but **I'm staying** with my
   sister in Glasgow at the moment.
9. When **he spoke** to me, I realised that **I had
   seen** him before.
10. **He's been** to East Africa several times, so he
    speaks quite good Swahili.
11. When we were children, **we** usually **went** to
    the seaside for our summer holidays.
12. What **were you doing** this time yesterday?
13. **I'm seeing** a lot of Mary these days.

> simple present
> present progressive
> (simple) present perfect
> present perfect progressive
> simple past
> past progressive
> (simple) past perfect
> past perfect progressive

2 Look at the diagrams and descriptions, and
compare the examples in Exercise 1. Which tense
goes with each diagram?

A
PAST XXXXXXXXXXXXXXXXXXXXX FUTURE
NOW
repeated or permanent: past, present and future

B
PAST — — — — — XXXXX — — — — FUTURE
NOW
just now, or just around now

C
PAST —X–X–X–X–X–X–X–X–X–X NOW
repeated 'up to now'

PAST — — —X RESULT NOW
past, but with a result now

PAST — — — — —X NEWS NOW
past, but still 'news'

D
PAST XXXXXXXXXXXXXXXXXXX NOW
continuing 'up to now'

E
PAST — — —X–(X)·(X)— — — — — — NOW
one or more times in the past

F
10 p.m.
PAST — —XXXXXXXX— — — — — NOW
happening around a particular time in the past

X
PAST — —XXXXXXXX— — — — — NOW
already happening when something else happened

G
PAST — —X— — — —X— — — NOW
'second', earlier past

H
PAST — —XXXXX X— — — — NOW
repeated or continuing 'up to then'

3 What tenses would you choose for the following situations?

1. to talk about one of your habits
2. to talk about one of your childhood habits
3. to give news of an examination success
4. to answer a question about your movements at midday yesterday
5. to explain that you are tired because of a game of football
6. to explain that you were tired yesterday evening because of a game of football
7. to say that you can't go dancing because of an accident

4 Can you explain these two exceptions?

1. **I don't want** to go home. (NOT I'm not wanting to go home.)
2. How long **have you known** Debbie? (NOT How long have you been knowing Debbie?)

5 Pronunciation and spelling. Look at the following pairs of words. What difference does the letter *e* make to the pronunciation of the vowel before it?

mad made   win wine   hop hope
cut cute

Now read these pairs of words. You can pronounce them correctly even if you don't know them.

sin sine   cap cape   lop lope
run rune   pip pipe   pan pane

6 Look at these pairs of words. Why does the second word in each pair have a double letter?

big bigger   run runner
mad madder   hot hotter
sit sitting   begin beginning

How would you pronounce these words if they didn't have double letters?

dinner   happy   butter   summer
middle

How would you pronounce these words if they had double letters in the middle?

inviting   amusing   voted   hated
writer

7 Some of these words are written with *k*; others are written with *ck*. Why? Can you find a rule?

back   break   sick   look   luck   thank
rock   wake   neck   work   stuck   think
walk   like   sack   week   joke

8 Some of these words are written with *ch*; others are written with *tch*. The rule is the same as for *k* and *ck*, but four of the words are exceptions. Which?

catch   reach   coach   rich   fetch   each
much   arch   bench   such   hitch   search
which   couch   brooch   hutch

9 Listen to the song. (The words are on page 153.) The word *so* is used several times. Can you write down any of the words that come after *so*? Can you write down the words that come after *such*? What is the difference between *such* and *so*?

Study the Lesson Summary at the back of the book.

"Why wait till Father's Day? Give it to him now."

B Situations

Listening comprehension; giving directions; telephoning; other situational language.

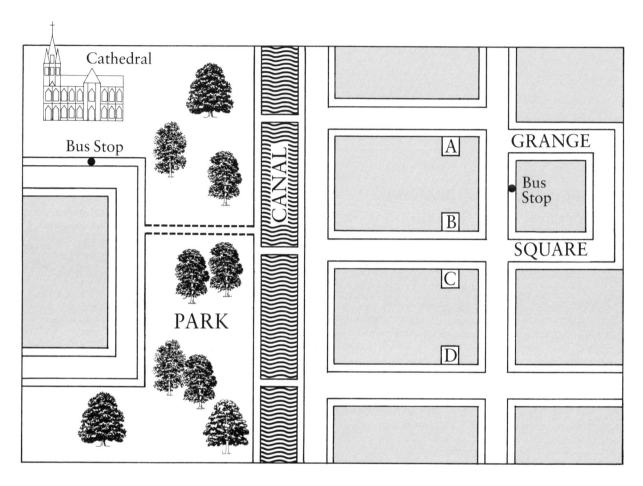

1 Do you know all of these expressions? All except one are commonly used in telephone calls. Which one is the exception?

Trying to connect you.
His/Her line's busy.
Can you hold?
Do you know his/her extension?
I'll see if I can transfer you.
I'm sorry. I've/You've got the wrong number.
His/Her number's ringing for you.
I'll put you through.
This is (name).
Who are you?
Who is that?
Speaking.
We got cut off.
This is a very bad line.
I'll ring you back.

2 Listen to the telephone conversations. You will hear all except three of the expressions from Exercise 1. Which three?

3 Now listen again to the final conversation between Stuart and Margaret. As you listen, look at the map. Stuart tells Margaret how to find a restaurant called Lacy's. Where is the restaurant – at A, B, C or D?

4 Do you know these words and expressions? (They are all used in giving directions.)

across   along   down   in front of
opposite   past   through   towards

roundabout   traffic lights   T-junction
fork   bend

Go straight ahead for . . . yards/metres.
Take the first/second/etc. on the right/left.
Turn right/left at . . . It's on your right/left.
You can't miss it.

5 Work in pairs. Imagine that you are standing in the centre of a town or city that you know well. One of you lives there, the other is a tourist asking for directions to somewhere. Act out the conversation.

6 What situations would the following expressions be used in? Choose one of the situations and see how many more typical expressions you can think of.

What would you like to start with?
Three first-class, please, and this one is to be registered.
Do you mind if I look round?
A hundred in fives and the rest in tens, please.
Is it direct or do I have to change?
Day return to London, please.
Could you check the oil and the tyres?

7 Work in small groups. Prepare and practise a conversation which takes place in one of the situations from Exercise 6. The conversation must include the following: 1) a problem; 2) a telephone call; 3) directions about how to get to a place. When you are ready, act out your conversation for the rest of the class.

Study the Lesson Summary at the back of the book.

"First left over the bridge, second right past the church, then straight on until you come to the roundabout, third exit out of that, keep left at the fork and it's the fourth turning on the right after you pass the milk depot."

"Excuse me, is this the second street on the left?"

Language

A Learning a language

1 Which aspects of English are the most difficult, in your opinion? Copy the list, and for each aspect write VD (= *very difficult*), D (= *difficult*), N (= *neither difficult nor easy*), E (= *easy*) or VE (= *very easy*). When you have done this, compare notes with other students.

pronunciation   spelling   grammar   vocabulary   speaking fluently   writing fluently
understanding speech   reading fluently   other

2 Use the words in the box to answer the questions.

```
consonant   culture   functional language
grammar   intonation   pronunciation
situational language   spelling   stress
vocabulary   vowel
```

1. A foreigner asks for 'fire' instead of 'a light' for a cigarette. What kind of mistake is he making?
2. A foreigner is asked 'How long are you here for?' She replies 'Since April' (the correct reply would be 'Till November'). What kind of mistake is this?
3. A foreigner tries to buy paper and is given pepper. What is the problem here?
4. The verb *record* is pronounced differently from the noun *record*. Do you know what the main difference is?
5. These two sentences don't sound the same if you hear them. What makes the difference?
   That's Mrs Lewis.
   That's Mrs Lewis?
6. If you don't know whether to write *necesary*, *necessary*, *neccesary* or *neccessary*, you have a problem with – what?
7. Which is the odd one out: *b, m, a, c, f, z*? Why?
8. A foreigner is asked 'How are you?' and replies with a long description of her health problems. She needs to learn more about – what?
9. A foreigner knows a lot of grammar and vocabulary, but doesn't know what to say in a shop or when making a phone call. What does he need to learn?
10. A foreigner knows a lot of grammar and vocabulary, but doesn't know how to apologise, complain, interrupt politely, give warnings or change the subject. What does she need lessons in?

3 Choose one of these questions and ask the other students. Make notes of the answers, and tell the class what people have said.

1. What do you think is the most important thing to learn in English?
2. Can you think of something in English that it is not important to learn?
3. How important is it to speak correctly?
4. What is the most interesting aspect of English, for you?
5. What is the most boring aspect of English, for you?
6. Do you think that musical people are good at learning pronunciation?
7. What do you think is the best way to learn pronunciation?
8. What do you think is the best way to learn grammar?
9. What do you think is the best way to learn vocabulary?
10. How long do you think it takes to get a good working knowledge of a language?
11. Do you prefer British English, American English, or another kind of English? Why?
12. Can you think of one thing in English that you dislike (for example a word, a sound or a grammatical rule), and one that you like?
13. What is the most important job of a language teacher?
14. Would you like to be a language teacher?
15. Do you think your language is easy or difficult for foreigners to learn? Why?
16. Do you think it is possible to learn a foreign language perfectly?

4 Here are three different explanations of the origins of writing. Which one do you think is probably most correct?

1. According to archaeologists, the first writing was religious. 5,000 years ago, people in the Middle East invented signs for the names of their gods, and wrote them on clay tablets. Later, people started using writing for other purposes – for example, for keeping records and accounts.

2. Writing began 5,000 years ago in the Middle East with pictures on tablets made of baked clay. As time went by, more and more pictures were invented, until there was a picture for each word in the language.

3. About 10,000 years ago, people in the Middle East used small objects made of baked clay to keep records and accounts. Later, they made pictures of the objects on clay tablets, instead of using the objects themselves. Finally, this picture writing was used for other things besides accounting.

5 Listen to the recording. You will hear a talk about the origins of writing. After you have heard it, decide whether you want to change your answer to Exercise 4.

6 Listen to the talk again and make brief notes. (The first few notes are written for you below.)

first writing Sumerians
pictures : 1500 signs
wood on clay
baked

7 Work in groups of three or four. Try to produce a more detailed summary of the talk in 100–150 words.

Study the Lesson Summary at the back of the book. Do some of the Practice Book exercises.

Signs used 5,000 years ago in Sumerian picture writing on baked clay tablets		Baked clay objects (accounting tokens?) found in Middle East – up to 10,000 years old
⊕	SHEEP	
	WOOL	
	COW	
	OIL	
	METAL	
	SEAT	
	ONE	

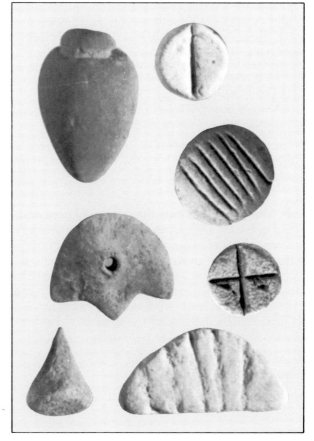

B Guess what the accents are

Understanding different accents; intonation; grammar; formal and informal language; vocabulary.

THIS LESSON HAS EXERCISES ON FIVE DIFFERENT ASPECTS OF LANGUAGE:
1. UNDERSTANDING DIFFERENT ACCENTS
2. INTONATION AND MEANING
3. GRAMMAR: DIFFERENT WAYS OF USING WORDS
4. STYLE: FORMAL AND INFORMAL LANGUAGE
5. VOCABULARY AND IDIOM: LANGUAGE FUNCTIONS.

CHOOSE EXERCISES ON THE ASPECTS OF LANGUAGE THAT INTEREST YOU MOST.

1 Can you understand English spoken with different accents? Listen to each person on the recording. How much can you understand? Do you think English is the speaker's mother tongue? Can you guess where he or she is from?

2 Intonation and meaning. Listen to the recording. You will hear a child say that she doesn't like colouring; you will then hear an adult say that she wants to ask some questions about the child's teacher. While answering, the adult says 'OK' three times. What do you think 'OK' means each time? Choose your answers from this list.

1. I have heard and understood your answer.
2. You're right.
3. Do you understand and agree?
4. I am going to change the subject.

One of the examples of 'OK' has a different intonation from the other two. Which? Does it rise or fall? Can you imitate it?

3 Many words in English can be used in more than one way. For example, *snow* can be a noun (*There's a lot of snow on the ground!*) or a verb (*Do you think it will snow?*); and *warm* can be a verb (*Shall I warm the milk?*) or an adjective (*The house isn't very warm!*). The following words can all be used in at least two ways: can you make sentences with them? Can you think of any other words that can be used in two ways?

cold   empty   land   light   look   open
past   play   rain   walk

"*Has phar la houdla seel vo plate?*"

"*Glhup hwow you shoul do da?*"

4 Can you divide these words and expressions into two groups: informal and formal? Can you 'translate' any of them from formal to informal, or from informal to formal? Can you think of any other words and expressions that are very formal or very informal?

Hi!
It's a pleasure to meet you.
What?
Great!
Pass me the bread, would you?
Excuse me, have you got the time?
Sleep OK?
I think you may be mistaken.
I'm afraid I have no idea.
Let's dance.
I don't think we've met before.

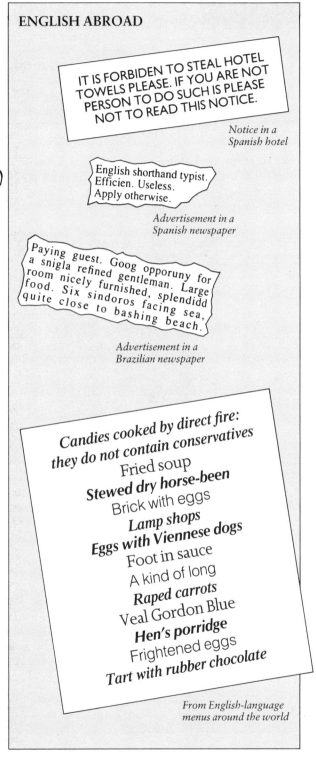

5 Here are some 'language functions' – things that we do with language. Do you know how to do all of these things in English? Can you add some more functions to the list?

asking for information
offering something
offering to do something
apologising
inviting
accepting an invitation
asking for something to be repeated
giving reasons
interrupting

6 Work in pairs or small groups. Prepare and practise a conversation which contains three or more of the language functions from Exercise 5, and some of the expressions from Exercise 4.

Study the Lesson Summary at the back of the book. Do some of the Practice Book exercises.

Unit 12

News

A The voice of democracy

Reading and listening comprehension; linking expressions; grammar (simple past, present perfect); pronunciation (stress).

1 Read the text of the news broadcast. Choose the correct tenses, and fill in the missing words and expressions from the box. Then listen to the recording and check your answers.

| according to | approximately | at least | due to |
| following | in spite of | which | with |

Free Fantasian Radio – the voice of democracy. It's ten o'clock, and here is Lucy Voronesk with the latest news.

Figures released today show that average earnings (*have gone up/went up*) by 60% over the last twelve months. Official sources say that this is .... the government's successful economic policies, which (*have led to/led to*) more efficient management and greater productivity. Industrial output (*has risen/rose*) by 43% during the last year, and exports (*have gone up/went up*) by 52%. Inflation is down to .... 3%.

.... police figures, about 5,000 people (*have taken part/took part*) in yesterday's anti-government demonstration. .... police efforts to maintain order, (*there has been/there was*) violence throughout the march. Stones and petrol bombs (*have been thrown/were thrown*) at government buildings, and .... 200 people (*have been hurt/were hurt*) in fighting .... (*has broken/broke*) out after speeches by opposition leaders in Wesk Square.

(*There has been/There was*) flooding in the south of the country, ... last week's heavy rains. Prompt action by local army units (*has limited/limited*) the damage, and the few people affected (*have now been able/were able*) to return to their homes.

Dr Joseph Brodsk, Deputy Governor of Stranvegan from 1976 to 1981, (*has died/died*) yesterday at his home in Banhooly. He was 78. The President (*has sent/sent*) a message of sympathy to Mrs Brodsk.

News (*has just come in/just came in*) of a plane crash at East Mork Airport. First reports say that two aircraft were involved, and that several people were killed, but no further details are available for the moment.

And now the weather forecast. It (*is/will be*) warm, ... continuous sunshine in all parts of the country. The outlook for the weekend is similar, with temperatures in the high thirties.

2 Here are some rules for the use of the present perfect and simple past tenses. Only one of them is true. Which? (The examples in Exercise 1 may help you decide.)

A. When the time of an action is given:
1. The present perfect is used when the time is finished; the simple past is used when it is not finished.
2. The present perfect is used when the time is not finished; the simple past is used when it is finished.
3. The present perfect is used for longer periods of time; the simple past is used for shorter periods.
4. The present perfect is used for repeated actions; the simple past is used for actions that are not repeated.

Here are some more rules. This time, three of them are true. Which?

B. When the time of an action is not given:
1. The present perfect is often used to report news.
2. The present perfect is often used with the word *just*.
3. The present perfect is often used to talk about past actions which have a present result.
4. The present perfect is used most often in informal conversation.
5. The present perfect is used for longer actions; the simple past is used for actions that happened quickly.

3 Listen to the recording. You will hear the ten o'clock news broadcast on another Fantasian Radio station – Democratic Fantasian Radio. There are some differences in the information given in the two broadcasts. What do you think is the main reason for the differences? Copy the table and try to complete it.

	FFR	DFR
Number of demonstrators:		
Was march violent?		
How many hurt?		
Average earnings up/down by:		
Industrial output up/down by:		
Exports up/down by:		
Inflation:		
Number of homeless due to flooding:		
Weather:		

4 Pronunciation. Contrastive stress. Look at the sentences. Which of the words in italics is stressed in each one? Say the sentences.

1. Democratic Fantasian Radio has a different political position from *Free Fantasian Radio*.
2. Free Fantasian Radio has a similar position to *Free Fantasian Television*.
3. Export figures are rising faster than *import figures*.
4. I've never met the President, but I've met the *President's wife*.
5. I don't usually vote in elections, but *this one*'s important.
6. First reports referred to two aircraft, but it is now believed that *three aircraft* were involved.

5 Contrastive stress. Here are some sentences from a newspaper report, with corrections in brackets. Make corrections as in the examples. Be careful to stress the right words.

1. The President's husband is 48 today. (46)
   'The newspaper said that the President's husband was 48 today, but actually he's 46.'
2. He is visiting the south of France. (*north*)
   'The newspaper said he was visiting the south of France, but in fact he's visiting the north of France.'
3. The President is leaving for China on Sunday afternoon. (*Monday*)
4. She will be accompanied by two senior officials from the Ministry of Technology. (*four*)
5. While in China, she plans to meet officials from the Ministry of Education. (*Foreign Trade*)
6. She will rejoin her husband before her visit to China. (*after*)
7. On her return, the President will take a long holiday. (*short*)
8. The President is not planning to stand again at the next election. (*is planning*)

6 Work in small groups. Invent a news item, and then report it to the class by mime (acting without words). The other students must guess what you are reporting and put it into words.

Study the Lesson Summary at the back of the book.
Do some of the Practice Book exercises.

B The Swiss have voted

Listening comprehension;
vocabulary; pronunciation;
speaking practice.

1 Here are the subjects, verbs and some other words from the first sentences of seven radio news items. They have been mixed up. Try to decide what is probably reported in each news item.

SUBJECT	VERB	OTHER WORDS
Four black people	are investigating	cloudy start
Police in Swindon	are tunnelling	collision, police car, mini car
Raiders	becoming brighter	home, pop star, antiques
The Swiss	have been killed	police, South Africa
The weather	have been shot	retain neutrality, United Nations
Two Britons	have smashed their way	suspected arson, fire
Two men	have voted	wreckage, hotel, Singapore

2 Listen to the news items. (They were broadcast on British radio in March 1986.) Some of the difficult words and expressions are given below. Look up the ones you don't know before you listen, or try to guess their meanings while you listen, as you prefer.

FIRST ITEM
overwhelmingly   reject   proposal   major
in isolation   maintain

SECOND ITEM
unrest   mining   district   injured
funerals   alleged

THIRD ITEM
equipment   painting   mess   halt   album

FOURTH ITEM
damage   estimated   flames   swept
in the region of   dustbin   hurled
newsagents   the scene

FIFTH ITEM
emergency   vehicle

SIXTH ITEM
collapsed   rescue   crawl   gap   concrete
rubble   basement   high-pressure   water jet
project

SEVENTH ITEM
drizzle   Celsius   Fahrenheit   southerly
moderate   overcast

3 Choose one of the items and listen again two or three times. Write down as much as you can of the text. Then work with one or two other students and see if you can get the whole of the text.

4 Choose some words and expressions from the news items to learn. Discuss your choices with other students.

5 Pronunciation. You will hear some extracts from the news broadcasts. Listen particularly to the phrases below. Notice how the ends of the words are pronounced, and how one word is joined to the next. Then say the phrases yourselves.

government proposals
wanted Switzerland to become
preferred to keep
have smashed their way
best known for his song
left by the raiders
he's had to halt work
last night
flames swept through a garage
a dustbin was hurled through the front window
police were called to the scene
a cloudy start to the day
sunshine in most parts
top temperatures
rain and drizzle

6 Work in small groups. Make up short news broadcasts about things (real or imaginary) that have happened in your school, town or country. Use some words and expressions that you have learnt in this lesson. Practise, and then read your news broadcast to the class.

Study the Lesson Summary at the back of the book.
Do some of the Practice Book exercises.

Fears

A The Lonely One

1 Look at the map and pictures. Three single women, Lavinia, Helen and Francine, went out on the evening of July 20, 1928. At some time that evening, some or all of them were: at Lavinia's house, at Helen's house, at Francine's house, in the ravine, at the cinema, at the drugstore. Work in groups to find out as much as you can about their movements that evening, and about the Lonely One.

– Write to the teacher, asking five questions.
– When you get your answers from the teacher, compare them with another group's. Did the other group find out anything you didn't?
– Each group can then ask another five questions. Don't waste your questions: listen to what the other groups ask.

2 You will hear five recordings of people from the story. Who is speaking in each recording? Where does each recording happen?

3 Grammar revision. Here are some sentences from the story. Can you choose the correct verb form in each sentence? Can you give a grammar rule for each sentence or group of sentences?

1. Maybe we shouldn't *go* / *to go* to the show tonight.
2. The Lonely One might *follow* / *to follow* us and *kill* / *to kill* us.
3. Logically, the Lonely One can't *be* / *to be* around.

4. *To think* / *Thinking* about the Lonely One terrified Francine.

5. Francine wanted Lavinia *spend* / *to spend* the night with her.
6. Lavinia told Francine not *be* / *to be* silly.
7. The police asked the cinema manager *close* / *to close* early that night.

8. Lavinia laughed at Francine for *to be* / *being* so afraid.
9. Lavinia couldn't get home from Main Street without *to cross* / *crossing* the ravine.

10. Before they went to the cinema, the three women stopped at the drugstore to get something *eat* / *to eat* / *eating*.
11. Helen didn't have anything *drink* / *to drink* / *drinking* at the drugstore.
12. There was no one *walk* / *to walk* Lavinia home.

4 Look at these sentences.

As Lavinia was walking towards the ravine, she heard a dog bark in the distance.
As she started across the bridge, Lavinia heard someone walking behind her.

Why do you think *bark* is used in the first sentence and *walking* in the second? Work in groups and try to suggest a rule. Check your rule against the following sentences; if it works, make four more sentences about what people saw, watched, heard, or felt in the story. You can use your imagination. If your rule doesn't work, try again or ask your teacher for help.

The stranger saw Lavinia open her purse to pay for the chocolate soda.
Francine saw a man leaning against a wall smoking a cigarette.

5 Which sentences do you hear?

1. It'll be you alone on the path.
2. It'd be you alone on the path.
3. I thought, My God, what have I done!
4. I thought, My God, what had I done!
5. The show would be over at eleven.
6. The show will be over at eleven.
7. I make hot chocolate.
8. I'll make hot chocolate.
9. I promise I'll phone.
10. I promised I'd phone.

6 What do you think happens next in the story of the Lonely One? Work in groups to write ten or more sentences to end the story.

7 Read the text on page 154 to see how the original author (Ray Bradbury) ended the story.

Study the Lesson Summary at the back of the book.
Do some of the Practice Book exercises.

B I was terrified

Listening comprehension; vocabulary; discussion.

1 What were you frightened of as a child? Help your teacher make a list of common childhood fears. Then show how you felt about a few of them by moving to a place in the room: start with fear of the dark, and if you were terrified of the dark stand at the front of the room; if the dark didn't bother you at all stand at the back of the room; if you were a little bothered by it stand almost at the back of the room, and so on.

2 Listen to a six-year-old talking about his fears. Which things in the box is he afraid of?

big dogs	the dark	flying
ghosts	lions	machines
snakes	spiders	tigers

3 Make sure you know the meanings of the words and phrases in the box. Then read the sentences with help from your teacher or a dictionary. Which fear do you think each person is talking about? Listen to the tape to see if you were right.

agoraphobia	claustrophobia	fear of birds
fear of flying	fear of heights	fear of mice
fear of snakes	fear of spiders	phobia

JEANETTE CABELDU
'I couldn't bear to live in the house with it.'
'I couldn't face going in the room where I knew the ∗∗∗ had been.'
'It's, it's totally irrational, but – I hate ∗∗∗.'

TONY ROBINSON
'And it was a fear that I hadn't been a-, able to admit to myself, but had to then.'
'On the ground it wouldn't have been terrifying, but ∗∗∗ there it was terrifying.'
'But I was terrified, I couldn't move, and I was clutching at, clutching at grass.'

H. A. SWAN
'I went on a ∗∗∗ for the first time erm, when I was about in my, my late twenties, and then for ten years I couldn't get on another one at all.'
'It's sheer blind panic, and the physical symptoms are you shake, you, hands are damp, erm, you can't breathe properly, erm.'

FRAN SEARSON
'I always thought I was going to be sick.'
'I never was; but to get on a train or be with strangers, and I used to just freeze up.'
'But then I overcame that, and I was fairly, you know, outgoing.'
'. . . if somebody said "How are you?", I'd burst into tears.'

MARILYN NORVELL
'I don't go in lifts at all. There is noth-, nobody could get me into a lift.'
'I also don't like being in a room er, without seeing an exit.'
'I don't have any fear of any animals or spiders or water or flying, but I find that terrifying.'

4 Vocabulary exploration. Look back at Exercises 1–3, or use your dictionary, to help you answer the questions.

1. Copy the list below, and:
   – circle the word which is the strongest
   – put a square around the word which is the weakest
   – of the words which are left, if there is one that is stronger than the others, underline it.

afraid   bothered   frightened   scared   terrified

2. Look at the words and expressions in the box below. Find:
   – four expressions that describe what happens when people are frightened
   – two verbs that mean the same
   – one word that can be used as a noun or a verb
   – a word that describes what all phobias are
   – a verb that says what most people would like to do about their phobias.

afraid (of)   agoraphobia   be sick
bother   burst into tears   can't bear
can't breathe properly   can't face
claustrophobia   fear (of)   freeze up
frighten   hands get damp   heights
irrational   overcome   panic   scare
shake   snakes   spiders   terrify

3. In groups of two or three, make 'Find . . . ' questions for some of the words in the box and try them on other groups.

5 Read the text and fill in the blanks with some of the words and expressions from the box in Exercise 4. Compare your answers with another student's. You may have to make some small changes, and sometimes more than one word or expression may be appropriate for a blank.

I'm not afraid of very many things: snakes and .... don't .... me; I have no fear of ...., even on very high mountains, and I'm not .... of most animals. But I do suffer from .... I am just .... of small closed spaces. I used to be much worse; I have .... the fear to some extent, and now I can take lifts or ride a crowded underground train with only a little discomfort. But last winter when our water pipes in the attic froze, I just .... crawling up into the narrow roof space to melt the ice with a hair dryer. I tried for a few minutes, but then I just .... My hands got damp, I ...., and I'm sure if I had stayed in there I would have started screaming. I know it's ...., and I'd really rather not be this way, but I don't think I'm going to get much better.

6 In groups of three or four, make up a short scene about a phobia. Act it out for the rest of the class and see if they can guess what the phobia is.

Study the Lesson Summary at the back of the book. Do some of the Practice Book exercises.

"Fear? He doesn't know the meaning of the word!"

Politics

A Labour and Conservative

Listening practice; summary writing; vocabulary work; reading practice; discussion.

Robert Jackson

Clare Short

1 You will hear two Members of Parliament, Clare Short and Robert Jackson, answering some of the following questions, but not in order. Listen, and decide which questions they are answering. Write down the letters of the questions next to the numbers you hear. Be careful: there is one extra question.

a. What made you decide to go into politics?
b. Have you got a job outside Parliament?
c. What is the most enjoyable or satisfactory part of your job?
d. What's the least enjoyable or least satisfactory part of your job?
e. What do you hope to achieve in your present term in Parliament?

2 Make sure you understand the words and expressions in the box. Then listen to the two politicians again, and make a one-line summary of each answer.

> brewing   candidate   career
> catch (my) fancy   civil servant   civil service
> constituency   get rid of
> House of Commons   issue   lawyer
> neutral   represent   response   strain
> superficiality   worthwhile

3 Work in groups. Decide which of the two people you have heard is a member of the Labour Party and which is a member of the Conservative Party. Be ready to give reasons for your answer.

4 We asked Robert Jackson and Clare Short, 'What are the most important qualities for a successful politician – one who gets to the top?' Each mentioned three or more qualities. Look at the list below and try to guess who chose what. Then read their answers and see if you were right.

ability to make decisions quickly
ability to organise people
belief in things they're working for
clarity
energy
intelligence
openness
physical attractiveness
relationship with people that elect them
sensitivity

ROBERT JACKSON

Well, I think the most important quality is energy; er, I think particularly in the British political system. We have a parliamentary system which is intensely demanding on the physical and nervous energies of the top people. Parliament sits for much longer each year than do the parliaments of other countries, er, around the world. Er, ministers are expected to take part in debates, face questions – on an everyday basis. And so a senior minister not only has all the stress and strain of the work of his department, and er, obviously in government departments now we're dealing with enormous numbers of people, large sums of money, very important issues; but also he has the stress and strain of maintaining his position, maintaining his, his face, his status, in Parliament. And so I think the main quality is energy. I would say the next quality is intellect. Erm, there's a, a great many intellectual demands involved in this kind of life, and I think people have got to have the intellectual capacity to cope with the issues. Erm, I think a third quality which is important is sensitivity and responsiveness. You have to be able to sense the way in which people are thinking and moving, the way in which their views, their beliefs, their ideas, their aspirations, their hopes are evolving, er, so that you can respond to that evolution. This is absolutely necessary in a democracy; that's the way in which democracy works. Erm, but it's also necessary for political survival and for political success.

CLARE SHORT

Well, I don't kn–, I think there are different qualities that take people to the top. I personally think the most important qualities for a, a good politician, which might not mean the same thing, is to sincerely believe in the things that they're working for; to really have some relationship with and care about the people that elect them; 'cause that's the learning base. I mean, it's what's happening to people that should shape erm, everything you stand for. And then to speak up clearly and openly and not kind of calculate personal advantage. Erm, I think that's the best formula; and I think it makes you very strong, 'cause you're not sort of trying to plot things or think of what will go down with whom. But I think, you know, like in any institution, people rise to the top through all sorts of devious means; and maybe some honest straightforward people rise to the top, but there are others who are creeps who rise to the top, and who calculate to keep in with the powers that be at any given moment.

Have you got to be intelligent?

Well, I think it depends what the word 'intelligent' means. I, er, really think that all human beings are capable of being intelligent and all human beings are capable of being stupid. It isn't this notion like IQ, you've either got it or you haven't, it's whether people face up honestly to questions, think about the problems and look honestly for the facts that will help to explain them. Erm, and if intelligence is interpreted in that way, then yes, I would agree.

5 Work in groups of four or five. Each group member must take responsibility for the discussion of one question, and make sure that everyone else expresses an opinion on it.

1. Which of the two politicians in this lesson do you feel the most sympathy for? Why?
2. What do you think are the two or three most important qualities for a successful politician?
3. Do you think politicians should have jobs other than their political jobs?
4. Do you think politicians should vote the way their party expects them to vote, even if their own opinion is different?
5. Should Members of Parliament be paid more or less than: doctors, heads of universities, senior executives in industry?

HOUSE OF COMMONS
LONDON SWIA OAA

Study the Lesson Summary at the back of the book.
Do some of the Practice Book exercises.

B Neither left nor right

1 We talked to three people who don't believe in traditional politics. Read what they said; try to fill in the blanks with words from the boxes.

RICHARD LAWSON
(doctor, Green Party member, local councillor)

administer	economics	economy
environment	philosophy	right values

We in the Greens say we're neither left nor .... but in front. We go right back to the root of the problem in our .... And the problem as I see it is first that erm, everything is, all values are monetary ....; that .... is about money, erm, and market values. So we say, no, look at that economy and what is .... about, and what is ecology about, and you see that they are sis-, they have to be sister disciplines. Economy, eco-nomy, means our administration of our habitat, of the world, the ...., and eco-logy means the study of the environment. So how can you .... something if you don't know what it's about?

NICK GREGOR
(therapist, ex-prisoner)

choices	decisions	extreme	individual
Labour	left-wingers	politics	
right-wingers			

I do believe that the trouble with the .... and Conservative thing is that we've got two extremes. And I think, you know, some of these .... left-wingers are just as bad as the extreme .... You've got the extreme .... saying, you know, 'The Conservatives are too dictatorial', and, you know, 'They're pushing people around and people don't have ....' But at the same time these left-wingers are saying 'This is what people want.' And I'm a, I'm a firm believer in rather than changing people's environment, looking at the ...., and then the individual can make their own choices about their own environment. They don't need people running around for them and telling them what they want. So I, I think .... for me is about giving people real choices to make .... for themselves.

GEORGE MELLY
(jazz singer, writer)

impractical	political	politicians	relied
responsible	weapons	world	

Are you interested in politics at all?

I hate them. I mean, interested in them in that they affect one. But I really detest politics and .... When I was young I called myself an anarchist, because I believed that politics was .... for most of the dreadful things that go on in the world, and that if we .... more on ourselves as individuals and on self-help and the help of others without a .... structure, it would be a better .... People say that is ....; but one looks around at er, at leaking atomic bases and at er, the endless build-up of .... and wonders what sort of impractical it would be!

"And above all, madam, my party is endeavouring to bring honesty back into politics."

2 How do *you* feel about politics and politicians? Write two to four sentences. You can use words and expressions from Exercise 1. The teacher will read out students' sentences and you can try to guess who wrote what.

3 Listen, and notice how the words are linked in the first three phrases. Then try to pronounce the following phrases, linking where necessary.

1. our administration of the environment
2. just as bad as the extreme right-wingers
3. most of the dreadful things that go on in the world
4. the problem as I see it
5. we've got two extremes
6. I'm a firm believer in looking at the individual
7. the individual can make their own choices about their own environment
8. interested in them in that they affect one
9. if we relied more on ourselves as individuals

"What's the Government trying to do – run the country?"

4 Here are two political speeches from the country of Fantasia. Work in groups to guess which words go in the blanks, and then listen to the recording to see if you were right.

Take a deep breath. Can you .... the exhaust fumes? Listen quietly for a moment. You should be .... birdsong, not brakes and horns. Look at the historic buildings all around us. .... how their stone is being blackened and eaten away? And unless something is done about it quickly, it's not going to get ....; it's only going to get worse.

There is only one answer, and the Fantasian Pedestrians' Party has it: ban all .... If you .... us, we will change your lives. Silent electric trams will take you to your .... and shopping. The streets will be clean, the air will be .... Your children will be safe walking home from .... There will be no more car accidents, so our national medical bill will go .... dramatically. With no more oil ...., our currency will be strong, and inflation will stop.

The Fantasian Pedestrians' Party will give you all this and more. So take the big step – vote for the FPP.

Fantasians! Can you face a challenge? Are you ready for the twenty-first ....? Are you willing to show the courage that has made our .... nation great? Why should the superpowers be the only ones to create the humans of the future? Vote for the Fantasian Nuclear Party and we will build a new .... power station every month, guaranteed to leak radioactive gases. Your grandchildren will not .... much like you – a few more eyes perhaps, the odd extra ....; but our country will remain a great .... power. There will be no place at the conference tables of the future for the humans of the .... Don't let Fantasia become a third-rate country. Mutate and be great – .... for the FNP.

5 In groups, invent a political party and write a campaign speech for it. Choose one person to give the speech and help him or her practise it. Listen to the other groups' speeches; then vote for the party of your choice.

Study the Lesson Summary at the back of the book. Do some of the Practice Book exercises.

Schooldays

Listening comprehension; vocabulary; discussion.

A I don't like playtime 'cause it's cold outside all the time sometimes

1 Can you think of at least ten different subjects or activities that you did at primary school? (Ask the teacher if you don't know the English names.) Which ones did you like, and which did you dislike?

2 Listen to the recording. Do the children mention any things that are not on your list?

3 Listen to the next part of the recording. What eight things do the children say they dislike?

4 Now you are going to hear the children saying what they like about their teacher, Mrs Cabeldu. Can you guess what they will say? Listen and see if you were right.

Mrs Cabeldu by Anita Bryon, age 5½

5 Vocabulary and dictionary use.

1. Which of these words can be used to describe typical primary schoolchildren, in your opinion? If necessary, use your dictionary to check the exact meanings.

> careful   constructive   co-operative
> critical   disciplined   enthusiastic
> happy   patient   respectful   sensitive

2. The opposite of *happy* is *unhappy*. You can change the other words to their opposites by using *un-*, *in-*, *im-*, *dis-* or *-less*. Use your dictionary to find out which is correct.

3. Which of the opposites do you think could be used to describe typical teenage schoolchildren?

6 These sentences are taken from a conversation with some teenagers about school. Listen to the recording: which four sentences do you *not* hear?

1. If you don't understand it then some teachers don't explain anything.
2. Nobody ever listens to them.
3. They're not fair.
4. They think that they're teaching, you know, but they ain't.
5. Blow it up.
6. They give you too much work to do.
7. It's a dump.
8. Some of the teachers there still treat you like a little kid.
9. They keep on at you for not doing your homework.
10. Most of the time the teachers are on strike anyway.
11. There's no point in going to school.
12. I'd keep school down to one day a week – or private lessons at home.
13. He asks you what you think, but he never listens to the answers.
14. She can't explain anything to you.
15. She can't teach . . . she can't do things: she's useless.

DO EITHER EXERCISE 7 OR EXERCISE 8.

7 Make a list of the subjects that you studied (or are studying) at school, with the ones you think are most useful at the top and the ones you think are least useful at the bottom. Use a dictionary or ask the teacher for help if necessary. Write *I* against the subjects you found (or find) interesting, and write *B* against the boring ones. Then work in small groups and discuss your lists. Which are the most and least popular school subjects?

8 Work in groups. Each group is a committee, which has to work out a plan for secondary education reform. Write a list of the changes that you would like to make. You may want to consider some of the following:

subjects
organisation of the school day
size of classes
examinations
teacher training
teacher–pupil relationships
the aims of secondary education

Study the Lesson Summary at the back of the book. Do some of the Practice Book exercises.

B Should children have more freedom?

Vocabulary; grammar (past and perfect tenses; *let* and *make*);
pronunciation; language of discussion.

*"Oh, by the way . . .
according to my
teacher I'm
suffering from a
lack of discipline
in the home. See to
it, will you . . . ?"*

*"Girls, girls! – A little less noise,
please."*

1 Vocabulary revision. Use these words and expressions to help
you complete the text. You may need to make some small changes.
If necessary, look back at Lesson 15A to see what they mean and
how they are used.

critical	each	enthusiastic	examination	explain
fair	job	least	on strike	no point in . . .ing
patient	popular	private	size	subject
unco-operative	useless			

Caroline's favourite .... at school was maths: she enjoyed
solving problems, and was .... about the teaching methods.
But most of her friends tended to find maths very difficult, and
because they thought it was a .... subject they saw no ....
in working at it, and were .... and .... in the lessons.
Maths was, in fact, the .... subject in Caroline's class.
    During Caroline's last year at school the teachers went ....
for two months, to protest against the .... of classes (30–35
was typical). .... morning, Caroline gave .... maths
lessons to three of her friends, so that they would have a chance of
passing their .... She's ...., and good at .... things to
people, and the lessons went well: Caroline and her three friends all
passed. They offered to pay her for the lessons, but she refused: she
sympathised with the teachers' strike, and did not think it would be
.... if she took money for doing their ....

2 Grammar. Simple past or
present perfect progressive?

1. Paul is 14. Alice is 50. Which of
them do you think probably
said each of these sentences?
Why?

 – 'I did English at school for
 three years.'
 – 'I've been doing maths at
 school for seven years.'
 – 'I've been doing chemistry for
 a year.'
 – 'I didn't do physics at school.'
 – 'I've been going to school for
 eight years.'
 – 'I went to school for eight
 years.'

2. Ask other students (or the
teacher) two questions
beginning *How long have you
been studying . . . ?* and two
questions beginning *How long
did you study . . . ?*
Before you start, practise the
pronunciation of *How long
have you been studying . . . ?*

3 Grammar. Look at the examples to see how *let* and *make* are used. Then say:

a. what your parents let you do when you were small.

b. what your parents made you do when you were small.

c. what you will let (let/would let) your children do.

d. what you will make (make/made/would make) your children do.

Examples:

'She lets us do anything we like.'
'My parents never made me help with the housework.'

4 Pronunciation. These words all have the letter *e* in the first syllable. They are divided into two groups. Can you see why? Can you pronounce them?

depend   enthusiastic
examination   explain   prepare

definite   educate   enter
expert

5 Here are some expressions which are often used in discussions. Do you know what they mean and how to pronounce them?

Definitely.
Certainly.
Of course.
Do you think . . . ?
Yes, I do.
I certainly do.
I agree.
Yes, I think so.
I'm not sure.
It depends.
What do you mean by . . . ?
I suppose so.
I don't know.
Perhaps.
I don't think so.
I don't agree.
Definitely not.
Certainly not.
Of course not.

6 Say what you think about some of the following questions. Use a dictionary or ask for help if necessary.

1. Do schools do a good job of preparing people for life? Should education be more practical?
2. Should all children have to learn maths?
3. Should all children have to learn English?
4. Should all education be free?
5. Should teachers be paid more?
6. Who should be paid most – the teachers of small children or the teachers of older children?
7. Should school classes be smaller?
8. Should children have more freedom at home and at school? Or do children have too much freedom these days?
9. At what age should children be free to leave school?
10. At what age should children be free to make their own decisions about smoking, drinking, drugs, sex etc.?
11. Is it ever right to smack a child?
12. Should parents let small children watch violent films and cartoons on TV?
13. Should boys have more freedom than girls?
14. Which is more important – a good upbringing or a good education?

7 Work in groups of three or four. Choose one of the following problems and try to agree on a solution.

1. Anna is sixteen. She is working at a children's holiday camp, and is in charge of a group of eight-year-olds. One of the children in her group comes to her and says that all his money has been stolen. It was probably taken by one of the children in the group. What should Anna do?

2. Carol is six. She wants to watch a violent TV serial. Her parents say that she can't watch it, because they think it will give her nightmares. Carol cries, and says that all her friends watch it. What should the parents do?

3. John is fifteen. He goes out one Saturday night and comes back drunk. What, if anything, should his parents do about it?

4. Jilly is seventeen. She finds out that she is pregnant. She has a very warm and loving relationship with her parents, and they have always trusted her. But she knows that if she tells them, it will be a terrible shock to them, and they will probably not understand. Should she tell them or not?

Study the Lesson Summary at the back of the book.
Do some of the Practice Book exercises.

Places

A Australia

Listening comprehension; vocabulary (describing places); speaking practice.

1 How much (or how little) do you know about Australia? Close your books, and see how many facts you can write down in exactly three minutes.

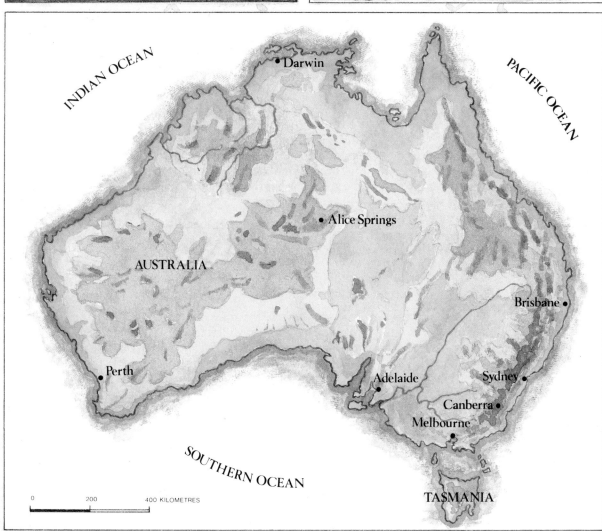

INDIAN OCEAN

• Darwin

PACIFIC OCEAN

• Alice Springs

AUSTRALIA

Brisbane •

• Perth

Adelaide •

Sydney •

Canberra •

Melbourne •

SOUTHERN OCEAN

0   200   400 KILOMETRES

TASMANIA

2 You are going to hear a discussion about Australia between three people: Annemarie and Tony (two Australians living in Britain), and an American interviewer. The complete discussion lasts for several minutes. You will not follow everything, but if you listen carefully you should understand most of the main ideas. Some of the difficult words are in the box below – have a look at these before you start. Then choose one or more of the next three exercises. Exercise 3 is easy, Exercise 4 is moderately difficult, and Exercise 5 is difficult.

bother	climate	coast	culture	desert	desire
direct	environment	harsh	interior	physical	
push	space	subtropical	vegetation	Wales	Welsh

3 Listen to the first half of the discussion only, up to the words 'They don't talk to one another, do they?' Which of the following places and things are mentioned?

Sydney	plants	gold mines
fishing	kangaroos	Perth
small towns	mountains	Melbourne
light	snow	
Adelaide	New South Wales	

4 Listen to the whole of the discussion, and see how many of these questions you can answer.

1. Why does Tony like Sydney?
2. Does Annemarie like big cities?
3. What does she feel about small towns in Australia?
4. Where can you ski in Australia?
5. Where did Tony first see snow? When?
6. What city does Tony say he has never been to in Australia?
7. How far is it from his home in Sydney?
8. What expression do people in Perth use when they are talking about the rest of Australia?
9. Why?
10. How do Australians talk, according to Tony?
11. Annemarie and Tony don't like the English climate because there isn't enough – what?
12. Do Australians stand closer to each other when talking than British people, or not? Why?
13. What do Australia and Russia have in common?
14. Who finds British 'lack of push' and 'lack of desire' more depressing – Annemarie or Tony?
15. Does Tony like living in Britain?

5 Listen to the discussion and take notes. Then give short answers to the following questions:

1. What different kinds of landscape are there in Australia?
2. What differences between Australia and Britain are mentioned in the discussion?
3. What differences between Australian and British people are mentioned?

6 Work with two or three other students. Choose one of the following subjects, and talk about it for at least two minutes to the other people in your group.

1. What do you like about your country, and the place where you live? What do you dislike? Why?
2. Compare two different places that you know well.
3. Talk about a place that you like very much.

Study the Lesson Summary at the back of the book.
Do some of the Practice Book exercises.

B A beautiful place

Reading comprehension; vocabulary (describing places); grammar (past perfect); writing descriptions.

1 Read the text and look at the pictures. Which place do you think is described in each section?

EXTRACTS FROM THE REPORT OF ZARGON, A SPACE EXPLORER, WRITTEN IN THE YEAR 2050

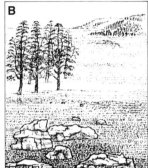

1

As I approached the planet, my thermoanalytic detectors told me that there was a great variety of plant life, but no animal life at all. In my three hundred years of space exploration, I had never before come across a world where there were no animals. It was so strange that I wondered whether something had happened – some war or natural disaster which had killed off all animal life on the planet . . .

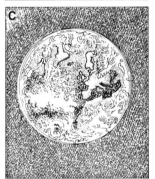

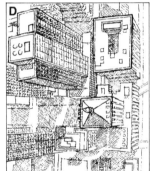

2

I made my first landing on soft ground near a group of red rocks. As soon as I had tested the atmosphere, I stepped out and began to look round. In front of me there were large plants, on which grew a kind of fruit like none that I had ever seen before. On my left, not far away, the ground rose gently to some low hills. On my right and behind me the ground was level, stretching away into the distance. It was an impressive but monotonous landscape . . .

3

After I had rested and written my report I flew to another part of the planet. Detecting a high level of radioactivity, I did not land; but I flew over the area several times. It was a place of deep valleys with vertical walls; in them regular square or rectangular openings had been made, whose purpose I was not able to guess. There was little vegetation, but my instruments showed a good deal of metal. Not far away there was a great expanse of water containing various chemicals . . .

4

It was impossible to see very far, and movement was very difficult. I could tell that many different kinds of animals had lived here, and I collected some bones in the hope that our analysts would be able to find out what had killed them . . .

5

The temperature was very low, and the oxygen thin. There were few plants, and those I found were small. In front, the horizon was very close; behind, I could see for a long way. Far below, a stretch of water shone in the sun. It was a beautiful place, and I was sorry to leave. But my time had run out, and I had to return to Rozul . . .

(Translation copyright Swan and Walter)

2 Grammar. Choose the right tense (simple past or past perfect).

1. When I was a child, I (*often dreamed*/*had often dreamed*) of being a space explorer.
2. When I was 25 I (*applied*/*had applied*) for a place at the space training academy.
3. I will never forget the day when the Principal (*told*/*had told*) me that I (*passed*/*had passed*) my final exams.
4. On my first mission, I (*went*/*had gone*) to visit a small planet in star system 18B.
5. The planet (*stopped*/*had stopped*) sending out radio signals some months before, and my orders were to find out what (*happened*/*had happened*).
6. It was early morning when I landed. As soon as I (*found*/*had found*) somewhere to leave the space-ship, I (*started*/*had started*) to explore the surrounding countryside.
7. There was no sign of life, and I (*wondered*/*had wondered*) what (*happened*/*had happened*) to the people.
8. I (*found*/*had found*) several kinds of plant that I (*never saw*/*had never seen*) before.
9. Not far from my landing place, I (*discovered*/*had discovered*) a small house.
10. It was in a very poor condition; obviously nobody (*lived*/*had lived*) there for years.
11. Suddenly I (*heard*/*had heard*) a footstep, and a woman (*appeared*/*had appeared*) from behind the house.
12. I asked her what (*happened*/*had happened*), but she (*just looked*/*had just looked*) at me with a strange smile.

3 Vocabulary: describing places. As quickly as you can, write down:

1. something that is on your right
2. something that is on your left
3. something that is in front of you
4. something that is behind you
5. something that is in front of the building where you are now
6. something that is opposite the building where you are now
7. something that is a long way away
8. something that is not far away
9. something that is very close
10. something that you can see that is level
11. something you can see that is not level
12. something you can see that is square
13. something you can see that is rectangular
14. something you can see that is round
15. something you can see that is oval
16. something you can see that is vertical
17. something you can see that is horizontal
18. something that is directly above your head
19. something that is high above you
20. something that is far below you

4 Pronunciation. Listen to the sentences. You will hear either a present perfect, a past perfect or a simple past verb (for example *I've heard*, *I'd heard* or *I heard*). Write down the verbs that you hear.

5 Work individually or with other students, as you prefer. Write a paragraph from a space explorer's report (like Exercise 1), about a well-known place. Show your paragraph to other students and see if they can guess where it is. Use some of the words and expressions from Exercise 3, and some of the structures in the box. Include some examples of the past perfect tense.

| in front (of me) |
| on my left/right |
| behind (me) |
| high above |
| far below |
| in(to) the distance |
| not far (away) |
| a long way (away) |
| I could see |
| There was/were |
| I had never . . . |
| I wondered whether . . . |
| As soon as I had . . . |

6 Listen to the song. (The text is on page 154.)

Study the Lesson Summary at the back of the book. Do some of the Practice Book exercises.

Getting things done

A Coffee, toothpaste and pencils

1 Read the three texts. In each text, two sentences have been added which should not be there. How quickly can you find them?

INSTANT COFFEE

When coffee arrives at an instant coffee factory, it has already been roasted and ground. In the factory, water is slowly passed through the coffee. The resulting liquid is then repeatedly pumped through tubes at a very high temperature and pressure. The liquid is boiled, and sugar, salt and a variety of chemicals are carefully added. This makes some of the water evaporate, leaving very strong 'coffee liquor'.

To make instant coffee powder, the coffee liquor is poured through large cylindrical driers at a temperature of 250°C. The heat evaporates the liquid, leaving instant coffee powder which is collected and put into jars.

Granulated coffee is made by freeze-drying. The process is a secret one, and is passed from one family of manufacturers to the next. The coffee liquor is rapidly frozen into blocks. After these have been broken up into very small pieces, they are dried in a vacuum. This removes the water without heat, leaving instant coffee granules.

STRIPED TOOTHPASTE

How are the stripes put into striped toothpaste? The toothpaste is not striped when it is put into the tube, as some people imagine. At the factory, red paste and white paste are put into the tube separately, with the red paste completely filling the part near the cap. This has several different effects. A short hollow pipe is also put into the toothpaste tube. When the toothpaste tube is squeezed, the white paste is pushed down the inside of the small pipe, while the red paste is pushed into five grooves on the outside. Compressed air is then pumped between the two 'skins', forcing the water out and making it lighter. In this way, strips of red paste are mixed into the white paste as it comes out of the tube.

PENCIL LEAD

A well-made pencil looks like a single piece of wood, but actually it is made from two pieces of wood which have been carefully glued together. The manufacturing process is the same as that used for making plastic telephone receivers. Strips of wood are sent through a machine which cuts grooves in them. Pencil lead, which is made from graphite, clay, water and wax, is cut into lengths and inserted into the grooves in one strip. A second strip is put on top of the first so that the grooves meet, with the lead inside, and the strips are glued together. They are then cut and shaped into separate pencils. These are packed up and sent to all the company's staff.

2 Pronunciation. How many different ways are there to pronounce -ed at the end of a verb? Look at the following words, listen to the recording if you wish, and try to work out the rules.

added   boiled   collected   compressed
dried   glued   inserted   mixed   packed
passed   poured   pumped   pushed
removed   roasted   shaped   squeezed
striped

3 Grammar: present progressive passive. Look at the picture. It shows a busy hotel kitchen at 11 a.m. Can you say some of the things that *are being done*? Examples:

'Coffee is being made.'
'Vegetables are being prepared.'

Can you suggest things that are being done in other parts of the hotel?

4 Grammar: present perfect passive. Imagine that the following newspaper report is about a town or city that you know well. Read the report, and then make up two or three sentences which could appear in the next paragraph, to say what *has been done* to put things right after the disaster. Use the words in the box to help you.

clear away (re)build (re)connect remove repair replant

A few months ago, this town was a smoking ruin. In the volcanic eruption of June 17, most of the houses were badly damaged. The Town Hall, the railway station and a number of other public buildings were completely destroyed. The central library was burnt down, with the loss of all the books. Electricity, gas and water supplies were cut off, and the railway line was buried under tons of rock and earth. Roads and open spaces were covered under 20 cm of volcanic ash.

Today, the transformation seems miraculous. The town has been completely restored. A new concrete and glass Town Hall, several times as large as the old one, has been put up in the central square.

FARMERS

5 Grammar: *can* + passive infinitive. Work in groups. How many ways can you find of using the following things? Examples:

'*A coin can be used as a screwdriver.*'
'*A bath can be used to hold drink for a party.*'

a bicycle   a bra   a car   a chair an English textbook   a fridge   a glass a lampshade   a sheet   an umbrella

6 Imagine that you are writing a letter to a visitor from another planet. He/she/it understands English, but knows very little about our world. Write a paragraph explaining (very briefly) one of the following things. Use your dictionary, or ask the teacher for vocabulary, if necessary. When you have finished, exchange letters with another student. Now imagine that you are the visitor. Read the letter you have received, and write three or more questions asking for more information.

How a house is built.
How coffee or tea is made.
How glass is manufactured.
How a table is made.
How a woollen sweater is made.

Study the Lesson Summary at the back of the book. Do some of the Practice Book exercises.

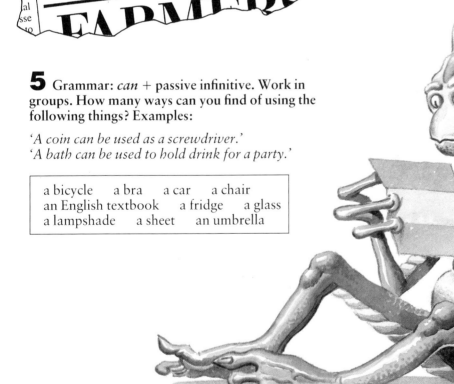

Instructions, explanations and suggestions; *do* and *make*; grammar (position of adverbs); listening comprehension; speaking practice.

B Make it yourself

1 Here are the things that are needed to make a kind of food. Work in groups: see if you can guess what kind of food it is, and how to cook it.

garlic
onions
herbs
tomatoes
salt
pepper
butter, margarine or oil
water

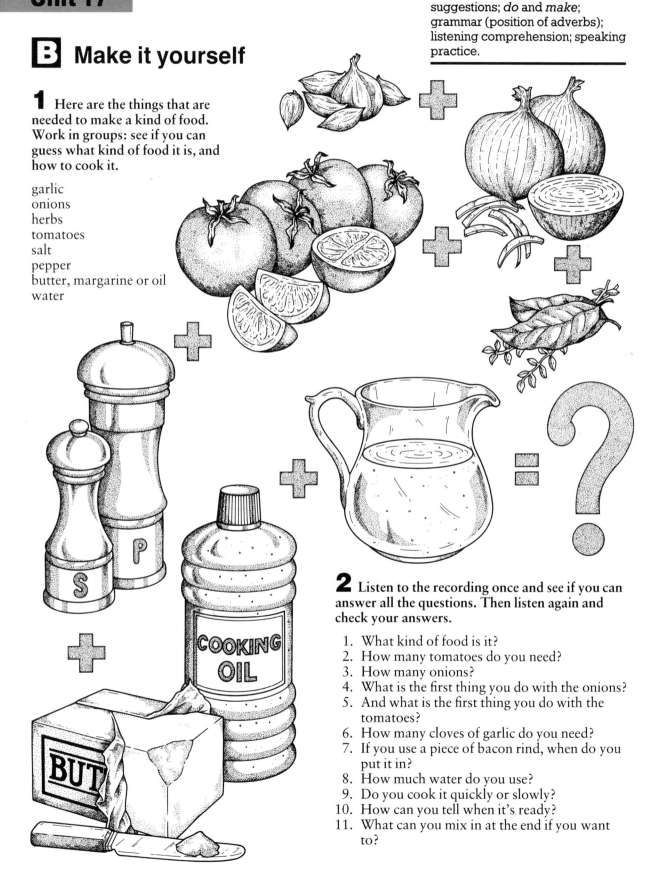

2 Listen to the recording once and see if you can answer all the questions. Then listen again and check your answers.

1. What kind of food is it?
2. How many tomatoes do you need?
3. How many onions?
4. What is the first thing you do with the onions?
5. And what is the first thing you do with the tomatoes?
6. How many cloves of garlic do you need?
7. If you use a piece of bacon rind, when do you put it in?
8. How much water do you use?
9. Do you cook it quickly or slowly?
10. How can you tell when it's ready?
11. What can you mix in at the end if you want to?

3 Vocabulary. Do you know when to use *do* and when to use *make*? Look at the examples and see if you can find a rule.

Why not **make** your own vegetable soup?
In his spare time he **makes** wooden toys for his children.
I've got too much work to **do**.
I've just **done** something very stupid.

4 Put in *do/does/did* or *make/makes/made*.

1. Do you ever .... your own bread?
2. The first thing to .... is to cut up the onions.
3. Don't just stand there – .... something!
4. She .... all her own clothes.
5. I .... no work at all yesterday.
6. It's really boring to .... housework all day.
7. We need to .... a plan for the holidays.
8. Can I .... a phone call from your office?
9. The children have to .... their own beds in the morning.
10. A person who never .... a mistake never .... anything.

5 Grammar. Can you put adverbs in the right places? Put one of these adverbs into each sentence.

badly	carefully	gently	quickly
slowly	thoroughly	well	

1. Stir the soup.
2. Please check your ticket.
3. He speaks French.
4. She washed the plates.
5. I read the letter.
6. He picked up the child.
7. The coffee is passed through pipes at high pressure.
8. The liquid is frozen.
9. Everything is dried before being packed.
10. My car was damaged in a crash last week.
11. The kitchen needs to be cleaned.

6 Imagine that you have to explain how to do one of the following things, to somebody who doesn't know what to do. Prepare an explanation, using some of the expressions in the box. Look in a dictionary or ask the teacher if you need other vocabulary. When you are ready, work with three or four other students and give them your explanation.

How to cook something (you choose what).
How to drive a car.
How to change a wheel on a car.
How to change a fuse.
How to make a paper aeroplane or hat.
How to plant bulbs, or some other kind of flower.
How to get a passport.
How to play a card game or other game.

Why not . . . ? You need . . . The first/next/last thing to do is to . . . Then you . . . I usually . . . If . . . , you can always . . . You *must* have . . . When you've done that, . . . OK. So you . . . Sorry – I should have said. You . . . You might like to . . . Keep . . .ing. It's best if you . . . You know what I mean? You can . . . , but I don't bother.

Study the Lesson Summary at the back of the book.
Do some of the Practice Book exercises.

Needs

A People going hungry

Listening comprehension; discussion; vocabulary.

1 Work in groups of four or five to decide on the answers to these questions.

1. Compared to the situation ten years ago, do you think more or fewer people in your country regularly give money to help people in need?
2. What are the main causes of poverty and hunger in the Third World? Try to put these (and any other) causes in order of importance: droughts, floods, armed fighting, debts to other countries.
3. Who do you think are the poorest of the poor people in the world: poor farmers, poor women, poor factory workers, . . . ?
4. How much of a charity's money should be spent on administration and how much should get to the people the charity is helping?

2 Look at the grid and make sure you understand all the words and expressions. Then listen to the man from Oxfam and the woman from War on Want talking about their organisations, and try to complete the grid.

	Oxfam	War on Want
Charity		
Mentions small-scale projects		
Has a women's officer		
Has field officers overseas		
Involves local people		
Works in almost every Third World country		

3 Make sure you understand the words in the box, and divide them into two or three groups, based on their meanings.

capital	cattle	consumption
debt	interest	lend	milk
peanuts	repay	rise	surplus

Now use the words from the box to fill in the blanks in these texts.

When a bank .... you money, your .... usually consists of two things: the .... (the sum you originally borrowed), and the .... (a percentage of the original sum). If you are unlucky, ... rates may .... before you finish .... the entire sum.

*   *   *

.... are raised for meat and for .... This is not as economical a way of using land as growing foods like wheat or .... Additionally, production is much greater than .... in many Western countries, and the result is a .... of .... and butter.

4 Listen to Roger Elbourne of Oxfam talking about international economics and world hunger. Then look at the pictures and try to fill in the blanks in the labels.

1. 1970s: oil money flooded to Western ...., who .... money to Third World countries.

2. Later: interest rates .... Third World countries couldn't pay back the .... or the ....

3. West African farmers sold .... (their food) to the West.

4. Money from food sales was used to .... the debt.

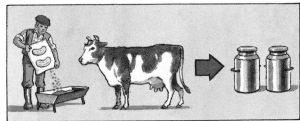

5. Western farmers fed the .... to their .... A .... of milk was produced.

6. The .... dried milk was sent to hungry West African children.

5 Do this exercise in groups of four or five. Imagine a rich woman has just died and left your committee £1 million to start a charity to help hungry people in the Third World. Plan your charity, making sure you cover all of the points below.

1. Choose a country or countries to help.
2. Will you concentrate on certain sorts of projects? How will you decide which individual projects to support?
3. About how much of the £1 million will go on setting up your head office? How much on administration? How much on raising more money? How much on educating people in the West to help change government policies that hurt the Third World?
4. Of the money that goes directly as aid to the Third World, what percentage will be used for emergency relief and what percentage for long-term projects?
5. How many employees will your charity have?
6. Give your charity a name, and think of a motto for it.

Study the Lesson Summary at the back of the book. Do some of the Practice Book exercises.

B In a bit of a panic

Listening comprehension; vocabulary; grammar (complex sentences); pronunciation; speaking practice.

1 Use the words in the box to say what's wrong with this picture.

| enough   lack   missing   need |

2 Work in pairs. Your teacher will give you the page number of a dialogue to complete (either A or B). Don't copy the lines from the book; you must both write down ONLY the new lines that you invent. Then leave your partner and find someone else who has worked on the other dialogue. Read your lines together to see if they work.

3 Which sentences do you hear? All of the sentences below would be correct English in the dialogue you will hear. Listen carefully to see which sentences are actually in the dialogue.

1. a. Could I speak to Alistair, please?
   b. Is that Alistair?
   c. Is Alistair there, please?

2. a. How can I help you?
   b. What can I do for you?
   c. Is there something I can do for you?

3. a. There are two glasses missing.
   b. Two glasses are missing.
   c. There seem to be two missing glasses.

4. a. Could I borrow a set from you, by any chance?
   b. Have you got a set you can lend me, by any chance?
   c. Could you lend me a set, by any chance?

5. a. When do you want them by?
   b. When do you want them?
   c. When do you need them by?

6. a. Well, shall I come over in a quarter of an hour?
   b. Well, can I come over in a quarter of an hour?
   c. Well, suppose I came over in a quarter of an hour?

7. a. I need some of that as well.
   b. I'm right out of that as well.
   c. I've run out of that as well.

8. a. Is that all you're out of?
   b. Is that all you need?
   c. Is that all you're short of?

9. a. No, I think I'm OK otherwise.
   b. No, I think I'm all right otherwise.
   c. No, I've got what I need otherwise.

4 Grammar. In these two sentences, somebody telephones and somebody borrows something. Which happens first in each sentence?

Before I lend them to you I'd like to ring her.
I'll phone Alistair about the glasses before I come by for the sugar.

Make sentences beginning 'Before . . . ' for these situations.

1. Duncan will put the champagne in the fridge. Then he will go to Marilyn's. (Begin 'Before Duncan goes . . . ')
2. Duncan will go to Marilyn's. Then he will go to Alistair's.
3. Duncan will get the glasses and icing sugar. Then he will start getting dinner ready.
4. Duncan will have finished preparing dinner. Then his wife will come home.

5 For each sentence, the recording will give you one word. Does the recorded word come in the sentence in your book? After you have listened, pronounce the sentences in the book.

1. Well, in a bit of a panic, actually.
2. I wouldn't dream of it, then.
3. You haven't got six champagne glasses you can lend me, have you?
4. Heaps of it.
5. Leave it on the doorstep.
6. Hello, could I speak to Alistair, please?
7. I wondered if I could borrow some pepper.
8. I've run out of that as well.
9. Do get back to me if you can't find any.
10. I'll be going out later.

6 In groups of three to five, write and practise your own dialogues about borrowing something. Use at least six of the words and expressions from Exercises 1, 2 and 3.

Study the Lesson Summary at the back of the book.
Do some of the Practice Book exercises.

Relationships

Listening comprehension;
discussing relationships; grammar
(*have* and *have got*).

A They love each other a lot

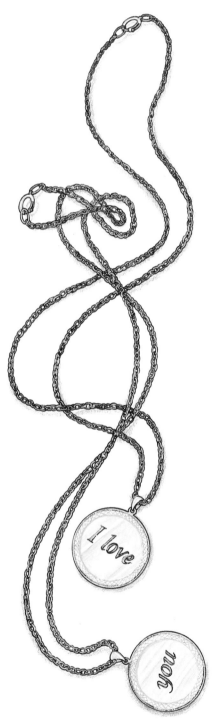

1 You are going to hear some people talking about relationships.
First of all, make sure you know the words and expressions in the
box. Then copy the table, listen to the recording and try to fill in
the spaces.

argue   bright   decision   dull
get on well (with somebody)
have something in common (with somebody)
make something work   marriage
sense of humour   tolerant

COUPLE	GOOD OR BAD RELATIONSHIP?	WHAT IS GOOD OR BAD ABOUT IT?
Lyn's parents		They love each other a lot.
Jill and her boyfriend		
Jill's parents		
Anne and her husband		
Anne's daughter and her boyfriend		
Mike and his wife		

2 Make sure you know the words in the box. Then listen to some or all of the extracts and answer the questions below.

| argument   faithful   moody   personality   trust   waste |

1. A boy says what he thinks is the most important thing for a couple to agree on. Do you agree with him?
2. A girl says what qualities she looks for in a boyfriend. What do *you* think are the most important qualities in a partner?
3. Two girls talk about marriage. What do you think of their opinions?

4. Two girls say what they think are the most important qualities in a good relationship. Do you agree with them?
5. A woman talks about the fact that her 18-year-old daughter has left home to live with her boyfriend. What do you think of the woman's point of view?

3 Grammar. *Have* and *have got*.

1. Sometimes *have* and *have got* are both possible, with the same meaning. (*Have got* is less common in formal speech or writing.) Here are some examples.

We have a good relationship.
OR
We've got a good relationship.

We have a lot in common.
OR
We've got a lot in common.

He has a terrific sense of humour.
OR
He's got a terrific sense of humour.

2. *Got* cannot be used in the following examples. Why not? Can you find the rule?

It's important to have a lot in common.
I don't like having too many close relationships at the same time.

3. *Got* is not used in these expressions. Can you find the rule? And can you add some more expressions to the list?

to have an argument   to have a talk
to have a good time   to have a dream
to have a holiday   to have a drink
to have breakfast   to have a bath

4 Work in groups of three or four. In each group, choose one of the following subjects. Prepare some more questions. When your questionnaire is ready, go round the class asking your questions. Note the answers. Then report to the class on what people think. Give your own opinions as well.

FRIENDSHIP
How important are your friends to you?
....

LOVE AND SEX
Do you think you can love more than one person at the same time?
....

MARRIAGE
Do you think marriage is a good thing?
....

PARENT–CHILD RELATIONSHIPS
Do you think most children can communicate well with their parents?
....

HOMOSEXUAL RELATIONSHIPS
Do you think homosexual relationships are wrong?
....

RELATIONSHIPS IN WORK AND SOCIETY
Do you ever start conversations with strangers?
....

Study the Lesson Summary at the back of the book.
Do some of the Practice Book exercises.

B I'm shy of girls

Reading, writing and speaking practice; suggestions and advice; grammar (frequency adverbs).

1 Read the six letters. Which do you think describes the most serious problem? Which writer do you think is the most sensible? Do you think any of the letters is silly?

I don't remember the last time I had a conversation with a girl.

I am in my twenties, and other people my age seem able to talk to girls. Sometimes I wonder if I ever will.

The Sun

For the ten years of my marriage, my husband has gone after other women, sometimes merely flirting but sometimes sleeping with them.

I left him twice and went back when he begged me to. But you can imagine how unhappy and humiliated I have been.

You may wonder why I've stuck to him. Well, I love him and I believe that in his own peculiar way, he loves me, too.

He has improved since I left the last time, about six months ago.

But there's no feeling of security for me and I'm always on tenterhooks.

Some time ago I met a very nice man who would like me to live with him. I know I'd have peace with him and I'm very tempted though I don't love him.

Which should I choose – a man like my husband or the one who'd never give a woman a moment's worry?

The Daily Mirror

I am married to a super man – very kind and considerate and loving to me and our two children. He would do anything in the world for us, until he gets behind the wheel of his car. Then he becomes a totally different man.

He's aggressive, bad tempered and drives too fast.

We're on tenterhooks when we're in the car and thankful to get out of it.

What makes otherwise lovely men like him turn into beasts on the road?

The Daily Mirror

When I was a teenager I slept around, as they say.

Then I got married to a good man and have had 16 years of happiness and two fine sons.

But all the while I dread meeting any boyfriends from the past, in case my husband gets to know.

The Sun

Dear Cathy & Claire – I hope you can help me. I can't seem to make friends. If I speak to anyone in my class, they just say, "'bye," or ignore me. I have one friend in the year above me, but that's it.

I do have quite a lot of penfriends, but no-one I can go out with.

I have talked to my form teacher, but she said she couldn't do anything and that I should have a word with my mum. I did that, but she said, "Don't be silly."

Jackie

I've been going out with Peter for eight months. A few weeks ago, he packed me in for another girl, even though he said he loved me and we'd never part. Then, a week later, he asked me out again. Of course, I said yes. But he still keeps talking about her and making excuses to see her. He's being very moody and snaps at me when I ask him about her. I'm so miserable, what should I do?

Oh, Boy

2 Choose one of the letters. Work individually or in groups and decide what advice to give the writer. Useful expressions:

Why don't you . . . ?
Why not . . . ? (e.g. *Why not try to forget him?*)
What/How about . . .ing?
I/We think you should . . .
You could/might . . .
If I were you, I would . . .
A good way to . . . is to . . .
The best way to . . . is to . . .
I think it's a mistake to . . .
Stop . . .ing and start . . .ing.

3 Grammar: frequency adverbs. Do you often ask other people for advice? Who do you ask? Say how often you ask some of the following people for advice: your father, your mother, your husband/wife, your boyfriend/girlfriend, your friends, your boss, your teacher, other people (say who). Use the words and expressions in the box. Examples:

'I often ask my wife for advice.'
'I never ask people for advice.'
'I sometimes ask my mother for advice.'
'I have often asked friends for advice.'
'I would never ask my father for advice.'

always	usually	very often	often
quite often	sometimes	occasionally	
hardly ever	never		

4 Pronunciation. How many words do you hear in each sentence? (Contractions like *don't* count as two words.)

5 Write a short letter asking for advice about a real or imaginary problem. Don't put your name on it. When you have finished, give it to the teacher.

6 Work in groups. Each group will receive some of the letters that were written in Exercise 5. Write answers giving advice. Then show or read the letters and the answers to the rest of the class.

Study the Lesson Summary at the back of the book. Do some of the Practice Book exercises.

"Just a minute, Smedley – are you having an affair with my wife?"

Tony Husband

"My family's all grown up now – except my husband, of course."

DONEGAN

"But you're special to me, darling."

HOW TO PICK UP WOMEN

WRONG   RIGHT

Revision and fluency practice

A You don't mind, do you, Bill?

Conversational expressions; words that are often confused; pronunciation; grammar (reported speech).

Dürer: Piper and drummer

1 Grammar: reported speech. Look at the picture for two minutes. Then close your book and listen to the recording. There are a number of mistakes in the description. Can you say what they are? Example:

'She said the sky was grey, but actually it's blue.'

2 Vocabulary revision: words that are easily confused. Choose the right word for each sentence. (You may have to change the words slightly.)

(*Say* or *tell*)
1. He .... that he would be late.
2. He .... me that he would be late.
3. Please .... us when you're ready.

(*Listen (to)* or *hear*)
4. I like to .... the radio when I'm driving.
5. Speak a bit louder – I can't .... you.
6. ....! I can .... somebody moving about downstairs.

(*Look (at)*, *watch* or *see*)
7. ....! I've had my hair done. Do you like it?
8. I don't .... TV much: I haven't got the time.
9. '............ that big bird!' 'Where? I can't .... a bird.'

(*Good* and *well*)
10. You speak very .... English.
11. You speak English very ....
12. 'She's got a new job.' 'That's ....'
13. He's always very .... dressed.

(*This* and *that*, *here* and *there*)
14. 'Hello. Bridgewater 31062.' 'Hello. Is .... Jake?' 'No, ... is Phil. Who's ....?' 'It's Mike. Is Olivia ....?' 'No, sorry, Mike. She's not .... just at the moment.' 'OK. I'll try a bit later.'
15. Could you go over .... and get .... file and bring it to me, please?
16. 'Hello. Come in and take your coat off.' 'Thanks. .... is a nice house. How long have you lived ....?'

(*Borrow* and *lend*)
17. 'Could you .... me your cassette player for a couple of hours?' 'OK, but don't forget to give it back. Last time you .... it you kept it for six weeks.'
18. I don't like .... money from people and I don't like .... money to people.

(*Journey* and *travel*)
19. Did you have a good ....?
20. Air .... in Europe is extremely expensive.

3 Pronunciation. Look at the following pairs of words and then listen to the recording. Do you hear A or B?

A	B
hear	ear
hold	old
hand	and
high	I
howl	owl
hair	air
hungry	angry

Now say some of the words and see if other students can decide whether you are saying A or B.

4 Pronunciation. Practise saying the following expressions.

He said that he'd be late.
He told Helen that he'd be late.
I can't hear you.
I've had my hair done.
I haven't got time to watch TV.
She's not here just now.
They live in a nice house.
How long have they lived there?
Hello.
It's hard work.
Are you having fun?
You wait here for a moment.

5 Conversational expressions. Complete the following dialogue and then act it out.

(Alice is waiting in front of the station for Bill.)
CAROL: Hello, Alice. What are you doing?
ALICE: Waiting for Bill.
CAROL: Yeah. He's always late, isn't he?
(Alice agrees.)
ALICE: .... But he's nice.
CAROL: Yes, I know.
(Carol explains why she can't go on talking to Alice, and leaves.)
CAROL: ....
(Steve, a stranger, tries to get into conversation with Alice.)
STEVE: ....
(Alice gets rid of him.)
ALICE: ....
(Joe, another stranger, starts talking to Alice.)
JOE: ....
(He is successful.)
ALICE: ....
(Joe asks Alice about her job.)
JOE: ....?
ALICE: I'm a nurse.
(Joe expresses interest.)
JOE: ....? Do you like it?
ALICE: Well, it's hard work. But it's interesting. I only started –
(Bill turns up. Alice greets Bill, asks Joe's name, and introduces Bill and Joe.)
ALICE: ....
JOE: ....
ALICE: ....
BILL: ....
(Joe greets Bill and goes back to his conversation with Alice.)
JOE: .... You only started –
ALICE: Yes. I only started six weeks ago –
(Bill apologises for interrupting.)
BILL: ....
(He reminds Alice that they are going to a party.)
BILL: ....
ALICE: Oh, dear. I didn't realise it was so late. Time flies when you're having fun, doesn't it?
(Alice invites Joe to come to the party along with them.)
ALICE: ....? You don't mind, do you Bill?
(Joe accepts.)
JOE: ....
(Bill agrees, not very enthusiastically.)
BILL: ....
(Joe says he's going to get a bottle of wine, and promises to be back shortly.)
JOE: You wait here a minute. I'm just going to get a bottle of wine. ....
ALICE: OK.
(You finish the conversation.)

83

B I don't see the joke

Situational language; speaking practice; listening practice; grammar (revision of tenses).

1 Look at the cartoons. Talk to other students and say what you think about them. Find out which are the most and least popular cartoons. Useful expressions:

'I don't see the joke.'
'What do you think of this one?'
'That one's really funny.'

'It isn't funny at all.'
'I think it's stupid.'
'It doesn't make me laugh.'

"Anything wrong, dear? You don't sing in the bath anymore."

*"You sold my **what** to **who**?!"*

"Steak too tough, sir?"

"Was the train very crowded, dear?"

"I'm afraid you've got the wrong number. This is Louis XV."

2 Grammar: revision of tenses. Put in the correct word or words. Do you know the rules for each group of sentences?

1. If I arrive before you, ... wait for you. (*I'll/I'd*)
2. Suppose you had to change your job. What .... you do? (*will/would*)
3. If I were you, ... try to save some money. (*I'll/I'd*)

4. I'll telephone you as soon as I .... something. (*know/will know*)
5. We can't go out until the rain .... (*stops/will stop*)

6. I would have helped her if she .... me. (*asked/had asked*)
7. If I'd known you were coming, ... some champagne. (*I'll buy/I'd buy/I'll have bought/I'd have bought*)
8. It would have been better if you .... anything. (*didn't say/hadn't said/wouldn't have said*)

9. As soon as I saw him, I knew that we .... before. (*met/have met/had met*)
10. Excuse me. I .... a coffee half an hour ago. Is it ready yet? (*ordered/had ordered*)

11. 'How long are you in this country for?' '...........' (*Until May./Since January.*)
12. 'Is she an old friend of yours?' '........... her since we were children.' (*I know/I've known*)

13. A friend of mine .... in a car crash yesterday. (*was hurt/has hurt/has been hurt*)
14. I'm afraid I can't come and see you. My car .... today. (*is repaired/is being repaired/is repairing*)

3 Pronunciation. Practise saying the following words and expressions.

isn't   doesn't   hasn't   wasn't
It isn't funny.
It doesn't make me laugh.
She hasn't been to see me.
I wasn't there yesterday.

4 Pronunciation. Listen to the recording. Do you hear the singular or plural of these words? Practise saying the plurals.

hand   bank   desk   crisp   act   camp
pint

Do you hear the present or past of these words? Practise saying the past forms.

hope   look   beg   watch   fix   bank
help   ask   gasp

5 Situations. What situations would the following expressions be used in? Choose one of the situations and see how many more typical expressions you can think of.

Boarding at 3.15, Gate 6.
What size are you?
Could you pass the salt?
How many kilometres does it do to the litre?
Double, with bath, please.

6 Work in small groups. Prepare and practise a conversation which takes place in one of the situations from Exercise 5. The conversation must include the following: a problem, a misunderstanding, an interruption. When you are ready, act out your conversation for the rest of the class.

7 Listen to the song, 'Fiddling Across the USA'. Try to write down two place names, two forms of transport and two kinds of weather that are mentioned in the song. Then look at page 155 and check your answers.

Study the Lesson Summary at the back of the book.

85

Grammar (*need + -ing* form with passive meaning; *have something done*); vocabulary (changes; houses); pronunciation; listening and speaking practice.

Somewhere to live

A A lot needs doing to it

1 Match the words with the pictures and say what needs doing to the outside of the house. Use the verbs in the box. Example:

'*Some bricks need replacing.*'

bricks   chimney   doors   garage   garden
gate   hedge   path   roof   steps
TV aerial   window frames   window pane

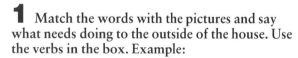

| clean up   cut   paint   rebuild   repair |
| replace   straighten |

2 Ask the teacher about the inside of the house. Find out how many rooms there are on each floor, how they are arranged, and what size they are. Work in pairs; each student should draw a plan of one of the two floors.

3 Listen to the recording. You will hear somebody being shown round the house. Write the names of the different rooms on your plan.

4 When the owners of the house first moved in, they had a lot of things done. Can you remember any of them? Listen to the recording again, if necessary, and complete the sentences. Use the words in the box to help you.

build	ceiling	convert	cupboard
lower	make	put in	raise	redecorate
take down			

1. In the dining-room, they had a new .... put in.
2. And they .... the dining-room decorated.
3. They had the study doorway ....
4. In the main bedroom, they had ....
5. In the kitchen, ...
6. They had the downstairs store-room ....
7. (staircase)
8. (living-room)
9. (upstairs ceilings)
10. (upstairs bedroom)
11. (upstairs bathroom)

5 Pronunciation. Listen to the recording and decide whether the words you hear come from list A or list B. Say some of the words and see whether other students can decide which ones you are saying.

A	B
pane	pen
gate	get
main	men
paper	pepper
late	let
shade	shed
fail	fell
whale	well
wait	wet

6 Listen to the recording and practise these words and sentences.

afraid   change   decorate   escape   frame
ladies   make   paint   raise   replace
straighten   take

I'm afraid it's rather a mess.
We changed the bedroom into a store-room.
It needs decorating.
Where's the fire escape?
The window frames need painting.
The ladies is on the first floor.
We had new windows made.
I had the ceiling raised.
Some bricks need replacing.
They're going to straighten the road.
We'll have to take that wall down.

7 Work in groups. Your task is to convert the house into one of the following:

– a casino
– a hotel
– a clothes shop
– a health club and gymnasium
– a language school
– a residential hostel for six physically handicapped people (who will go out during the day to work) and their full-time caretaker

Say what changes you will make. Use some of the new words and expressions from the lesson. The following may also be useful:

add   car park   change (into)   divide
emergency exit   entrance   fire escape
gents (toilet)   improve   increase
ladies (toilet)   strengthen   turn (into)
widen

Study the Lesson Summary at the back of the book.
Do some of the Practice Book exercises.

B More houses should be built

Listening comprehension; vocabulary work; taking notes; pronunciation; speaking practice; grammar (*should* and *ought to* with passives).

1 Who's speaking? Listen to the recording and decide which of the five people is speaking in each case.

Alwyn Anchors, self-employed house builder.

James Bethell, racehorse trainer; some of his lads live in tied accommodation.

Debra Freechild, a tenant about to become a single parent; her private landlord cannot make her leave or raise her rent.

Barbara Gatehouse, adviser at the Housing Aid Centre, Oxford.

Susanna Harsanyi, originally from Hungary, now living in Oxford.

2 Look at the sentences from the recording, and try and find words to fit the definitions in the box.

> - loan to pay for a home
> - person who invites other people for a meal, a party, or other entertainment
> - made to fit its purpose
> - place to live (a general word)
> - limits
> - one room that serves as bedroom and sitting-room

1. When I was a student, and we were living four in a house, it would have been nicer to have a house that was more suitably designed for that.
2. I've persuaded the better paid ones to try and get on a rung of the mortgage ladder and buy their own accommodation, which seems to be working better. I mean it pays me to put their salaries up enough, you know, by sort of £25 to £30 a week, for them to be paying a mortgage.
3. And the person whose house it is is the host, and they entertain them quite generously . . .
4. The worst housing problems, in my personal view, are being in a room, a bedsit, with one or two children . . . something we ought, all ought to try and do something about as soon as possible.
5. But certainly more houses should be built. Erm, and, er, they should be built in the price range so that people can actually afford to live, you know, buy and live in a house.

3 Make sure you know what the words in the box mean. Then copy the partial notes below, leaving big blanks where the dots are. Listen to Claire Booker from Shelter (a national campaign for the homeless) and complete the notes.

> budget   divorce   poverty
> recession   sell off   structure

1. because of ...., increase in ....
   - more than .... below poverty line
   - governments have .... for housing budget ....
     in last 5 years
   - results: little building, no ....
   - council housing has been ....
2. families becoming ...., but ....
   - more young and old ....
   - more divorce means ....
3. summary
   - not enough ....
   - more ....
   - change in actual ....
   - result: ....

4 Pronounce the following sentences, paying special attention to the pronunciation of *w*, *v*, and *b*. Check your pronunciation with the recording or your teacher.

1. My ideal would be to be able to live in the kind of house I needed at a particular time of my life.
2. They entertain them quite generously – good food and a lot of wine, it's very . . . And the house gets built.
3. The worst housing problems, in my personal view, are being in a room, a bedsit, with one or two children.
4. They should be built in the price range so that people can actually afford to buy and live in a house.

5 Choose ten or more words or expressions to learn from Exercises 1–4. Tell another student the reasons for your choices.

6 Work in groups of four or five. Each group member takes responsibility for one question, making sure that everyone else expresses a view on it. Try and use words from the previous exercises. Then write one other sentence about housing with 'ought to be' or 'should be' and give it to another group to discuss.

1. More housing should be owned by the government and rented to people with low incomes.
2. People who are going to live in government housing should be consulted about the design of new housing.
3. Tied housing ought to be declared illegal.
4. Tenants ought to be allowed to make any improvements they want to accommodation where they are living.

Study the Lesson Summary at the back of the book.
Do some of the Practice Book exercises.

Describing people

Grammar and vocabulary for descriptions; listening, speaking and writing practice.

A What do they look like?

1 Listen to the song. (The words are on page 155.) Each verse describes one of the four people in the pictures. Which picture goes with which verse?

A

B

C

D

2 Here are some words, expressions and structures that can be used for describing people's appearance. Do you know all of them? Can you think of any important words that have been left out?

Hair: long, medium-length, short; straight, curly, wavy; blond(e), fair, dark, brown, black, red, grey, going grey, white, thinning; a beard, a moustache, bushy eyebrows
He's (going) bald. He's got a bald patch.
Eyes: green, blue, brown, greenish-blue, grey
Nose: long, turned-up
Mouth: wide, generous; thin lips, full lips
Chin: pointed, firm, weak
Face: oval, round, long; high cheekbones; a scar
Forehead: high, low
Ears: big, small
Shoulders: broad, narrow
Build: thin, slender, muscular, heavily-built, plump, overweight, fat
Height: tall, of medium height, short
Age: young, middle-aged, elderly, old; in his early thirties; in her mid-fifties; in their late forties
Expression: serious, cheerful, worried, friendly
General appearance: good-looking, pretty, beautiful, attractive, plain; well dressed, casually dressed
He looks old. She looks like a businesswoman.

Structures:
She has (She's got) blue eyes and brown hair.
a woman with blue eyes and brown hair
a blue-eyed, brown-haired woman

a man with a beard
a girl with glasses

a woman in a blue dress
a man in a grey jacket

3 A person with fair hair is *fair-haired*. Somebody who writes with his or her left hand is *left-handed*. What are the adjectives for these people?

1. a person with grey hair
2. a person with a thin face
3. somebody with broad shoulders
4. somebody with long legs
5. people who write with their right hands
6. a person with green eyes

Now say these in another way.

1. a brown-eyed man
   'a man with brown eyes'
2. a grey-haired old lady
   'an old lady .... ,
3. a left-handed child
   'a child who .... ,
4. a thin-faced person
   'somebody who has .... ,
5. a dark-eyed woman
   ' .... ,

4 Prepare and give a short description *either* of one of the people in the pictures *or* of somebody in the class. (Don't be rude!) See if other students can guess who it is.

5 Complete the text with words from the box.

I'm in my .... fifties. I'm very tall, and quite .... built, but I have rather .... shoulders. I'm a little overweight.
   I have .... medium-length .... hair, but I'm going ...., so there isn't a lot of it left. I have a grey .... and moustache. My eyes are ...., and I wear .... I've got a rather long face, with a .... chin, a big nose and big .... I have .... lips, and I usually have a .... expression; my face changes a lot when I .... I have a high forehead; I like to think that it looks intelligent.
   Clothes are not very important to me, and I'm usually very .... dressed.
   I don't think I'm very ...., but I'm not all that bad-looking either. I probably .... a bit younger than I am.

bald	beard	blue	casually	early
ears	fair	glasses	good-looking	
heavily	look	narrow	serious	smile
straight	strong	thin		

6 Write a description of yourself; don't put your name on it. When you are ready, give it to the teacher.

7 Listen to the descriptions as the teacher reads them out. Can you guess who wrote each one?

Study the Lesson Summary at the back of the book. Do some of the Practice Book exercises.

B What are they like?

Vocabulary (personal characteristics);
pronunciation; speaking practice.

A

B

C

D

1 Vocabulary. Do you know all these words? If
not, use a dictionary or ask your teacher. Can you
find words from the list to describe the people in
the pictures?

affectionate   aggressive   bad-tempered
calm   cheerful   cold   easy-going
emotional   friendly   generous   honest
kind   mean   moody   nervy   optimistic
pessimistic   polite   practical   reserved
rude   self-confident   sensitive   serious
shy   sociable

E

2 Do any of the words in Exercise 1 describe you? Are there any words that definitely don't describe you?

3 Pronunciation: stress. *Affectionate* is stressed on the second syllable. Can you find any other words in Exercise 1 that are stressed on the second syllable? Can you find any that have the main stress on the third syllable? Practise saying the words.

4 Make up three questions that you could use in a questionnaire to find out how sociable people are. Use some of these structures.

Do you ever . . . ?
Have you ever . . . ?
How often . . . ?
If . . . , would . . . ?

F

G

5 Now choose another characteristic, and make up questions for it. Ask the teacher for help if necessary.

6 Go round the class asking your questions. Speak to as many people as possible. Don't forget to note each person's answers.

7 Tell the class some of the things you have found out. Use some of these words and expressions.

extremely   very   quite   not very   not at all

(nearly) everybody   most people
some people   several people
a few people   hardly anybody   one person
nobody   the majority
two out of nine   three out of fourteen

H

Study the Lesson Summary at the back of the book. Do some of the Practice Book exercises.

Keeping healthy

A They lose all of their rights

Listening comprehension; note-taking;
pronunciation; speaking practice.

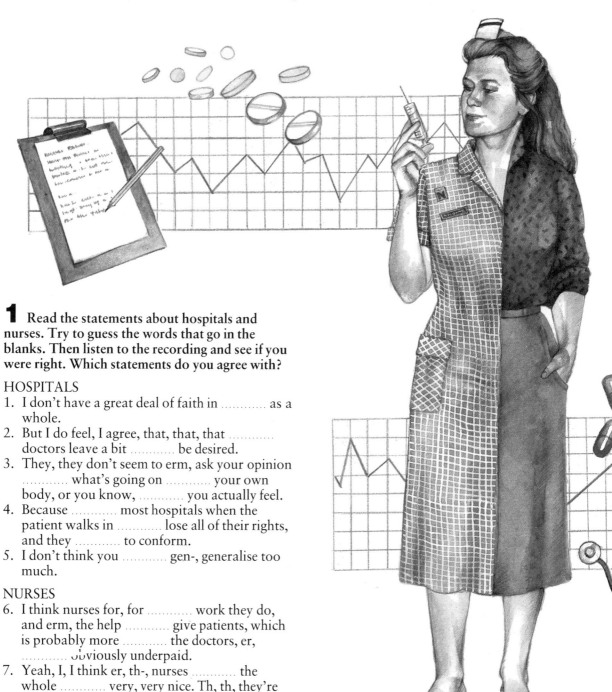

1 Read the statements about hospitals and
nurses. Try to guess the words that go in the
blanks. Then listen to the recording and see if you
were right. Which statements do you agree with?

HOSPITALS

1. I don't have a great deal of faith in .... as a
   whole.
2. But I do feel, I agree, that, that, that ....
   doctors leave a bit .... be desired.
3. They, they don't seem to erm, ask your opinion
   .... what's going on .... your own
   body, or you know, ... you actually feel.
4. Because .... most hospitals when the
   patient walks in .... lose all of their rights,
   and they .... to conform.
5. I don't think you .... gen-, generalise too
   much.

NURSES

6. I think nurses for, for .... work they do,
   and erm, the help .... give patients, which
   is probably more .... the doctors, er,
   .... obviously underpaid.
7. Yeah, I, I think er, th-, nurses .... the
   whole .... very, very nice. Th, th, they're
   very erm, very good, erm, ... you know,
   reassurance and whatnot.
8. I think nurses always .... the best they can.

2 You are going to hear about a National Health Service hospital at Burford in Oxfordshire, where the experience of being a patient is very different from that in an average hospital. Before you listen, work in groups of three or four to try and predict what might be different about this hospital and the way the nurses work there.

3 Now listen to the recording once and take notes about how the hospital is organised. You needn't note down the examples. Compare your notes with another student's, and negotiate a common set of notes. You can listen a second time if you want to.

4 Pronunciation. There are two different ways to pronounce *th*:
1. 'voiced' (as in *the* /ðə/, *mother* /ˈmʌðə(r)/)
2. 'unvoiced' (as in *thing* /θɪŋ/, *earth* /ɜ:θ/).
Can you divide the following words into two groups according to the pronunciation of *th*?

there   teeth   those   faith   think
them   then   whether   together   clothes
something   thirsty   thirty   rather   than
third   fourth   truth

5 Work with another student to act out a patient's first interview ('nursing assessment') at Burford Hospital. One of you will play the nurse, and another the patient. When you have finished find a new partner and change roles.

Study the Lesson Summary at the back of the book. Do some of the Practice Book exercises.

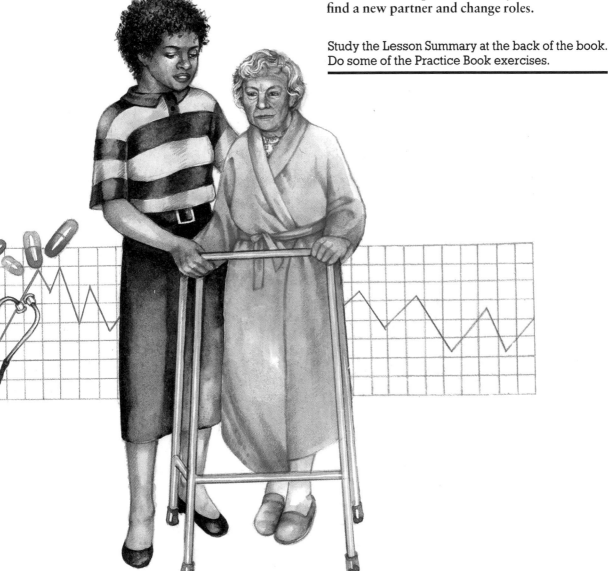

95

B Bed rest is bad for you

Reading practice; vocabulary work; grammar (passives, imperatives); speaking practice.

1 Look quickly through the texts and decide which text is the easiest and which is the most difficult. Then answer the questions below as quickly as you can.

1. What happens to your bones if you stay in bed too long?
2. What is the best drink to give to someone who has had an accident?
3. The average 55-year-old man sleeps longer each night than the average 55-year-old woman: how much longer?
4. What groups of people are most likely to survive near-drowning without brain damage?

ZZZZZZ...

Insomnia isn't good for you. Complete lack of sleep will kill you more quickly than complete lack of food. Elephants and dolphins can survive happily with 2 hours of sleep out of every 24, but the average night's sleep among normal human beings is now reckoned to be 7 hours 36 minutes.

People in their fifties tend to sleep less than those in their twenties, but people in their sixties get more sleep than at any time since childhood. Men sleep ten minutes more than women, and the difference rises to 20 minutes more in the fifties and 50 minutes more in the seventies.

(by Gyles Brandreth – adapted)

'Drowned' people could recover safely

STORIES about seamen, apparently drowned, staying under water for far longer than the traditional four minutes and coming back to life without any brain damage, may be true.

Doctors at St Bartholomew's Medical College in London have discovered that human beings have a "diving response", like that of sea mammals, which is triggered by a surprise fall into water – especially cold water. By closing off most of the needs of the body for blood supply, reducing the heart rate and power to a very low level but concentrating the emergency blood supply on the brain, humans can survive being under water for more than half an hour – and probably much longer – without brain damage.

In infants and children, it seems, the diving response is especially powerful.

(from *The Guardian* – adapted)

WHEN A CUPPA COULD KILL

A screech of brakes, a deafening crash...and you realise there's a road accident just outside your front door. You've phoned for the police and an ambulance. What's your next step – put on a pot of tea or break out the brandy bottle? That could be the most dangerous thing possible, say the experts who deal with accidents.

Nothing at all must be taken by mouth – not even tea. Mr D.J. Fuller, consultant orthopaedic surgeon at the Radcliffe Infirmary, Oxford, said: "Anyone involved in an accident, even injured in a fall down the stairs, may need an operation. To give a general anaesthetic after drinking or eating could be very dangerous."

(source unknown)

BED REST IS BAD FOR YOU

Ever noticed how you seem to take longer to get over an illness if you take to your bed for a few days instead of struggling on? The reason, according to the leading American health magazine *Prevention*, is that a whole range of bodily functions begin to weaken after as short a time as one day in bed.

Muscle tissue starts to break down, robbing the body of important minerals and leading to substantial weakness in just a few days; bones start to break down and lose calcium; the body is unable to use food efficiently; heart and blood vessels get weak after a couple of days, which can lead to a rise in pulse rate and a drop in blood volume; joint stiffness and constipation are also common.

'Prolonged bed rest is not to be taken lightly,' says Dr Benjamin Natelson, professor of neurosciences at New Jersey Medical School. And that's why doctors these days make every effort to get patients up and moving as soon as possible after heart attacks and operations.

(from *Living Magazine* – adapted)

2 Choose one of the texts to read in detail. Try and guess the meaning of words you don't know, and check your guesses with a dictionary or your teacher. Then choose five new words to learn. Find one or two other students who have chosen the same text; compare your lists of words to learn and the reasons you have chosen them.

3 How much do you know about treating bruises? Try and match the beginnings (which are in order) and the ends of the sentences. Use your dictionary to look up new words.

Bruises are very
They normally get
Parents sometimes worry that a bone may
If a child gets
it is unlikely that a bone has
But the child may
Severe bruising can
In the case of a badly bruised leg, the limb should
Lying in bed
A cold compress may
This

be raised.
been broken.
be broken.
is the easiest way to do this.
is made by soaking some material in water and
    applying it to the bruise.
common in children.
up at once after a fall and moves about normally,
ease a bad bruise if applied at once.
be treated by rest for 24 to 48 hours.
better in seven to ten days.
be stiff the next day because of the bruising which
    has occurred.

4 How much do you know about treating cuts and grazes? Use the verbs in the box to complete the texts. Put each verb into an appropriate form; you can use words like *be, have, do, can, must,* and *may.* You may use some verbs more than once. Use your dictionary to look up new words.

apply	bleed	cause	clean out
consult	cover	dry	enter	fall off
inspect	keep	make	pull	stick
stop	wash

CUTS
Bleeding can usually ……….. by applying pressure to the cut for two minutes. The cut can then ……….. carefully ……….. . If it has ……….. freely, any germs will normally have ……….. away by the blood.
    ……….. a bandage firmly, bringing the edges of the cut together so that it heals quickly. ……….. it dry for one to two days.
    If the cut is deep and the edges cannot ……….. together with a bandage, ……….. a doctor or a nurse.

GRAZES
Dirt will often ……….. a graze caused by falling on a hard or rough surface. It must ……….. carefully with an antiseptic solution.
    After cleaning, ……….. not ……….. the graze. Exposure to the air will ……….. a scab to form. This will gradually ……….. and ……….. .
    ……….. not ……….. a bandage. This may ……….. to the graze or ……….. it soggy and infected.

5 Work in groups of three or four. Prepare and perform a (serious or funny) three-minute television demonstration of how to deal with one of these:
– back injuries
– drowning
– bee or wasp stings
– a broken bone
– a nosebleed

Study the Lesson Summary at the back of the book.
Do some of the Practice Book exercises.

Describing things

A Medium-sized, not small

The language of descriptions; listening and speaking
practice; pronunciation.

1 Some people were asked to describe the
butterflies from memory. Here are some of the
things they said about one of the butterflies. Can
you complete the sentences with words from the
box? (There are too many words.) When you have
finished, listen to the recording and check your
answers. Which butterfly were the people
describing?

'............-sized, brown ...., black markings
with a bright red –'

'Well, er ...., er brown, some white, on the
wing-tips I think, and, er, yes, medium-............,
not small, not ....-large like a peacock, er,
can't remember anything ....'

'I don't think I could .... anything to that. No,
that's .... what I'd say, that it was red and
white, sort of ....-red, with two white eyes in
the larger wings.'

'I think it has a sort of pattern of ...., doesn't
it, of some sort, in the sort of – at the top of its
wing.'

'There's a red – black and red .... going along
the top and there's a .... of white blobs
somewhere.'

'The actual bulk of it was brownish, with red on the
.... of the wings, the fore-wings. I think
there was eyes on the lower wings, in the ....,
and there's white as well.'

about	add	background	centre	couple
dots	else	extra	medium	orangey
outside	red	sized	stripe	

2 Close your book and describe one of the other
butterflies from memory.

Peacock

Red Admiral

Small Tortoiseshell

3 Look at the list of words and expressions. Find out the meanings of any that you don't know (look them up in a dictionary or ask somebody). How many pairs of opposites can you find? (For example *hard/soft*.)

big   blunt   cheap   cold   dull   expensive   fast
flat   flexible   fragile   hard   heavy   light   long
medium-sized   narrow   pointed   rigid   rough   sharp
shiny   short   slow   small   smooth   soft   transparent
unbreakable   warm   waterproof   wide

4 Do you know the names of all the things in the pictures? Choose one of the pictures and write down all the words from the list in Exercise 3 that could be used to describe what is in the picture (or part of it).

5 Listen to the recording. Which picture is each person talking about?

6 Pronunciation. Say the following expressions, making sure that you link the words correctly where shown.

very expensive
as heavy as a car
fairly easy

rather expensive
neither expensive nor cheap

too expensive

not at all
made of metal
small enough

not very expensive
not quite so heavy
quite big

7 Make up your own descriptions of things in the classroom, or things that you can see through the window. See how long you can talk before other students can decide what you are describing. The following words and expressions may be useful.

extremely   very   rather
quite   fairly   not very
neither . . . nor . . .   not at all
about the size of a . . .
a bit bigger than a . . .
not quite as heavy as a . . .
small enough to hold in your hand

Study the Lesson Summary at the back of the book.
Do some of the Practice Book exercises.

B Guaranteed used cars

Vocabulary and grammar (comparison, similarities, differences and identity); pronunciation (contrastive stress); fast reading; listening; speaking practice.

1 Fast reading practice. Choose one of the first two cars advertised below. Then look quickly at the rest of the advertisement, and find the cheapest car with all of these:
– a similar colour to yours
– the same number of doors as yours
– similar accessories to yours
– a much lower mileage than yours

★ ★ ★ EVAN STABETSI ★ ★ ★

GUARANTEED USED CARS

Not just as good as new – BETTER than new!

★ THIS MONTH'S ★ BARGAINS

FORD ESCORT 1600, 5 door, powder blue, radio-cassette, sunroof, 34,000 miles, price £2,600.

BMW 318i, 4 door, red, electric windows, fog lamps, radio-cassette, 14,000 miles, price £6,250.

★ ★ ★ ★ ★ ★ ★ ★ ★

Renault 11 TSE, 5 door, white, sunroof, radio-cassette, electric windows, 17,000 miles, £4,200.

Mercedes-Benz 500SEL, 4 door, diamond blue metallic, electric sunroof, air conditioning, 28,000 miles, £22,500.

Volvo 340DL, 5 door, deep red, sunroof, radio-cassette, 8,000 miles, £7,000.

Nissan Stanza 1.6GL, 5 door, sky blue, radio-cassette, sunroof, 34,000 miles, £2,100.

MG Maestro 1.6i, 4 door, cherry red, air conditioning, 5,500 miles, £6,200.

Saab 900 Turbo, 5 door, Admiral blue, electric sunroof, radio-cassette, only 1,500 miles, £9,200.

Nissan Sunny 1.5GL, 4 door, green metallic, fog lamps, radio-cassette, 35,000 miles, £3,200.

Jaguar XJ6 3.4 automatic, 4 door, ruby red, stereo radio-cassette, electric sunroof, electric windows, fog lamps, only 4,000 miles, £15,650.

Volvo 245DL, 4 door, deep red, radio-cassette, fog lamps, sunroof, electric windows, 6,000 miles, £8,500.

Peugeot 505, 5 door, royal blue, sunroof, radio-cassette, 4,200 miles, £6,850.

Ford Capri 2.8i, 4 door, dark red, fog lamps, radio-cassette, 125,000 miles, £900.

Metro 1.3L, 5 door, light blue, fog lamps, 17,000 miles, £3,800.

2 Copy the table. Then listen to the recording and fill in the missing details.

	UNITED MOTORS BANGER	MASSCAR BURNUP
Number of doors	5	
Engine capacity		
Number of gears		
Petrol consumption		
Acceleration 0–60		
Top speed		
Number of seats		1
Accessories		
Number of colours		
Price		

3 Here are some ways of comparing things. Study the examples.

MORE/LESS

Car A uses | much far | more/less petrol than car B.
Car B is | a lot rather slightly | faster/slower than car A.

THE SAME

Car A uses the same amount of petrol as car B.
Car B uses as much petrol as car A.
Both car A and car B do 18 miles to the gallon.
Car A and car B both do 18 miles to the gallon.
Neither car A nor car B is very economical.

SIMILAR

Car A's design is similar to car B's.
Car A's bonnet looks very like car B's.
Car A and car B have similar styling at the back.

DIFFERENT

Car A's headlamps are not at all like car B's.
Car B's engine design is different from car A's.
Car A doesn't use as/so much petrol as car B.
Car A is very/rather/quite different from car B.

4 Now write a comparison of the Banger and the Burnup, using information from Exercise 2 and structures from Exercise 3.

5 Pronunciation: contrastive stress. Listen to the examples and imitate them.

The Ford has better acceleration than the Ferrari, but its top speed isn't so high.
The Ford has better acceleration than the Ferrari, but it's not so good as the Porsche.

Now listen to the beginnings of the following sentences, and decide how they will continue.

1. The Ford has more passenger space than the Nissan,
   a) but not so much as the Toyota.
   b) but less luggage space.
2. Our new car's more comfortable than the old one,
   a) but it's much noisier.
   b) but it still isn't as comfortable as it might be.
3. The Ford's cheaper than the Volvo,
   a) but it isn't so fast.
   b) but it costs more than the Citroen.
4. The engine's been well looked after,
   a) but the body's very rusty.
   b) but it *has* done 120,000 miles.
5. I enjoy driving big cars,
   a) but I hate driving small ones.
   b) but I hate having to park them.

6 EITHER: Write an advertisement for something very cheap, trying to make it sound attractive and interesting. Use some of the vocabulary and structures from this lesson.

OR: Prepare a one-minute talk in which you try to sell something strange to the class. Use some of the vocabulary and structures from this lesson. Some suggestions:

an electric eyebrow-brush
a musical mousetrap
gramophone records that you can eat
a pocket lie-detector
a portable folding lavatory
perfumed books
anti-yawning pills
a bicycle-seat warmer

Study the Lesson Summary at the back of the book.
Do some of the Practice Book exercises.

Telling the truth

A Freedom of information

Reading comprehension; vocabulary; discussion; pronunciation.

1 Read the text. Use a dictionary if necessary.

FREEDOM OF INFORMATION IN THE USA AND BRITAIN

1. GOVERNMENT RECORDS

THE USA

The federal *Freedom of Information Act* says, in general, that any US citizen can inspect and copy any of the records of the various federal government departments. There are some exceptions – many defence and foreign policy matters are kept secret, for instance. And people are not allowed to obtain information about other citizens' private affairs.

The Freedom of Information Act only applies to federal records. State governments do not have to open their records to the public, and the majority do not.

BRITAIN

The *Local Government (Access to Information) Act* says that local government meetings must be open to the public (with a few exceptions), and that the public may inspect any documents which were consulted at the meetings. But at the time of writing (1987), Britain has no law similar to the Freedom of Information Act. So there is at present no general right to inspect national or local government records, though this may change during the next few years.

2. PERSONAL FILES

THE USA

Under the Freedom of Information Act, people can find out whether federal authorities hold files on them, and can inspect and copy their files.

State governments are not obliged by law to show individuals their personal files.

BRITAIN

From November 1987, the *Data Protection Act* gives people the right to see, check and if necessary correct any information about themselves which is kept in computerised records. But people have no right to see personal information which is held in non-computerised records.

British local government authorities keep files on large numbers of people – for instance, all those who have had anything to do with the local authority housing, social services or education departments. Some local authorities allow people to see their own files. (In Barnet, in London, for instance, schoolchildren are allowed to see their own files, and from the age of ten they can stop their parents seeing them.) But many local authorities keep people's files secret. So unless these files are computerised, individuals may not be able to check the truth of what is written about them.

However, an *Access to Personal Files Bill* is going through Parliament, and may become law in 1987. If this happens, British people will be able to see what is written about them in some kinds of records (though they will still not be allowed to see their medical or banking files unless these are computerised).

2 Now see how many of these questions you can answer in ten minutes. (You can look back at the text if you want to.) Write *Yes* or *No* – if the information is not given in the text, write *Don't know*.

1. An Englishman changed doctors in 1986. Could he read his last doctor's notes on his medical records?
2. An American wonders why the government has cut the National Parks budget. Can she see records of official discussions on the subject?
3. In 1985, there was a British government report into educational standards in city-centre schools. It was not published. Were journalists able to consult the documents?
4. An American state government has been giving road-building contracts to a firm belonging to a friend of the governor. Can citizens see records of the official meetings at which these decisions were made?
5. A British schoolboy of fourteen wants to see his school record. Will he have the right to do this if the Access to Personal Files Bill becomes law?
6. An American wants to see his file at his bank. Has he the right to do so?
7. A British housewife is refused credit to buy a car. Has she the right to inspect information about herself on the credit company's computer?
8. An American wonders how much the Defense Department spends on preparations for chemical warfare. Can he find out?
9. A mentally-handicapped British woman has difficulty in looking after her children. A local authority committee decides to put them in the care of the local authority. Can the woman see the information on which the committee based its decision?

3 Pronunciation: stress and rhythm. Practise the following words and phrases, and then practise reading aloud the first paragraph of the text about freedom of information.

freedom   information   freedom of information
general   in general
inspect   inspect and copy
record   any of the records
federal   government   department
federal government departments
exception   There are some exceptions
defence   foreign   policy
defence and foreign policy matters
instance   for instance
obtain   to obtain information
citizen   private   affairs
other citizens' private affairs

4 Choose some words and expressions to learn. Compare your list with another student, and explain the reasons for your choices.

5 Work in groups of three or four. Imagine that your group is a committee; your job is to plan a Freedom of Information Act (it can be for your country, for Britain, or for another real or imaginary country). Decide what kinds of information you will allow the public to obtain, and what kinds will be kept secret. Include the following kinds of information in your discussion (and other kinds as well, if you want). When you are ready, report to the class.

– personal medical records
– personal educational records
– personal credit records
– personal job records
– local authority files
– national government files

Study the Lesson Summary at the back of the book. Do some of the Practice Book exercises.

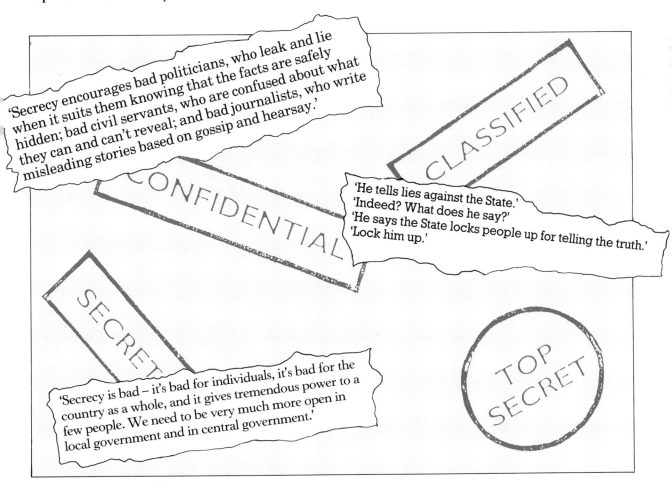

'Secrecy encourages bad politicians, who leak and lie when it suits them knowing that the facts are safely hidden; bad civil servants, who are confused about what they can and can't reveal; and bad journalists, who write misleading stories based on gossip and hearsay.'

CLASSIFIED

CONFIDENTIAL

'He tells lies against the State.'
'Indeed? What does he say?'
'He says the State locks people up for telling the truth.'
'Lock him up.'

SECRET

'Secrecy is bad – it's bad for individuals, it's bad for the country as a whole, and it gives tremendous power to a few people. We need to be very much more open in local government and in central government.'

TOP SECRET

B Would you ever lie?

Listening; discussion; grammar ('unreal' past tenses); vocabulary; letter-writing.

1 Are there any situations where you would not tell the truth to somebody? If so, how many can you list? Useful expressions:

I would/might lie to . . .
I would/might lie if . . .
I would/might say that . . . was . . .

2 Listen to the recording. The people talk about four or five situations in which one might lie. One situation is: if the children were looking for their Christmas presents before Christmas Day. Write a few words summing up each of the other situations. (Begin *If* . . .)

3 Listen again to the person who says 'I think lying is a very basic sin.' How far do you agree with her attitude? Why?

4 Listen again to the last part of the discussion. Would you want to know if you only had a short time to live?

5 Grammar: 'unreal' past tenses. Look at the following sentences from the recording. Can you fill in the missing verbs? Listen to the recording and check your answers.

1. You might tell untruths and say that it .... not in the loft.
2. If somebody .... me a present for the baby, a piece of clothing or something that I .... dreadful, I would say how pretty it .... and how much I .... it.
3. Perhaps if some-, they .... something wrong with them, I wouldn't tell them.
4. You wouldn't tell somebody that they .... dying, for instance?

6 Now complete these sentences by putting one or more words in each gap.

1. I would never tell somebody that I .... like their clothes, even if they .... terrible.
2. But I would always tell somebody if I ....
3. If I was really in love with somebody, I would tell them everything that I ....
4. Suppose you were invited to dinner and the meal .... really terrible. Would you tell the people how good it .... and how much you .... it, or .... them the truth?
5. If you .... married to somebody who .... much cleverer than you ...., would it upset you?
6. If animals could tell us what they .... about us, we would get some surprises.
7. Suppose a bank clerk .... you an extra £10 note by mistake. .... you tell her?
8. Suppose you .... certain that you only .... two days to live. What ....?
9. If you .... completely free to do what you ...., ... English?
10. If I could have anything that I ...., I'd start by getting a new house.

7 Here are the interviewer's notes on a job applicant, together with three possible letters to the applicant. Which letter do you think is the best? Why?

> Post: bilingual secretary/receptionist
> Applicant: Alice Prior, age 23
> July 14, 2.30
> nervous, unconfident; silly laugh
> physically unattractive — spots
> French not very good
> slight stutter
> lacks experience
>
> NO!

Ms A Prior
10a Silver Street
Cosfield DO7 4BQ

TEL 9162 34455

July 17,1987

Dear Ms Prior,

Thank you for coming for interview on July 14.
We have considered your application carefully,
but regret that we are unable to offer you the
post.

You

A.

Ala
Per

BATSFORD & STAPLETON

17 Mews Lane
Cosfield
DO7 6AJ

Ms A Prior
10a Silver Street
Cosfield DO7 4BQ

TEL 9162 34455

July 17,1987

Dear Ms Prior,

Thank you for coming for interview on July 14.
We regret that neither your linguistic
qualifications nor your interpersonal skills are
up to the level we require. We are therefore
unable to offer you a post.

BATSFORD & STAPLETON

17 Mews Lane
Cosfield
DO7 6AJ

Ms A Prior
10a Silver Street
Cosfield DO7 4BQ

TEL 9162 34455

July 17, 1987

Dear Ms Prior,

Thank you for coming for interview last Tuesday.
We have considered your application carefully,
but regret that we are unable to offer you the
post. While your secretarial skills are well up
to the standard required, I did not feel that
your command of French was sufficiently good
for our purposes. In addition, you seem to lack
confidence in dealing with people, which would
certainly be a handicap if you were to work as
a receptionist. May I suggest that you might do
better to look for a job involving routine
office work?

With kind regards.

Yours sincerely,

A. Lomax

Alan Lomax
Personnel Director

---

8 You work for a publishing
firm. An old friend of your
mother's has sent you his collected
poems and asked you to consider
them for publication. A typical
poem goes:

'While I was eating a fried egg
I thought of you
and began to cry.
Life is so sad.'

**You do not feel able to publish the
poems. Write a letter to your
mother's friend telling him so.
Useful expressions:**

Thank you for . . .ing
I/We have considered . . . very
   carefully
but (I) regret that . . .
I am unable to . . .
While . . .
I do/did not feel that . . .
In addition . . .
May I suggest that . . .

**Study the Lesson Summary at the
back of the book.
Do some of the Practice Book
exercises.**

Sport

Reading comprehension; vocabulary; pronunciation; speaking practice.

A They are incredible runners

1 See how quickly you can find the answers to the following questions in the advertisement on the opposite page.

1. The man in the top picture has 'BR' on his shirt. What does this stand for?
2. How high are the valleys of the Occidental?
3. What colour did the Tarahumaras dislike?
4. Where did the American visitors cross the Mexican border?
5. What is the name of the wall of mountains that keeps the Tarahumaras isolated from the outside world?
6. How far did a Tarahumara run in four days and three nights, according to a story?
7. Who helped the Americans make contact with the Tarahumaras?
8. How well did the best Tarahumara girl do in the Kansas marathon?
9. Does Augustino Duran speak English?
10. What are the runners' shoes made of?

2 Do these statements say the same thing as the advertisement or not? Write *S* if they say the same, and *D* if there is a difference.

1. Bill Rodgers and Company make clothing for runners, footballers and tennis-players.
2. The Tarahumaras live in Northern Mexico.
3. They are all incredible runners.
4. Some people from Bill Rodgers and Company made a trip to see the Tarahumara runners.
5. They wanted the Tarahumaras to try out their running clothes and shoes.
6. They flew from El Paso.
7. The man in the top picture ran a distance of over 50 miles in around six hours.
8. He liked the Bill Rodgers clothes.
9. The next day, he tried out the Bill Rodgers Nor'Easter winter suit in the mountains.
10. There was one colour which the Tarahumaras refused to wear.
11. The reason was that it was unlucky.
12. The people from Bill Rodgers say that the Tarahumara civilisation is 3,000 years behind modern American civilisation.

3 Look at the advertisement again and choose some words and expressions to learn. Compare notes with other students, and talk about the reasons for your choices.

4 Pronunciation. In standard British English, the following words are all pronounced with the same vowel (/ɔː/). Can you say them? And can you think of ten more words with the same vowel that are written with *or*, *aw* or *al*?

all	border	course	four	more
northern	saw	shorts	stories	wall
warm				

5 Pronunciation. In standard British English, the following words are all pronounced with the same vowel (/ɜː/). Can you say them? And can you think of ten more words with the same vowel that are written with *er*, *ir*, *wor* or *ur*?

first	girls	heard	hers	learned
turn	virtually	word	worked	world

6 Work in groups of three or four. Write a questionnaire which can be used to find out about people's interests in sports and games. Prepare at least twenty questions. Examples:

Do you do any sport?
Do you like watching sport?
Have you ever played golf?
Can you play bridge?
What's the farthest that you have ever run?

7 Find somebody from another group and ask your questions. Answer his or her questions.

8 Tell the class some of the things that you have found out. Example:

'Alice isn't very interested in sport. But I was surprised to learn that she likes watching chess matches.'

To find out how good our running clothes really are, we traveled 3,000 miles south. And 3,000 years backwards.

Stories about the Tarahumara foot runners of Northern Mexico had been filtering back to us for quite some time.

Incredible, unbelievable stories.

Oh, there's the one about the tribesman who ran continuously over a period of four days and three nights without sleep. No small feat. Especially when you consider he averaged 10 miles per hour during one three hour stretch. They say he ran 300 miles altogether.

Then there's the one about the Tarahumara chief who was invited to send some runners to a marathon in Kansas. When the chief learned the distance was a mere 26 miles, he sent three young girls.

One of them placed second.

The Tarahumaras ran in sandals made of old tires.

Augustino Duran, the finest runner we met on our trip. He ran over 50 miles in our clothes.

The tribesmen raced along this course. Our clothes kept them comfortable as the competition heated up.

We decided to make a trip to Mexico. For two reasons.

First, we saw an opportunity to meet what had to be the most extraordinary runners we'd ever heard of.

Second, we saw an opportunity to prove what we've been saying about our clothes all along: they'll keep you comfortable no matter how hard or how long you run.

So this last January, we flew to El Paso, crossed the border at Juarez, and worked our way through the wall of mountains that make up the Sierra Madre Occidental.

This "wall" has kept the Tarahumaras virtually isolated from the outside world for centuries.

We found the Tarahumaras to be friendly, gentle people. And, of course, incredible runners.

For example, we asked the tribesman pictured above to take our mesh top and pinstripe shorts out for a test run. The test lasted approximately six hours. And over 50 miles.

Through a translator, the tribesman told us that the clothes seemed to "breathe" with him.

Another tribesman took our Nor'Easter winter suit up to the chilly, 8,000 foot valleys of the Occidental. The air is very thin up there, and we found it hard to breathe just standing still.

The tribesman ran the hills for four hours. And said he liked the suit because it kept him warm without hindering his running.

At the 48-mile mark, the Tarahumaras ran into the hills. The air was thin, but our clothes breathed easily.

After 57.8 miles, the race ended. Nobody could agree on who won, but they all agreed the clothes were winners.

The Tarahumaras tried our whole line out. And most of the clothes passed their tests with flying colors. (We say most, because one of the suits was cranberry. And for reasons we're still not sure of, none of the tribesmen would wear cranberry.)

We could go on with more reminiscences about our trip. But space doesn't permit it. So let us leave you with a suggestion instead.

The next time you go running, wear the clothes that runners 3,000 years behind us like to wear.

We're confident that once you try us out, the clothes you're running in now will become ancient history.

Special thanks to Father Luis Verplancken, a Jesuit priest who helped us make contact with the Tarahumaras.

Bill Rodgers & Company

Bill Rodgers & Company (U.K.), 2, Eastville Close, Eastern Avenue, Gloucester GL4 7SJ. Tel: (0452) 423262

B 'Man of the Match'

Listening; grammar (reported speech); vocabulary; discussion.

1 You are going to hear extracts from an interview with Trevor Hebberd, a professional footballer. Before you listen, read the questions and make sure you understand them. Choose one or more questions and try to guess what Trevor Hebberd's answer might be.

(*Note:* At the time of the interview, Hebberd had just completed a very successful season with Oxford United, a first-division British football club. He was voted 'Man of the Match' for his performance in the Cup Final game at Wembley Stadium against Queen's Park Rangers, when Oxford won the 'Milk Cup'.)

1. Was there anyone who specially helped you in your career?
2. What was it like when you were a young professional footballer – when you were working as an apprentice?
3. What would you say is the biggest pressure in your job?
4. What's the most agreeable part of your job?
5. And what do you find disagreeable about your job?
6. What advice would you give to a talented young footballer, thinking of trying to turn professional?
7. What's important in your life besides football?
8. Has your life changed since you played in the Cup Final at Wembley?

2 Now listen to the recording. You will hear the answers to the questions in Exercise 1, but not in order. Write down the letters A–H (for the answers); against each letter, write the number of the question that goes with it.

3 Choose one of Trevor Hebberd's answers. Listen again several times and try to write down exactly what he said.

4 Next, you will hear Trevor Hebberd talking about what he plans to do when he retires from football, and about the amount of free time that he gets as a footballer. Before you listen, read the questions in Exercise 5. Then listen to the recording twice and take notes.

5 Grammar: reported speech. Answer the following questions. Example:

Did he say that he knew what he wanted to do when he retired?
'*No, he said he didn't know.*'

1. Did he say he had thought about opening a sports shop?
2. Did he say that he liked the idea of becoming a publican?
3. Did he say he wanted to work for somebody else?
4. Did he say that it would be easy for him to do a nine-to-five job?
5. What did he say about his hours of work during the season? ('*He said . . .*')

6 Make a list of the main advantages and disadvantages of the life of a professional sportsman or sportswoman. Then work with two or three other students and try to agree on a group list of the three most important advantages and the three most important disadvantages.

7 Listen to the song.

HIGH PRESSURE

Was a high flyer in the neighbourhood,
Had a dream and yes it felt so good.
The man said he would let me know.
He was a sharp dealer turning every stone.
But I was so young I didn't know the score.
I gave it all I got then he closed the door.

I got fire in my feet, want to see me go.
Yes, I'm ready for action when the whistle blows.
Now I've signed my name along the dotted line.
Guess that makes me a star – you're going to see me shine.
Come on, Primadonna, better watch your step.
Until we're face to face you ain't seen nothing yet.

Chorus
High pressure – you're building up to high pressure.
Don't give it up.
High pressure – you're building up to high pressure.

I was always told if you need to win,
You've got to keep shooting till your ship comes in.
One day you're just a face in the crowd,
But then you hear them shouting your name out loud.
But they don't know all the pleasure and pain.
If I lived my life over I would do it again.

Now you see it, now you don't.
In the game you've got to go for broke.
Now you're in it, now you're out.
You got no time to see what life is all about.

Study the Lesson Summary at the back of the book. Do some of the Practice Book exercises.

"*Excuse me, can you settle an argument? My colleague here says we've scored nine goals but I say it's ten!*"

Plans

Grammar (future perfect and future progressive tenses); pronunciation; writing practice.

A I'm afraid this is going to come as a shock

1 Here are some pieces of a letter. The person who received the letter was so upset that he or she tore it up. What do you think it might have been about? Work in groups of two or three and make up a complete version of the letter. Use as many of the pieces as you can – all of them if possible.

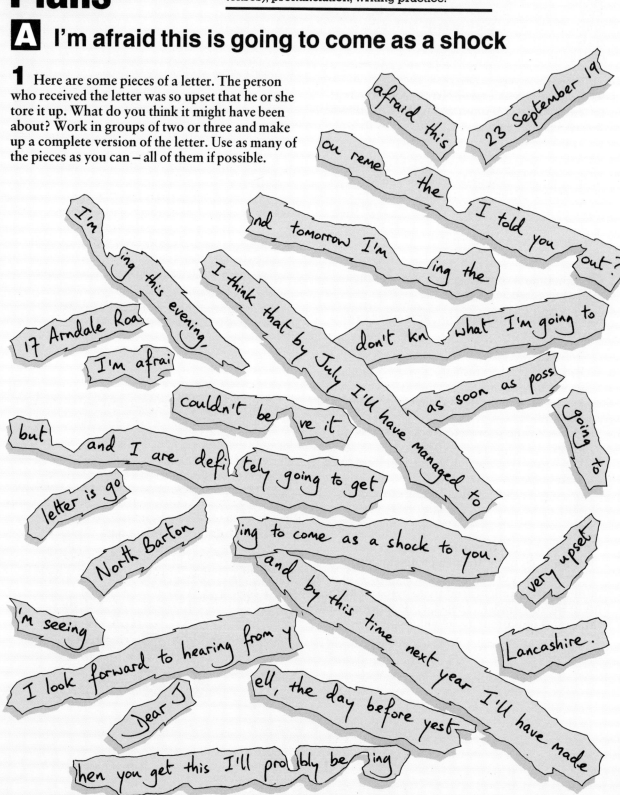

afraid this

23 September 19

ou reme

the

I told you

out?

I'm

ing this evening.

nd tomorrow I'm

ing the

I think that by July I'll have managed to

don't kn

what I'm going to

17 Arndale Roa

I'm afrai

as soon as poss

going to

couldn't be

ve it

but

and I are defi

tely going to get

letter is go

North Barton

ing to come as a shock to you.

very upset

'm seeing

and by this time next year I'll have made

Lancashire.

I look forward to hearing from y

Dear J

ell, the day before yest

hen you get this I'll pro bly be ing

2 Pronunciation. How do you think *have* and *for* are pronounced in the following sentences? Practise saying them, paying special attention to rhythm.

1. By next July I'll have been here for eight months.
2. When they get married they'll have known each other for three years.
3. When I retire I'll have been working for nearly 50 years.
4. Next summer we'll have been married for 30 years.

3 Grammar: future perfect tense. Change the sentences as in the examples.

In three years I'll be famous. (*become*)
'*In three years I'll have become famous.*'

In a couple of years her life will be very different. (*get married; settle down*)
'*In a couple of years she'll have got married and settled down.*'

1. When I'm 70 I won't be working. (*retire*)
2. By next summer I expect I'll be fully qualified. (*pass all exams*)
3. July 17th will be our tenth wedding anniversary. (*be married*)
4. I suppose in another few weeks the ice won't be there. (*melt*)
5. You say you love me, but a year from now I expect you won't even know my name. (*forget*)
6. We can't phone him at eleven o'clock. He'll be in bed. (*go to bed*)
7. Our house will be ready by next Thursday. (*The builders; finish*)
8. By the end of the week I won't have any more money left. (*spend*)
9. When I see her again, I'm sure she'll be very different. (*change*)

4 Choose one of the following questions, and ask as many people as possible in two minutes. Then tell the class what you have found out.

By next summer, how long will you have been learning English/at school/living in the same house/married?
Will you have finished studying English by next summer?
Ten years from now, will you have forgotten me?
When you're 70, do you think you will have changed a lot?
How many hours will you have worked by the end of this week?

5 Grammar: future progressive tense. Make sentences as in the examples. Use the words in the box to help you.

eight o'clock tomorrow morning / in the bathroom
'*At eight o'clock tomorrow morning I'll be brushing my teeth.*'
half past eight / in the car
'*At half past eight tomorrow morning I'll be driving to work.*'

1. ten o'clock tomorrow morning / in a meeting with the Sales Director
2. one o'clock tomorrow afternoon / in a restaurant
3. four o'clock tomorrow / on the tennis court
4. five o'clock tomorrow / in the swimming pool
5. six o'clock tomorrow / in the pub
6. eight o'clock tomorrow / in front of the TV
7. ten o'clock tomorrow evening / on the night train to Glasgow

brush teeth	drive	have a drink	
have lunch	play	swim	talk	travel
watch			

6 Ask as many people as possible what they will be doing at a particular time tomorrow. (You decide what time.)

7 Imagine that you are a young man or woman who has just arrived in an English-speaking country. Write a letter to a friend about your plans. Use the structures you have practised in this lesson. You must also use at least six of the following words and expressions.

actress   bathroom   cat   European
excellent   fetch   in bed   in time `   mad
promise   taxi   terrible   zoo

8 Exchange letters with another student. Write a short answer to the letter you have received.

Study the Lesson Summary at the back of the book.
Do some of the Practice Book exercises.

B I'm a bit short of time these days

1 Fill in the gaps in the two telephone conversations.

SUE: Hello. Porlock 8166.
JOE: Hi. Is that Sue?
SUE: ....
JOE: This is Joe. How are you?
SUE: ....
JOE: Listen, Sue. Are you doing .... this evening?
SUE: I'm not .... Why?
JOE: Well, I thought we might go out for a meal somewhere.
SUE: Oh, dear. I've just .... It looks as if I'm not .... this evening after all. I'm ....ing.
JOE: Well, how about tomorrow?
SUE: No. I really ought to stay in tomorrow. It's ages since I washed my hair.
JOE: What .... the day .... tomorrow?
SUE: No, I'm away then. Look, Joe. I'm really a bit short of time .... days. I've got a whole lot of work to finish by the end of the month. It's because of the reorganisation at the office. You know how it is. I'll .... you a ring when things get easier. OK?
JOE: OK. Bye.
SUE: Bye.

TOM: Hello. Porlock 1764.
SUE: Hello. .... ?
TOM: Yes, ... ?
SUE: .... is Sue.
TOM: Oh, hi, Sue. .... ?
SUE: Fine. What about you? Still working .... the same place?
TOM: Yes. They haven't found out about me .... In fact, they even say they're .... to give me a rise next month.
SUE: Look, Tom, I haven't seen you .... ages. .... this evening?
TOM: Don't think so.
SUE: .... to come out for a drink? That is, unless you're too ....
TOM: No, I'd love .... Where .... we meet?
SUE: How .... the King's Arms?
TOM: OK. .... ?
SUE: Say, about .... o'clock?
TOM: Eight o'clock's difficult. I don't get home .... half past seven. Could we make it a quarter past?
SUE: OK. Quarter past eight at the King's Arms. .... you then.
TOM: See you. Bye.
SUE: Bye.

2 Pronunciation. Divide these words into groups according to the pronunciation of the vowels. There are four groups.

all	clock	come	don't	go	got
home	Joe	lot	love	moment	month
not	OK	one	ought	phone	so
thought	Tom	wash			

3 Pronunciation. How are the words in italics pronounced? Listen to the recording and check your answers. Practise saying the expressions, with particular attention to rhythm.

Are you doing anything this evening?
I haven't seen you *for* ages.
a whole lot *of* work
the end *of* the month
Still working *at* the same place?
Would you like to come out *for* a drink?
Where *shall* we meet?
at the King's Arms

4 Imagine that you are going to invite a friend of yours, Ann, to go out with you. Decide where you want to go, and where and when you want to meet. Then answer the tape-recorder as follows:

ANN: Hello. Rainbow Hill 8180.
YOU: *Ask if it's Ann speaking.*
ANN: ....
YOU: *Answer.*
ANN: ....
YOU: *Answer. Ask how Ann is.*
ANN: ....
YOU: *Ask if Ann is doing anything this evening.*
ANN: ....
YOU: *Invite Ann to go out somewhere with you.*
ANN: ....
YOU: *Answer what Ann says. If she accepts, continue the conversation. If she refuses, keep trying (ask her out for tomorrow, the day after tomorrow etc.) until she accepts or ends the conversation.*

5 Work in pairs. Prepare and practise phone conversations in which one person asks the other out. Use some of the following expressions.

Are you free this evening?
Are you doing anything this evening?
I thought we might . . .
unless you're too busy/tired.

I'm not sure.
It depends.
Maybe, maybe not.
I can't remember.

Just a minute.
Let me just look in my diary.

It looks as if I'm not free.
I'm not free after all.
I've just remembered.
No, I'm afraid I'm baby-sitting/washing my hair/going to the theatre/working/playing bridge/. . .ing.
I really ought to wash my hair/write letters/. . .
I'm away tomorrow.
I've got a terrible headache.

What/How about tomorrow/the day after tomorrow?

I'm really a bit busy at the moment/for the next few weeks.
You know how it is.

It's ages since I . . .
I haven't . . . for ages.

I'll give you a ring one of these days/some time/when things get easier.

That would be lovely.
I'd love to.

Where shall we meet?
What time?
What time were you thinking of?

I'll come round to your place.
I might be a bit late.

That's difficult.
Could we make it a bit later?

See you then.

6 Improvisation. 'Telephone' somebody else in the class and ask him or her out.

Family and roots

A Exiles

1 What three things would you miss most if you had to live in a foreign country? (Or, if you are living in a foreign country, what three things do you miss most?)

2 Nighat is a young Pakistani woman who came to England two years ago to get married. Her husband, who is also a Pakistani, has lived in England for twenty years. Listen to the recording twice and then decide which of the following sentences give a true picture of her attitude.

1. She likes England but would rather be living in Pakistan.
2. She misses her family.
3. When she has children, she will bring them up to be bilingual.
4. She considers it important to keep her children in contact with their relations in Pakistan.
5. She thinks that if a European man marries a Pakistani woman, the Pakistani should change her religion.
6. She has a very positive attitude to Britain.
7. She can't wait for the holidays, when she can go back home and see her family.

3 Johnny is one of many Ukrainian refugees who were unable to return to their country (part of the Soviet Union) at the end of World War 2. Johnny settled in Edinburgh, which has a large Ukrainian community, and married a local woman. This is an extract from an interview with Johnny's son Phil, who is a young artist now living in England. Read what he says (and listen to the recording if you like, but Phil has a very strong Scottish accent which you may find difficult). Then write one- or two-sentence answers to the following questions.

1. What did the Ukrainian refugees do to preserve their culture and way of life?
2. How do they try to pass their culture on to their children?
3. How well has Phil's father Johnny succeeded in doing this?

Your father's generation came from the Ukraine and came to Scotland and tried to preserve as much as possible of their culture and of their way of life. How well do you think they succeeded for themselves in preserving their culture and their way of life?

Er. I think, the situation they were put into, they did really well. Because they didn't have any contact with people in the Ukraine for a long time. And so just from their memories – and to get the – they set up churches and clubs fairly quickly once they got here. And they seem to have quite a good organisation throughout the UK, of people – of their clubs and of dancing groups and various things.

So what do they do in these clubs?

They organise the youth, the young kids, to doing dancing, and they have mandolin orchestras, choirs, and they have the odd exhibition of crafts that they do, that there used to be in the Ukraine, and they get some of the kids to do, like, embroidery and various things. And the older people as well – I mean, they all do it as well, and they – a lot of them take part in the choir singing and making wood carvings and things.

How about the language?

Well, they have – they didn't succeed very well with me, as far as the language went. But they – in England they seem to have a lot more than in Scotland – they're a lot more keen, the youngsters, to learn the language, whereas up there, because there's a lot more intermarrying between Ukrainians and Scottish people in Scotland, – whereas in England they tend to marry within their own community. My sister speaks a lot of Ukrainian, fairly fluently. She feels very strongly for them I think. Much more so than I do.

You've gotten on to my second point in a way, which is, you know, how well do you think they've managed to pass their culture and traditions on to their kids?

Well, it varies a lot. It depends a lot on the enthusiasm of the kids, and whether they want to get concerned with it.

What did – how – when you were younger, what sort of things did you do?

What I used to do, I used to be in a dancing group. And we used to go all over Britain. Went to Ireland, performing concerts.

Do you feel Ukrainian?

No – to an extent – not greatly. I feel Scottish more than Ukrainian, I think. I don't know, really.

. . . Would you like to (go to the Ukraine)?

I'd love to go back. Love to go across and see what it's like.

What sort of special things do you feel you've got from the Ukrainian part of your heritage?

Stubbornness.

Stubbornness. If you have kids yourself some day, would you hope to be able to pass on some of the idea of being Ukrainian to your kids?

Oh, I hope so. Yeah, I hope so.

What do you think – I mean – how would you see yourself doing that?

I've no idea. It would depend a lot on how the clubs last. People are getting less involved in the club. In Edinburgh there's less interest paid to dancing and stuff now. And most of the first generation of Ukrainians will have died off by then. Because I'm not very – I don't have much time – I don't spend much time in the club at all any more; and I don't spend much time involved in Ukrainian events. I think it's mainly telling them where my dad came from and what happened, and – more that sort of thing – just let them know about the history.

4 Work in groups of three or four. Choose one or more of the following questions and discuss them.

1. Do you think Nighat will do better than Johnny in passing on her language and culture to her children? Why (not)?
2. Do you think people living abroad should try to bring up their children in this way?
3. Have you any experience of this kind of problem yourself? If so, can you talk about it to the group?
4. How would you react to marrying a foreigner and living in a new country?

5 Project. In your groups, prepare an interview with a person who has left his or her own country to live abroad. After the lesson, find somebody like this (a married person with children if possible) and ask your questions. Report to the class in the next lesson.

B I knew everyone

Reading and summarising; grammar
revision (position of prepositions);
vocabulary and discussion.

1 Read the text without using a dictionary.

PERSONAL ISOLATION

To the best of my knowledge, all my aunts, uncles and grandparents
spent most of their lives within thirty miles of Troy, Pennsylvania. They
were farmers, horse traders, merchants, mailmen. As a boy I believe I
knew everyone living within four miles of our farm. And I guess Dad knew
just about everyone in the county. He enjoyed talking. We met people as
families at suppers on Saturday nights. We met at church festivities, at
cattle auctions, at the milk station, at the icehouse pond, and at the
contests on the steep road leading to Granville Summit on Sunday
afternoons. The contest was to see who could drive his car the farthest
up the hill in high gear.

Today a number of my relatives still live near Troy, but several of my
cousins, my nieces, my brother and my sister are scattered in many
states. The nearest relative to my home in New Canaan, Connecticut, is a
niece who lives about a hundred and ten miles away. My two sons live in
Wisconsin and Pennsylvania; my mother-in-law, until her recent death,
lived much of the time in Florida.

When my wife Virginia and I moved to New Canaan twenty-four years
ago it was a semi-rural town and I soon knew most of the people living
within a mile of us. In recent years almost all the old neighbors have
moved and many dozens of new houses have sprung up near us, many
of them occupied by highly-mobile managerial and professional families.
One house very close by, for example, has been occupied by four
families in five years. Today I wouldn't even recognise half of the people
living within five hundred yards of our house. Virginia and I feel
increasingly isolated.

Personal isolation is becoming a major social fact of our time. A great
many people are disturbed by the feeling that they are rootless or
increasingly anonymous, that they are living in a continually changing
environment where there is little sense of community. The phrase 'home
town' may well fade from our language in this century. Already half of all
US heads of families live more than a hundred miles from where they
were born – and one out of every five lives more than a thousand miles
from his birthplace.

(Abridged from *A Nation of Strangers*, by Vance Packard)

2 Here are three summaries of the
text. Which one do you feel is the
most accurate?

Life used to be more fun when I was a
child: I lived in a happy family and
had lots of friends. Now there are
fewer opportunities for enjoying the
company of other people, because we
are all becoming rootless and
anonymous.

My family used to live close together,
but now they are scattered. We used
to know most of our neighbours, but
this is no longer the case. People
move around more now, and the old
kind of close community is
disappearing.

The population is growing and towns
are getting bigger. People are more
mobile, and they don't know each
other so well as they used to.
Personal isolation is a big problem
nowadays.

3 Grammar: word order. We often put prepositions at the ends of questions in English. Look at the examples and then make questions for the other answers.

1. I come from Burma.
   Where do you come from?
2. She lives with her aunt.
   Who does she live with?
3. I'm writing to my mother.
4. I'm thinking about my childhood.
5. We live in a small country town.
   (*What sort of . . . ?*)
6. We're talking about our families.
7. She comes from Scotland.
8. He works for an insurance company.

4 Grammar: word order. There are two ways of making relative clauses with prepositions. Look at the examples and then change the other sentences from formal to informal.

1. I did not like the people **with whom I was at school.** (formal)
   *I didn't like the people **I was at school with.*** (informal)
2. I have never been back to the place **in which I was born.** (formal)
   *I've never been back to the place **I was born in.*** (informal)
3. He is one of the people with whom I used to work.
4. I do not much like the place in which I live.
5. My family is the only thing for which I would fight.
6. John is the only person to whom I write.
7. The house in which I grew up no longer exists.
8. He has had a terrible quarrel with the woman with whom he lives.

5 Read through the questionnaire. Look up any words you don't know, and make sure you can answer all the questions in English.

1. Where are you from?
2. Where were your parents from?
3. Where have you spent most of your life?
4. Are you in close contact with your immediate family (parents/brothers/sisters/children)?
5. Is your family the most important thing in your life?
6. How important to you is your 'extended family' (aunts/uncles/cousins etc.)?
7. How many of your relations live within 30 miles of your home?
8. Is your family very scattered, or do they mostly live close together?
9. How many of your relations do you know personally?
10. Have you seen more or less of your family in recent years?
11. Do you think big families or small families are better?
12. Do you think it is a good thing for parents to live with their married children?
13. Do you know a lot of your neighbours?
14. Do you recognise all the people who live within a hundred yards of your home?
15. Would you rather live in: an isolated house; a village; a small country town; a medium-sized town; a big city?
16. Who do you get on best with?
    – people you are related to
    – people you went to school/college with
    – people you work with
    – other people (who?)
17. What places do you feel most at home in?
    – the place you were born in
    – the place(s) you grew up in
    – the place you live in now
    – other places (where?)
18. Do you consider yourself a) rootless b) well-rooted c) something between the two?

6 Choose one of the questions and ask as many people as possible. When you have finished, report to the class on what you have found out.

7 Listen to the song. (The words are on page 156.)

Study the Lesson Summary at the back of the book. Do some of the Practice Book exercises.

Looking forward; looking back

A When you are old and grey

Guessing unknown words; the language of prediction; grammar (*will* and *shall*); discussion.

1 Read the three poems without a dictionary, and listen to the recording. Say what you think of the poems. Do you like or dislike any of them? Do you have any other reactions?

When you are old

When you are old and grey and full of sleep,
And nodding by the fire, take down this book,
And slowly read, and dream of the soft look
Your eyes had once, and of their shadows deep;
How many loved your moments of glad grace,
And loved your beauty with love false or true,
But one man loved the pilgrim soul in you,
And loved the shadows of your changing face;

And bending down beside the glowing bars,
Murmur, a little sadly, how Love fled,
And paced upon the mountains overhead,
And hid his face amid a cloud of stars.

(W. B. Yeats)

When you are old and grey

Since I still appreciate you,
Let's find love while we may,
Because I know I'll hate you
When you are old and grey.
So say you love me here and now,
I'll make the most of that;
Say you love and trust me,
For I know you'll disgust me
When you're old and getting fat.

Your teeth will start to go, dear,
Your waist will start to spread.
In twenty years or so, dear,
I'll wish that you were dead.
I'll never love you then at all
The way I do today,
So please remember, when I leave in December,
I told you so in May.

(from a song by Tom Lehrer)

Warning

When I am an old woman I shall wear purple
With a red hat which doesn't go, and doesn't suit me,
And I shall spend my pension on brandy and summer gloves
And satin sandals, and say we've no money for butter.
I shall sit down on the pavement when I'm tired
And gobble up samples in shops and press alarm bells
And run my stick along the public railings
And make up for the sobriety of my youth.
I shall go out in my slippers in the rain
And pick the flowers in other people's gardens
And learn to spit.

(from a poem by Jenny Joseph)

2 Choose one of the poems and read it again, still without a dictionary. Write down all the words you don't know. Can you guess what any of them might mean? Underline the words you have guessed, and compare your guesses with another student who is reading the same poem. Then use a dictionary to check any words that you want to.

3 Write your own 'warning' or 'promise' about what you will do (and not do) when you're old. Use some or all of the following structures.

When I am old, I will . . .
I will . . .
I will not . . .
I will (not) be able to . . .
I will (not) have to . . .
I (don't) suppose I will . . .
I doubt if I will . . .
I am sure I will (not) . . .
I might . . .

(*Note:* Instead of *I will*, you can use *I'll* or *I shall* if you want to.)

4 Choose five of the following predictions, and say whether or not you agree with them. Add three more predictions of your own.

IN THE YEAR 3000
Everybody will speak the same language.
Books will no longer exist.
There will be no religion.
Most animals and birds will be extinct.
People will be taller and stronger.
People will live much longer than now.
Large parts of the earth will be uninhabitable.
The world will be seriously overcrowded.
Families will be limited to one child.
There will be a world government.
There will be no such thing as money.
There will be no shops.
Private houses will not exist.
Private cars will not exist.
Nobody will work.

BY THE YEAR 3000
War will have come to an end.
The world's climate will have changed.
Political systems will have become more democratic.
We will have colonised other planets.
The problem of world hunger will have been solved.

Useful expressions and structures:
I don't think . . . will . . .
I don't suppose . . . will . . .
I'm sure/certain that . . . will (not) . . .
It's likely / not very likely / unlikely / very probable / quite probable / possible — that . . . will . . .

5 Work in groups. Each group must choose one of the following subjects, and spend a quarter of an hour discussing it. Then a member of each group must tell the class what the group has decided.

What will the housing situation be like in 50 years' time?
What kind of games and sports will people play in 200 years?
How will shopping work in 50 years' time? Will people still use money? If not, what will they use instead?
What do you think education will be like 100 years from now?
What will . . . be like in 100 years? (Your choice of subject.)

POLITICS   HUNGER   POPULATION
COMMERCE   GOVERNMENT   TRAVEL
HOUSING   WILDLIFE
CONSE   WEAPONS
DEMO   FAMILIES
NUC   WORK
POLI   UNGER   ATION
COMMERCE   GOVERN   RAVEL
HOUSING   RELIGIO   DLIFE
CONSERVATION   MO   APONS
DEMOCRACY   MILIES
NUCLEAR PO   WORK
POLITICS   PULATION
COMMERCE   NT   TRAVEL
HOUSING   N   WILDLIFE
CONSERVATI   NEY   WEAPONS
DEMOCRACY   TE   FAMILIES
NUCLEAR PO   SPACE   WORK
POLITICS   POPULATION
COMMERCE   MENT   TRAVEL
HOUSING   RELIGION   WILDLIFE
CONSERVATIO   NEY   WEAPONS
DEMOCRACY   TE   FAMILIES
NUCLEAR PO   SPACE   WORK
POLITICS   H   POPULATION
COMMERCE   GOVERNMENT   TRAVEL
HOUSING   RELIGION   WILDLIFE

THE YEAR 3000 ?

Study the Lesson Summary at the back of the book.
Do some of the Practice Book exercises.

B I wish we'd never met

Wishes and regrets; grammar (tenses after *I wish*; *should/ought to have . . .*); speaking practice.

1 Can you write some of the thoughts of the person who received this letter?

14, Railway Gardens
South Wick.

Tuesday.

My Darling,

What has happened? You don't answer the phone; you aren't at home when I call; you don't write. Is something wrong? Have I upset you in some way?

We only met five weeks ago, but I feel as if I had lived a whole new life since then. So many wonderful memories!

I wish we'd never met!

That party when I first saw you. I asked you to dance. You said yes! You are so beautiful, you could have danced with anybody, but you chose me! I couldn't believe my luck.

I wish I'd never gone to the party!

Then you came back to my place for coffee, and I showed you my stamp collection, and told you all about my plans, my hopes, my life. What an evening!

Other memories flood into my brain. The day we went on the river. The weekend when we went shooting with Joe and Daphne. The time we went swimming – I got into trouble, and you pulled me to safety with your beautiful strong arms.

And then last weekend. We stood on the edge of the cliffs, looking down. You threw a stone into the sea, and I kissed you. You laughed with pleasure, and I told you I loved you, and you were so happy that you cried, and you couldn't say anything. What were you thinking?

Please write. I can't wait to hear from you.

I love you,

Alex

2 Here is a list of regrets. Choose three that you share, and add one or more of your own.

I wish I had been nicer to my parents when I was younger.

I wish my family had had more money when I was small.

I wish I had listened to my mother's advice.

I wish I had worked harder at school when I was younger.

I wish I had gone to a different school.

I wish I had stayed at school for longer.

I wish I had left school earlier.

I wish I had not started learning English.

I wish I had saved more money when I was younger.

I wish I had travelled more when I was younger.

I wish I had taken a different job.

I wish I had not got married.

I wish I had been born more beautiful.

I wish I had been born more intelligent.

I wish I had looked after my teeth better.

I wish I had never started smoking.

I wish I had gone to bed earlier last night.

120

3 Here are some other ways to talk about how the past might have been different. Practise saying the sentences; be careful about the pronunciation of *have* and *had*.

If only I had listened to my mother's advice!
I should have listened to my mother's advice.
I ought to have listened to my mother's advice.

If only I had never started smoking!
I should never have started smoking.
I ought never to have started smoking.

Can you use these structures to express some of the ideas in Exercise 2?

4 Pronunciation. Say these sentences.

You should have listened to me.
I ought to have got up earlier.
I wish I had never been born.
You should have told me you were coming.
He ought to have phoned.
If only I had realised what was wrong!
You should have been more careful.
She ought to have arrived by now.

5 Look at the pictures. What do you suppose the people in them are thinking? See if other students have the same ideas as you.

6 Here are some wishes for the present and future. Choose three that you share, and add one or more of your own.

I wish it was cooler/warmer.
I wish it was the end of the lesson.
I wish I was at home.
I wish I could sing.
I wish I could play the guitar.
I wish I had more money/time.
I wish I spoke better English.
I wish I knew more people.
I wish people were more honest.
I wish the government would do something about unemployment.
I wish somebody would write me a letter.

7 Write your most important wish on a piece of paper, but don't put your name on it. Give it to the teacher.

8 Work in groups. The teacher will read out all the class's wishes to you. Write them down and divide them into different kinds of wish. Report to the class: how many kinds of wish have you found, and what is the commonest kind of wish? What was the most surprising wish?

Study the Lesson Summary at the back of the book. Do some of the Practice Book exercises.

Revision and fluency practice

A Journey to Namur

Listening comprehension; discussion and speaking practice; story-telling; spelling and pronunciation; grammar (*should have* + past participle).

1 Here are some notes about a woman's journey from her home in England to Namur in Belgium. Read the notes and work out what happened. See if other students agree with you.

– supposed to be in Namur Sat p.m. for meeting
– decided leave early Sat
– taxi to station
– fast train to Reading late (floods)
– coach Reading – Heathrow Airport delayed (roadworks)
– airport just before take-off time
– only hand-baggage – ran
– handbag at security check – ran back
– plane late taking off
– late Brussels
– long queues passport control (Pope; terrorists)
– representative waiting
– taxi station
– picnic lunch train
– bomb scare
– waited new train
– Namur meeting

2 Now listen to the recording, and see if you can get the answers to the following questions.

1. What time was the meeting in Namur?
2. Was the taxi from her home to the station on time or late?
3. Did she catch a fast or a slow train to Reading?
4. Did she catch the coach that she was supposed to take from Reading to Heathrow?
5. How many minutes before take-off time did she arrive at the airport?
6. How late was the plane at Brussels?
7. Did she catch her train from Brussels to Namur?
8. How long did she have to wait for another train after the bomb scare?
9. Did she arrive in time for the Namur meeting, or was she late?

3 Can you think of a journey you have made when something went wrong, or when you had a lot of problems? Work in small groups and tell the other students about your experience.

4 Spelling and pronunciation. Practise saying these words. What is special about them? Can you add a word to each group?

wallet wander was wash wasp
watch what

wall waltz water war warm warn

one love other none money some
wonder come done

5 Read the story, and then say what you think the different people should or should not have done. Example:

'Annette shouldn't have gone to see Clive.'

ANNETTE AND CLIVE
Annette's boyfriend Clive went to the Far East for six months on business. Annette loved Clive desperately, and couldn't stand being away from him for so long. She wanted to go and see him, but she couldn't afford the air fare. So she telephoned Clive, asking him to come over to London for a few days to see her, but he said that he ccouldn't because of pressure of work. So then she went to see Ian, an old boyfriend of hers, and asked if he would lend her the money. He said that he would, but only if she would go to bed with him. Annette refused, and went to her father Jake. (Jake had plenty of money but didn't like Clive at all.) Jake said no. So Annette went back to Ian and agreed to his terms. They spent the night together, Ian gave Annette the money for the plane ticket, and the next day she flew to see Clive.

When Clive asked Annette how she had got the money, she told him the truth. Clive was furious and broke off their relationship. Annette flew back to London in despair. When she got home, she went to see her father and told him what had happened. Her father phoned a friend of his, and the two of them went round to Ian's place and beat him up.

6 Work in pairs. Make up the other half of this phone call and then act out your conversation for the class.

'Hello.'
....
'Yes, speaking.'
....
'I beg your pardon?'
....
'What?????'
....
'I see. Well, I'm sorry, but I haven't.'
....
'Who is that speaking anyway?'
....
'Oh, I see. Well, I would if I could, but I can't.'
....
'No, I'm afraid it's impossible. Anyway, I don't see why I should.'
....
'Where?'
....
'You're crazy!'
....
'No, I won't.'
....
'All right, that's different. I'll do it today.'
....

7 Work in pairs. Make up a conversation, lasting a maximum of 90 seconds, in which you use as many as possible of the following words.

asleep centimetre end go away
haircut menu pen purse quick rock
second sex taste tie towel zero

Study the Lesson Summary at the back of the book.

123

B Can you eat it?

Pronunciation and spelling; discussion and speaking practice; vocabulary.

1 Look at the cartoons. Talk to other students and say what you think about them. Find out which are the most and least popular cartoons. Useful expressions:

'I don't see the joke.'
'What do you think of this one?'
'That one's really funny.'
'It isn't funny at all.'
'I think it's stupid.'
'I think it's terrific.'
'It makes (doesn't make) me laugh.'

"That funny noise is getting louder."

"There goes a car with exactly the same number as ours."

"Nice legs!"

"Gloria, the travellers cheques! Throw out the travellers cheques!"

"I am standing under your foot."

2 Pronunciation. There is one vowel which comes in all of the following five words. What is it?

America   England   Europe   Japan
Belgium

Practise saying the five words, and then see if you can say these.

Germany   Brazil   Malawi   Singapore
Finland   Canada   Lebanon   Morocco

3 Vocabulary. Write down the English names of:

– four countries in Eastern Europe
– four countries in the Middle East
– four countries in the Far East
– four countries with an Atlantic coast
– four countries with a Pacific coast

4 Vocabulary: words that are easily confused. Choose the right word for each sentence (you may have to make some small changes), and then make a sentence using the other of the two words.

1. Would you like me to .... your letters to the post office? (*bring* or *take*)
2. 'Could you help me for a moment, please?' 'OK. I'm ....' (*come* or *go*)
3. Chess is a very complicated .... (*play* or *game*)
4. Shakespeare .... in 1616. (*dead* or *died*)
5. I've been studying French .... over six years. (*for* or *since*)
6. There's a flower shop .... our house. (*in front of* or *opposite*)
7. She works very .... (*hard* or *hardly*)
8. Who do you think will get the Nobel .... for physics? (*price* or *prize*)
9. The only traffic you ever get on our .... is tractors from the local farm. (*road* or *street*)
10. She's a very .... child – she loves nature and poetry and music. (*sensible* or *sensitive*)

5 Here is the script of a game of 'Twenty Questions'. The question-master is thinking of a common object, and the others are trying to guess what it is. What do you think the object is?

'Is it useful?'
'Yes.'
'Can you eat it?'
'No.'
'Is it manufactured?'
'Yes.'
'Does it cost more than £5?'
'Yes.'
'Does it cost more than £100?'
'No.'
'Is it made of metal?'
'Yes, partly.'
'Is it used in an office?'
'No.'
'In a kitchen?'
'No.'
'Outside?'
'Yes.'
'Is the metal part made of iron?'
'No.'

'Steel?'
'Yes.'
'Is it a means of transport?'
'No.'
'Can you hold it in your hand?'
'Yes.'
'Has it got a point?'
'Yes.'
'Is it bigger than a lighter?'
'Yes.'
'Is part of it made of string?'
'No.'
'Is part of it made of wire?'
'No.'
'Is it used at a particular time of day?'
'No.'
'Is it waterproof?'
'Yes.'
'Is it an . . .?'
'Yes.'

6 Play 'Twenty Questions' yourselves in groups of four or five. Try to use words and expressions from Exercise 5.

7 Work in groups of four, five or six. Prepare and practise a sketch for the following situation. When you are ready, perform your sketch for the class.

SITUATION
The group is a family. (Each student in the group should play the part of one of the family members.) Father has been offered a very well-paid job abroad; he wants to accept it and take the family with him. The rest of the family disagree about whether to go or not (each person should have a good reason for staying or going). In the middle of their discussion, the postman comes with a letter for one of the family (not Father).

Study the Lesson Summary at the back of the book.

Unit 1: Lesson A

Grammar and structures

Asking for help; getting things clear

How do you say . . . in English?
What's the English for . . . ?
What do you call a person who . . . ?
How do you pronounce . . . ?
Sorry, what did you say?
What do you mean?
Could you speak more slowly?

-ing forms after *like, mind* and prepositions

I like **meeting** people.
I like **being** with children.
Do you mind **working** long hours?
Are you good at **organising**?

Emphasising

What I like is **working outdoors**.
What I don't like is **the long hours**.
It's **working outdoors** that I like.
It's **the long hours** that I don't like.

Preference

Would you rather work indoors
or outdoors?
    (NOT ~~Would you rather to work . . . ?~~)

Adverbs of degree

extremely important
very important
quite important
not very important
not at all important

Words and expressions to learn

Nouns
organisation /ɔ:gənaɪ'zeɪʃn/
trade union /'treɪd 'ju:nɪən/
salary /'sæləri/
working conditions
    /'wɜ:kɪŋ kən,dɪʃnz/
chance /tʃɑ:ns/
waiter /'weɪtə(r)/

Verbs
add /æd/
grow up (grew, grown)
    /'grəʊ 'ʌp (gru:, grəʊn)/

Adjectives
patient /'peɪʃənt/
important /ɪm'pɔ:tənt/

Other words and expressions
anything /'eniθɪŋ/
outdoors /aʊt'dɔ:z/
on business /ɒn 'bɪznɪs/
extremely /ɪk'stri:mli/
altogether /ɔ:ltə'geðə(r)/
all day /'ɔ:l 'deɪ/
I imagine /aɪ ɪ'mædʒɪn/

Revision: do you know these words?

relationship /rɪ'leɪʃənʃɪp/
job /dʒɒb/
holiday /'hɒlədi/
factory /'fæktri/
office /'ɒfɪs/
responsibility
    /rɪspɒnsə'bɪləti/
memory /'meməri/
sense of humour
    /'sens əv 'hju:mə(r)/

noise /nɔɪz/
guess /ges/
meet (met, met) /mi:t (met)/
organise /'ɔ:gənaɪz/
retired /rɪ'taɪəd/
personal /'pɜ:sənl/
part-time /'pɑ:t 'taɪm/
on my own /'ɒn maɪ 'əʊn/
I suppose /aɪ sə'pəʊz/

Learn these words if you want to

promotion /prə'məʊʃn/
energetic /enə'dʒetɪk/

ambitious /æm'bɪʃəs/
artistic /ɑ:'tɪstɪk/

practical /'præktɪkl/
logical /'lɒdʒɪkl/

Unit 1: Lesson B

Grammar and structures

Should + infinitive without *to*

I (don't) think people **should start** work before the age of
    fifteen.
I don't think trade unions **should have** more power.
Teachers **should be paid** more.
Factory workers **shouldn't earn** more than nurses.

Start, put off + *-ing*

I start **working** about one o'clock.
They have decided to put off **selling** it.

After + *-ing*

After getting Sally ready and **driving** her to school, she
    starts on the housework.

Get + object + complement

I get the **house organised** for the evening.
. . . **getting Sally ready** . . .

Able

(*I am able = I can*)
They **are** just not **able** to save money.
I like **being able** to travel.
People should **be able** to start work at the age of fourteen.

By (the time) (= 'at or before', 'not later than')

By that stage I've finished my tea.
By the time I get out of the bath she's fully dressed.

Asking for help

What does . . . mean?
How do you pronounce . . . ?

Other structures

She's just **about to** go off to work.
another ten minutes
as quickly as possible

Words and expressions to learn

Nouns
branch /brɑ:ntʃ/
the country /ðə 'kʌntri/
the seaside /ðə 'si:saɪd/

Verbs
wander /'wɒndə(r)/
get rid of /'get 'rɪd əv/
put off . . . ing (put, put)
    /'pʊt 'ɒf/
look after /'lʊk 'ɑ:ftə(r)/

Adverbs
fortunately /'fɔ:tʃənətli/
hardly /'hɑ:dli/

Adjectives
able /'eɪbl/
tidy /'taɪdi/
careful /'keəfl/

Other words and expressions
anywhere between
    /'eniweə bɪ'twi:n/
get into trouble /'get ɪntə 'trʌbl/

Revision: do you know these words?

the ironing /ðɪ 'aɪənɪŋ/
the housework /ðə 'haʊswɜ:k/
the washing /ðə 'wɒʃɪŋ/
the cooking /ðə 'kʊkɪŋ/
the shopping /ðə 'ʃɒpɪŋ/
bag /bæg/
boss /bɒs/
public library
　/'pʌblɪk 'laɪbrəri/
politics /'pɒlətɪks/
history /'hɪstri/

trip /trɪp/
zoo /zu:/
problem /'prɒbləm/
income /'ɪŋkʌm/
parents /'peərənts/
iron (verb) /'aɪən/
spend time/money (spent, spent)
　/spend (spent)/
waste time/money /weɪst/
share /ʃeə(r)/
earn /ɜ:n/

(can't) afford /ə'fɔ:d/
retire /rɪ'taɪə(r)/
local /'ləʊkl/
unemployed /ʌnɪm'plɔɪd/
worried /'wʌrɪd/
upstairs /ʌp'steəz/
downstairs /'daʊn'steəz/
properly /'prɒpəli/
usually /'ju:ʒəli/
round /raʊnd/

Learn these words if you want to

landing /'lændɪŋ/
ironing board
　/'aɪənɪŋ ,bɔ:d/
reward /rɪ'wɔ:d/
involve /ɪn'vɒlv/

Unit 2: Lesson A

Words and expressions to learn

Nouns
fur /fɜ:(r)/
plant /plɑ:nt/
poison /'pɔɪzn/
Mediterranean /medɪtə'reɪnɪən/
lavatory /'lævətri/
continent /'kɒntɪnənt/

Verbs
destroy /dɪs'trɔɪ/
disappear
　/dɪsə'pɪə(r)/
hunt /hʌnt/
save /seɪv/

Other words and expressions
shocked /ʃɒkt/
in danger /ɪn 'deɪndʒə(r)/
nuclear /'nju:klɪə(r)/
chemical /'kemɪkl/
rare /reə/
international /,ɪntə'næʃənl/
natural /'nætʃərʊl/
almost /'ɔ:lməʊst/

Revision: do you know these words?

farm /fɑ:m/
death /deθ/
alive /ə'laɪv/
surprised /sə'praɪzd/
industrial /ɪn'dʌstrɪəl/

Learn these words if you want to

fertiliser /'fɜ:təlaɪzə(r)/
pesticide /'pestɪsaɪd/
power station /'paʊə ,steɪʃn/
oil tanker /'ɔɪl ,tæŋkə(r)/

North Sea /,nɔ:θ 'si:/
forest /'fɒrɪst/
climate /'klaɪmət/
agriculture /'ægrɪkʌltʃə(r)/

effect /ɪ'fekt/
mammal /'mæml/
whale /weɪl/
survive /sə'vaɪv/

atomic /ə'tɒmɪk/
extinct /ɪk'stɪŋkt/
tropical /'trɒpɪkl/

Unit 2: Lesson B

Grammar and structures

Quantifiers with and without *of*
most of the clothes
most of my clothes
most of these clothes
most of them
BUT: **most** clothes

several of the conversations
several of our conversations
several of those conversations
several of us
BUT: **several** conversations

Relatives: *which/that*
a farm animal **which** will eat anything
　　　　　that will eat anything
an animal **which** can run very fast
　　　that can run very fast
the **only** animal **that** lives in holes

Relatives: *whose*
an animal **whose** neck is longer than its legs
a snake **whose** bite can kill you
a bird **whose** eggs people often eat

Words and expressions to learn

Nouns
neck /nek/
stomach /'stʌmək/
skin /skɪn/
poem /'pəʊɪm/

Verbs
chase /tʃeɪs/
provide /prə'vaɪd/

Other words and expressions
valuable /'væljəbl/
gentle /'dʒentl/
ugly /'ʌgli/
normally /'nɔ:məli/

Revision: do you know these words?

insect /'ɪnsekt/
fish /fɪʃ/
chicken /'tʃɪkɪn/
flower /'flaʊə(r)/
plant /plɑ:nt/
camel /'kæml/

cow /kaʊ/
rabbit /'ræbɪt/
pork /pɔ:k/
egg /eg/
hole /həʊl/

jump /dʒʌmp/
useful /'ju:sfʊl/
useless /'ju:sləs/
afraid /ə'freɪd/
dangerous /'deɪndʒərəs/

Learn these words if you want to

spider /'spaɪdə(r)/
butterfly /'bʌtəflaɪ/
whale /weɪl/
crocodile /'krɒkədaɪl/
giraffe /dʒə'rɑ:f/
snake /sneɪk/
deer /dɪə(r)/

elephant /'elɪfənt/
frog /frɒg/
owl /aʊl/
parrot /'pærət/
tiger /'taɪgə(r)/
wolf (*plural* wolves) /wʊlf, wʊlvz/
mouse (*plural* mice) /maʊs, maɪs/

Unit 3: Lesson A

Grammar and structures

-ing forms for activities
bird-watching
collecting
dancing
gardening

-ed and -ing
I'm interested in chess.
I think chess is interesting.
She's bored by languages.
She says the lessons are boring.

So am I, etc.
Sarah is interested in money, and so is Richard.
Oliver likes animals, and so does Celia.
Sarah can't swim, and nor can Mark.
Sarah doesn't collect antiques, and nor does Richard.
Mark has got a home computer, but Richard hasn't.
Sarah plays golf, but Celia doesn't.

Used to (/'ju:stə/)
Oliver used to like pop music, and so did Mark.
Sarah didn't use to collect stamps.

Prepositions
I'm interested in travel.
I'm bored by football.

Talking about things in general: no article
She's interested in money.
(NOT … the money.)
Antiques are expensive.
(NOT The antiques …)

Asking for help
How do you spell . . . ?

Words and expressions to learn

Nouns
list /lɪst/
antiques /æn'ti:ks/
art /ɑ:t/
countryside /'kʌntrɪsaɪd/
sport /spɔ:t/
theatre /'θɪətə(r)/

recording /rɪ'kɔ:dɪŋ/
home computer /,həʊm kəm'pju:tə(r)/
golf /gɒlf/
economics /i:kə'nɒmɪks/
baby-sitting /'beɪbi,sɪtɪŋ/
bird-watching /'bɜ:d,wɒtʃɪŋ/
gardening /'gɑ:dnɪŋ/

Other words and expressions
collect /kə'lekt/
shoot (shot, shot) /ʃu:t (ʃɒt)/
Russian /'rʌʃn/
indeed /ɪn'di:d/

Revision: do you know these words?

jazz /dʒæz/
design /dɪ'zaɪn/
opera /'ɒpərə/
sign /saɪn/

pop music /'pɒp ,mju:zɪk/
classical music /,klæsɪkl 'mju:zɪk/
stamp /stæmp/
draw (drew, drawn) /drɔ: (dru:, drɔ:n)/

worry /'wʌri/
interview /'ɪntəvju:/
pronounce /prə'naʊns/
spell (spelt, spelt) /spel (spelt)/

Unit 3: Lesson B

Grammar and structures

-ing form after prepositions and conjunctions
He was interested in learning to become a parachutist.
He is thinking of taking up water-skiing.
. . . after giving him a series of tests . . .
It's better than being miserable.
I'm interested in mountaineering as well as running.

Sentences with if
If I had plenty of time, I would go round the world.
If I was/were twenty years younger, I would spend all my time skiing.

Words and expressions to learn

Nouns
expert /'ekspɜ:t/
parachute /'pærəʃu:t/
training /'treɪnɪŋ/
course /kɔ:s/
series /'sɪəriz/
chief /tʃi:f/
kilometre /'kɪləmi:tə(r)/

Verbs
manage /'mænɪdʒ/
successful /sək'sesfʊl/
prove /pru:v/

Other words and expressions
tough /tʌf/
common /'kɒmən/
so long as /səʊ 'lɒŋ əz/
as well as /əz 'wel əz/
during /'djʊərɪŋ/
below /bɪ'ləʊ/
all sorts of things

Revision: do you know these words?

lie /laɪ/
field /fi:ld/
stream /stri:m/
problem /'prɒbləm/
race /reɪs/
the mountains /ðə 'maʊntɪnz/
snow /snəʊ/
ice /aɪs/
turn up /'tɜ:n 'ʌp/
fall (fell, fallen) /fɔ:l (fel, 'fɔ:ln)/
climb /klaɪm/
give up (gave, given) /'gɪv 'ʌp (geɪv, 'gɪvn)/

enjoy /ɪn'dʒɔɪ/
run (ran, run) /rʌn (ræn, rʌn)/
solve /sɒlv/
share /ʃeə(r)/
surprised /sə'praɪzd/
fit /fɪt/
easy /'i:zi/
important /ɪm'pɔ:tənt/
especially /ɪ'speʃəli/
across /ə'krɒs/
and so on /ənd 'səʊ 'ɒn/
almost /'ɔ:lməʊst/
plenty of /'plenti əv/

Learn these words if you want to

hobby /'hɒbi/
motorcycling /'məʊtəsaɪklɪŋ/
mountaineering /maʊntɪ'nɪərɪŋ/
water-skiing /'wɔ:tə ˌski:ɪŋ/

hang-gliding /'hæŋ ˌglaɪdɪŋ/
athletics /æθ'letɪks/
the Alps /ði: 'ælps/
confess /kən'fes/

rescue /'reskju:/
take up /'teɪk 'ʌp/
on my mind /ɒn maɪ 'maɪnd/

Unit 4: Lesson A

Grammar and structures

Talking about possibility

I'm sure it's true.
It's probably true.
It may be true.

It might be true.
It's probably not true.
It can't be true.

Describing things

a thing with a hole/handle/etc.
a thing/tool/machine/ for making/cutting/...
material/liquid/powder/stuff for ...ing
a thing that you ... with/in/on/etc.
a thing that goes on top of/under ...

Words and expressions to learn

Nouns
nationality /næʃə'næləti/
ad /æd/
bargain /'bɑ:gɪn/
value /'vælju:/
video /'vɪdiəʊ/
body /'bɒdi/
point /pɔɪnt/
toe /təʊ/
lady /'leɪdi/

Other words and expressions
save /seɪv/
missing /'mɪsɪŋ/
pointed /'pɔɪntɪd/
for ever /fər 'evə(r)/

Revision: do you know these words?

advertisement /əd'vɜːtɪsmənt/
number /'nʌmbə(r)/
cottage /'kɒtɪdʒ/
party /'pɑ:ti/
bath /bɑ:θ/
price /praɪs/
choice /tʃɔɪs/
quality /'kwɒləti/
machine /mə'ʃi:n/
tool /tu:l/
stuff /stʌf/
liquid /'lɪkwɪd/
powder /'paʊdə(r)/

material /mə'tɪərɪʊl/
hole /həʊl/
handle /'hændl/
ankle /'æŋkl/
advertise /'ædvətaɪz/
sure /ʃɔ:(r)/
bored /bɔ:d/
free /fri:/
cheap /tʃi:p/
expensive /ɪks'pensɪv/
square /skweə(r)/
round /raʊnd/
sharp /ʃɑ:p/

Learn these words if you want to

poster /'pəʊstə(r)/
sale /seɪl/
gift /gɪft/
catalogue /'kætəlɒg/
for sale /fə 'seɪl/

Unit 4: Lesson B

Grammar and structures

Verbs with two objects
Can you lend **me** a ballpoint?
Could you bring **us** some water?
I've bought **myself** a new car.
Susan has written **John** a strange letter.
We've ordered **you** steak and chips.

Asking and offering; answering
See Lesson 4B, Exercise 5.

Asking for help
What's this called (in English)?

Words and expressions to learn

Nouns
soap /səʊp/
beef /bi:f/
sauce /sɔ:s/
photocopy /'fəʊtəʊkɒpi/
sandwich /'sæmwɪdʒ/
steak /steɪk/
pyjamas /pə'dʒɑ:məz/
spoon /spu:n/
the truth /ðə 'tru:θ/
ballpoint /'bɔ:lpɔɪnt/

Verbs
run out of /'rʌn 'aʊt əv/
offer /'ɒfə(r)/
rent /rent/

Other words and expressions
simple /'sɪmpl/
hard of hearing /'hɑ:d əv 'hɪərɪŋ/
bad-tempered /'bæd 'tempəd/
left /left/
give somebody a hand
just a moment
Have you got the time?
Have you got a light?

Revision: do you know these words?

dress /dres/
toothpaste /'tu:θpeɪst/
change /tʃeɪndʒ/
computer /kəm'pju:tə(r)/
timetable /'taɪmteɪbl/
come round /'kʌm 'raʊnd/
have a look /'hæv ə 'lʊk/
buy (bought, bought) /baɪ (bɔ:t)/
teach (taught, taught) /ti:tʃ (tɔ:t)/
tell (told, told) /tel (təʊld)/
order /'ɔ:də(r)/
show (showed, shown) /ʃəʊ (ʃəʊd, ʃəʊn)/
glad /glæd/
easy /i:zi/
kind /kaɪnd/
free /fri:/
in a hurry /ɪn ə 'hʌri/
a little /ə 'lɪtl/

Unit 5: Lesson A

Words and expressions to learn

Nouns
hammer /ˈhæmə(r)/
prison /ˈprɪzn/
crime /kraɪm/
criminal /ˈkrɪmɪnl/
success /səkˈses/
effect /ɪˈfekt/
punishment /ˈpʌnɪʃmənt/
advantage /ədˈvɑ:ntɪdʒ/
disadvantage /ˌdɪsədˈvɑ:ntɪdʒ/

Verbs
succeed /səkˈsi:d/
punish /ˈpʌnɪʃ/
prevent /prɪˈvent/
catch (caught, caught) /kætʃ (kɔ:t)/
commit (crime) /kəˈmɪt/

Other words and expressions
social /ˈsəʊʃl/
instead of /ɪnˈsted əv/
in your opinion /ɪn ˈjɔ:r əˈpɪnjən/
in prison (NOT in the prison)
to prison (NOT to the prison)

Revision: do you know these words?

society /səˈsaɪəti/
reason /ˈri:zn/
prisoner /ˈprɪznə(r)/
conditions /kənˈdɪʃənz/
carry /ˈkæri/
laugh /lɑ:f/
cry /kraɪ/
successful /səkˈsesful/

Unit 5: Lesson B

Grammar and structures

Past conditionals
If he **had attacked** me, I **would have hit** him.
If I **had been** the shop assistant, I **would have run** away.
If my parents **had had** more money, I **would have gone** to university.
If he **had not used** a gun, he **would not have gone** to prison.

Past modal verb constructions
He **should have been** more careful.
If I had had more time last year, I **could have travelled** to India.
If she hadn't screamed, the lorry driver **might not have come** to help.

Conversational pronunciations
going to = 'gonna' (/ˈgənə/)
want to = 'wanna' (/ˈwɒnə/)
got to = 'gotta' (/ˈgɒtə/)

Words and expressions to learn

Nouns
appearance /əˈpɪərəns/
dress /dres/
shop assistant /ˈʃɒp əˌsɪstənt/
lorry driver /ˈlɒri ˌdraɪvə(r)/
note /nəʊt/
victim /ˈvɪktɪm/
handbag /ˈhændbæg/
umbrella /ʌmˈbrelə/

Verbs
blame /bleɪm/
exchange /ɪksˈtʃeɪndʒ/
scream /skri:m/

Adjectives
little /ˈlɪtl/
ordinary /ˈɔ:dənri/
experienced /ɪksˈpɪərɪənst/

Revision: do you know these words?

knife /naɪf/
bicycle /ˈbaɪsɪkl/
policeman /pəˈli:smən/
policewoman /pəˈli:swumən/
fight (fought, fought) /faɪt (fɔ:t)/
steal (stole, stolen) /sti:l (stəʊl, ˈstəʊlən)/
hit (hit, hit) /hɪt/
escape /ɪsˈkeɪp/
exactly /ɪgˈzæktli/

Learn these words if you want to

incident /ˈɪnsɪdənt/   prison sentence /ˈprɪzn ˌsentəns/   vice versa /ˌvaɪs ˈvɜ:sə/
mugger /ˈmʌgə(r)/   grab /græb/   at the top of her voice

Unit 6: Lesson A

Grammar and structures

Past progressive tense
What **were** you **doing** at ten o'clock yesterday evening?
I **was eating.**
I can't remember what I **was doing.**

Weak pronunciations of auxiliary verbs, prepositions etc.
was = /wəz/   and = /ənd/   for = /fə(r)/
of = /əv/   to = /tə/   that = /ðət/
were = /wə(r)/   from = /frəm/

Words and expressions to learn

Nouns
story /ˈstɔ:ri/
the 1930s /ðə ˌnaɪnti:n ˈθɜ:tɪz/
World War 2 /ˈwɜ:ld ˌwɔ: ˈtu:/
scene /si:n/
camp /kæmp/

Verbs
hide (hid, hidden) /haɪd (hɪd, ˈhɪdn)/
go to sleep /ˈgəʊ tə ˈsli:p/
connect /kəˈnekt/

Adjectives
safe /seɪf/
convenient /kənˈvi:njənt/
pleasant /ˈpleznt/
unusual /ʌnˈju:ʒʊəl/

Other words and expressions
in order /ɪn ˈɔ:də(r)/
by myself /baɪ maɪˈself/

Revision: do you know these words?

tent /tent/	the future /ðə 'fju:tʃə(r)/
wood /wʊd/	happen /'hæpn/
plastic /'plæstɪk/	last /lɑ:st/
supper /'sʌpə(r)/	smile /smaɪl/
farm /fɑ:m/	travel /'trævl/
dream /dri:m/	strange /streɪndʒ/

Learn these words if you want to

camp-site /'kæmp saɪt/	barn /bɑ:n/
facilities /fə'sɪlətɪz/	telepathy /tə'lepəθi/
hedge /hedʒ/	coincidence /kəʊ'ɪnsɪdəns/
moped /'məʊped/	puzzled /'pʌzld/

Unit 6: Lesson B

Grammar and structures

Reported speech

She said 'I'm tired.'
She said that she was tired.

He asked 'Do you smoke?'
He asked if she smoked.

She asked 'Where's my coat?'
She asked where her coat was.

He said 'Oh, do stay.'
He asked her to stay.

She said 'Go and jump in the river.'
She told him to go and jump in the river.

Say and *tell*

She **said that** she was tired.
   (**NOT** She said him that . . .)
She **told him that** she was tired.
   (**NOT** She told that . . .)

Saying what you think of things

I think the first one is very good.
I don't think much of the second.
What do you think of the fourth one?

Words and expressions to learn

Nouns
trust /trʌst/
desk /desk/
space /speɪs/
crew /kru:/
frost /frɒst/
railway line
   /'reɪlweɪ laɪn/
washing machine
   /'wɒʃɪŋ mə,ʃi:n/

Other words and expressions
whisper /'wɪspə(r)/
annoy /ə'nɔɪ/
locked /lɒkt/
up to date /'ʌp tə 'deɪt/

Revision: do you know these words?

heart /hɑ:t/	drawer /drɔ:(r)/	share /ʃeə(r)/
gun /gʌn/	feelings /'fi:lɪŋz/	full /fʊl/
wine /waɪn/	sock /sɒk/	late /leɪt/
beer /bɪə(r)/	wedding /'wedɪŋ/	early /'ɜ:li/
whisky /'wɪski/	present /'preznt/	busy /'bɪzi/
coat /kəʊt/	apple /'æpl/	stupid /'stju:pɪd/
address /ə'dres/	pull /pʊl/	sad /sæd/
marriage	prefer /prɪ'fɜ:(r)/	else /els/
/'mærɪdʒ/	invent /ɪn'vent/	

Unit 7: Lesson A

Grammar and structures

Simple past and past progressive

While they **were sailing** up the west coast, they **ran** out of food.
Marco **became** ill while they **were crossing** Afghanistan.
When the emperor **was getting** old, they **decided** to return home.

Simple past and past perfect

When they **arrived** home, they **had been** away for over two years.
After they **had returned** from China, they **planned** a new journey.
Nobody **believed** their stories about the strange countries they **had visited**.

According to

According to an old story, they set off at the beginning of winter.

Words and expressions to learn

Nouns
route /ru:t/
market /'mɑ:kɪt/
ship /ʃɪp/
supplies /sə'plaɪz/

Verbs
plan /plæn/
control /kən'trəʊl/
set off (set, set) /'set 'ɒf/
sail /seɪl/
recover /rɪ'kʌvə(r)/

Other words and expressions
rough /rʌf/
amazed /ə'meɪzd/
civilised /'sɪvəlaɪzd/
roughly /'rʌfli/
according to /ə'kɔ:dɪŋ tə/
further /'fɜ:ðə(r)/
eventually /ɪ'ventʃəli/

➡

Revision: do you know these words?

travel /'trævl/   diary /'daɪəri/   follow /'fɒləʊ/   east /i:st/
coast /kəʊst/   business /'bɪznɪs/   avoid /ə'vɔɪd/   west /west/
boat /bəʊt/   experience /ɪks'pɪərɪəns/   report /rɪ'pɔ:t/   south-west /'saʊθ 'west/
journey /'dʒɜ:ni/   month /mʌnθ/   land /lænd/   ill /ɪl/
midday /'mɪd'deɪ/   run out of (ran, run)   reach /ri:tʃ/   away /ə'weɪ/
food /fu:d/   /'rʌn 'aʊt əv (ræn)/   north /nɔ:θ/
delay /dɪ'leɪ/   discover /dɪs'kʌvə(r)/   south /saʊθ/

Learn these words if you want to

sailor /'seɪlə(r)/   trader /'treɪdə(r)/   hire /haɪə(r)/
historian /hɪs'tɔ:rɪən/   rival /'raɪvl/   row /rəʊ/

Unit 7: Lesson B

Grammar and structures

Question tags
They're all the same, **aren't they?**
You **have** got a ticket, **haven't you?**
She **works** here, **doesn't she?**
You **can't** please everybody, **can you?**
You **don't** want to travel on Sunday, **do you?**
There's nothing I can do about it, **is there?**

Intonation in question tags
Asking for agreement:
They're all the same, aren't they?
Asking for information:
You have got a ticket, haven't you?

Short answers
'You do work here, don't you?' 'Yes, **we do.**'
'Can you help me?' 'I'm sorry, **I can't.**'

Reply questions
'He went to see one of his old girlfriends.' '**Did he really?**'
'I went to stay with my sister.' '**Did you?**'

Words and expressions to learn

Nouns
discussion /dɪs'kʌʃn/
guy /gaɪ/
waiting-room /'weɪtɪŋ rʊm/
safety belt /'seɪfti belt/
air hostess /'eə 'həʊstes/
misunderstanding /mɪsʌndə'stændɪŋ/

Verbs
expect /ɪks'pekt/
make up your mind /,meɪk ʌp jɔ: 'maɪnd/
stay (with somebody) /steɪ/

Other words and expressions
deaf /def/
frankly /'fræŋkli/

(See also list of conversational
expressions in Lesson 7B,
Exercise 2.)

Revision: do you know these words?

girlfriend /'gɜ:lfrend/   luggage /'lʌgɪdʒ/   meet (met, met) /mi:t (met)/
timetable /'taɪmteɪbl/   airport /'eəpɔ:t/   shout /ʃaʊt/
trouble /'trʌbl/   plane /pleɪn/   important /ɪm'pɔ:tənt/
record /'rekɔ:d/   meeting /'mi:tɪŋ/   dirty /'dɜ:ti/
manager /'mænɪdʒə(r)/

Unit 8: Lesson A

Grammar and structures

Complex sentences
When I was small I thought that . . .
I had the impression that . . .
I didn't realise that . . .
For some reason or other, I thought that . . .
The reason was that . . .
It seemed obvious to me that . . .
I wondered whether . . .
It looked as if . . .
I never believed in . . . , because . . .
This was because . . .
It's the tooth fairy that puts the money there.

Prepositions
Why do you **believe in**
  spacemen?
I've **heard of** people going
  to the moon.

Words and expressions to learn

Nouns
evidence /'evɪdəns/
Father Christmas /,fɑ:ðə 'krɪsməs/
tooth (*plural* teeth) /tu:θ (ti:θ)/
Easter /'i:stə(r)/
chimney /'tʃɪmni/
descendant /dɪ'sendənt/
impression /ɪm'preʃn/
detective /dɪ'tektɪv/

Other words and expressions
loss of memory /'lɒs əv 'meməri/
obvious /'ɒbvɪəs/
for some reason or other
  /fə 'sʌm 'ri:zn ɔ:r 'ʌðə(r)/

Revision: do you know these words?

ghost /gəʊst/   present /'preznt/   the seaside /ðə 'siːsaɪd/   realise /'rɪəlaɪz/
rabbit /'ræbɪt/   Christmas /'krɪsməs/   fish /fɪʃ/   wander /'wɒndə(r)/
the moon /ðə 'muːn/   bone /bəʊn/   wonder /'wʌndə(r)/   missing /'mɪsɪŋ/

Learn these words if you want to

spaceman /'speɪsˌmæn/   dragon /'drægn/
dinosaur /'daɪnəsɔː(r)/   sea monster /'siː ˌmɒnstə(r)/

Unit 8: Lesson B

Grammar and structures

Will-future: warnings; announcing decisions

If you do, I'll **kill** you.
I'll **have** to give you a ticket.
I think I'll **try** them again.

Non-progressive verbs

You **look** like a camel wearing a tent.
(NOT ~~You're looking like . . .~~)
I **don't think** this shade suits me.
(NOT ~~I'm not thinking . . .~~)
I **hope** it doesn't rain.
(NOT ~~I'm hoping . . .~~)

What do you want?

(NOT ~~. . . are you wanting?~~)
I **know** she's there.
NOT ~~I'm knowing . . .~~)
Other non-progressive verbs: believe, feel, fit, like, love, need, remember, seem, suit, understand.

Words and expressions to learn

Nouns		Verbs	Other expressions
brackets /'brækɪts/	uniform /'juːnɪfɔːm/	notice /'nəʊtɪs/	make sure /meɪk 'ʃɔː(r)/
motorist /'məʊtərɪst/	fool /fuːl/	tear (tore, torn)	Good heavens! /'gʊd 'hevənz/
thought /θɔːt/	shoe shop /'ʃuː ʃɒp/	/teə(r) (tɔː(r), tɔːn)/	
traffic warden /'træfɪk ˌwɔːdn/	shade /ʃeɪd/	stuff /stʌf/	

Revision: do you know these words?

line /laɪn/   customer /'kʌstəmə(r)/   wear (wore, worn)   fit /fɪt/
camel /'kæml/   park /pɑːk/   /weə(r) (wɔː(r), wɔːn)/   suit /suːt/
throat /θrəʊt/   kill /kɪl/   try on /'traɪ ɒn/

Unit 9: Lesson A

Grammar and structures

Relative clauses: *which* and *that*

1. *We can use both* which *and* that *before a piece of information which can't be left out:*
I sang a song **which/that** I had learnt from Bessie Smith.
The kind of music **which/that** excites me is 1930s jazz.

2. *Before a less important piece of information which can be left out, we use* which, *not* that:
They wanted to revive the jazz of the thirties, **which** was my favourite period.
Jazz, **which** had been popular, became very unpopular.

3. *We can only use* which *before a preposition. Compare:*
. . . the newspaper **which/that** I was working for
. . . the newspaper **for which** I was working

4. *We use* which *to refer to the whole idea that comes before:*
We decided to go professional, **which** we did in the early 1950s.

Words and expressions to learn

Nouns	Verbs
career /kə'rɪə(r)/	slide (slid, slid)
public house	/slaɪd (slɪd)/
/ˌpʌblɪk 'haʊs/	resign /rɪ'zaɪn/
movement /'muːvmənt/	relax /rɪ'læks/
period /'pɪərɪəd/	
subject /'sʌbdʒɪkt/	**Adjectives**
article /'ɑːtɪkl/	popular /'pɒpjələ(r)/
	unpopular /ʌn'pɒpjələ(r)/
	professional /prə'feʃnl/

Revision: do you know these words?

jazz /dʒæz/   seat /siːt/
journalist /'dʒɜːnəlɪst/   folk song /'fəʊk sɒŋ/
trumpet /'trʌmpɪt/   singer /'sɪŋə(r)/
interview /'ɪntəvjuː/   imagination /ɪmædʒə'neɪʃn/
rule /ruːl/   surprise /sə'praɪz/
pop music /'pɒp ˌmjuːzɪk/   in order /ɪn 'ɔːdə(r)/

Learn these words if you want to

art gallery /'ɑːt ˌgæləri/   revive /rɪ'vaɪv/
band /bænd/

Unit 9: Lesson B

Grammar and structures

Position of adverbs

He plays the instrument **beautifully**.
  (NOT ~~He plays beautifully the instrument.~~)

That person plays the synthesiser **very badly**.
  (NOT ~~... plays very badly the synthesiser.~~)

Words and expressions to learn

Nouns

sound /saʊnd/
ear for music /ˌɪə fə 'mjuːzɪk/
standard /'stændəd/
critic /'krɪtɪk/
talent /'tælənt/

fear /fɪə(r)/
taste /teɪst/
background music
  /'bækgraʊnd ˌmjuːzɪk/
judge /dʒʌdʒ/

Other words and expressions

insist /ɪn'sɪst/
decrease /dɪ'kriːs/
nervous /'nɜːvəs/
brilliant /'brɪlɪənt/

broad /brɔːd/
narrow /'nærəʊ/
reluctantly /rɪ'lʌktəntli/
however /haʊ'evə(r)/

Revision: do you know these words?

instrument /'ɪnstrəmənt/
concert /'kɒnsət/
aunt /ɑːnt/
cousin /'kʌzn/
ticket /'tɪkɪt/

piano /pi'ænəʊ/
violin /vaɪə'lɪn/
page /peɪdʒ/
classical music
  /ˌklæsɪkl 'mjuːzɪk/

increase /ɪŋ'kriːs/
low /ləʊ/
excited /ɪk'saɪtɪd/
comfortable /'kʌmftəbl/

favourite /'feɪvrɪt/
share /ʃeə(r)/
choose (chose, chosen)
  /tʃuːz (tʃəʊz, 'tʃəʊzn)/

Learn these words if you want to

melody /'melədi/
enthusiasm /ɪn'θjuːziæzm/
soloist /'səʊləʊɪst/

pianist /'pɪənɪst/
stage /steɪdʒ/
cassette /kə'set/

compact disc /ˌkɒmpækt 'dɪsk/
orchestra /'ɔːkɪstrə/

consequences /'kɒnsɪkwənsɪz/
accompany /ə'kʌmpəni/

Unit 10: Lesson A

Grammar and structures

The names of the present and past tenses

Simple present:
  I work
Present progressive:
  I am working
(Simple) present perfect:
  I have worked
Present perfect progressive:
  I have been working
Simple past:
  I worked
Past progressive:
  I was working
(Simple) past perfect:
  I had worked
Past perfect progressive:
  I had been working

Long and short vowels (1)

A vowel is usually long before consonant + e. Compare:

Short	Long
mad /mæd/	made /meɪd/
win /wɪn/	wine /waɪn/
hop /hɒp/	hope /həʊp/
cut /kʌt/	cute /kjuːt/

Long and short vowels (2)

But a vowel is usually short before two consonants. Compare:

Short	Long
dinner /'dɪnə/	diner /'daɪnə/
hopping /'hɒpɪŋ/	hoping /'həʊpɪŋ/
matter /'mætə/	later /'leɪtə/

Long and short vowels (3)

When we add an ending on to a short word, we may have to double the last consonant in order to keep the vowel short. Compare:
hop – hopping   big – bigger
run – runner

Long and short vowels (4)

We usually write ck after short vowels and k after long vowels and consonants. Compare:

Short	Long
back /bæk/	bake /beɪk/
lick /lɪk/	like /laɪk/
thick /θɪk/	think /θɪŋk/

We usually write tch after short vowels and ch after long vowels and consonants. Compare:

Short	Long
catch /kætʃ/	reach /riːtʃ/
fetch /fetʃ/	coach /kəʊtʃ/
hutch /hʌtʃ/	lunch /lʌntʃ/

Exceptions: rich, which, such, much.

Words and expressions to learn

tense /tens/
habit /'hæbɪt/
past /pɑːst/
present /'preznt/

repeated /rɪ'piːtɪd/
permanent /'pɜːmənənt/
just now /dʒʌst 'naʊ/
up to now /ʌp tə 'naʊ/

Revision: do you know these words?

result /rɪ'zʌlt/
childhood /'tʃaɪldhʊd/
examination /ɪgˌzæmɪ'neɪʃn/

accident /'æksɪdənt/
tired /'taɪəd/
still /stɪl/

Unit 10: Lesson B

Words and expressions to learn

Expressions used in telephoning

Can/could I speak to . . . ?
Speaking.
One minute/moment.
(I'm) trying to connect you.
The/His/Her line's engaged/busy.
Can/Will you hold?

I'll ring/call again in a minute.
Do you know the/his/her extension?
It's ringing for you.
I'll put you through.
I'll see if I can transfer you.
I've/You've got the wrong number/extension.

This is . . .
Who's that?
We were/got cut off.
It's a bad line.
I'll ring/call you back.

Giving directions (revision)

across /əˈkrɒs/
along /əˈlɒŋ/
down /daʊn/
in front of /ɪn ˈfrʌnt əv/
opposite /ˈɒpəzɪt/
past /pɑːst/

through /θruː/
towards /təˈwɔːdz/
roundabout /ˈraʊndəbaʊt/
traffic lights /ˈtræfɪk laɪts/
T-junction /ˈtiː dʒʌŋkʃən/
fork /fɔːk/

bend /bend/
Go straight ahead for . . . yards/metres.
Take the first/second/etc. on the right/left.
Turn right/left at . . .
It's on your right/left.
You can't miss it.

Unit 11: Lesson A

Words and expressions to learn

Nouns
pronunciation /prənʌnsiˈeɪʃn/
vocabulary /vəˈkæbjələri/
consonant /ˈkɒnsənənt/
vowel /vaʊl/
noun /naʊn/
verb /vɜːb/
culture /ˈkʌltʃə(r)/
foreigner /ˈfɒrənə(r)/

working knowledge
  /ˈwɜːkɪŋ ˈnɒlɪdʒ/
origin /ˈɒrɪdʒɪn/
explanation
  /ekspləˈneɪʃn/
record /ˈrekɔːd/
accounts /əˈkaʊnts/
object /ˈɒbdʒɪkt/

Adjectives
fluent /ˈfluːənt/
religious /rɪˈlɪdʒəs/

Revision: do you know these words?

spelling /ˈspelɪŋ/
grammar /ˈgræmə(r)/
stress /stres/
mistake /mɪsˈteɪk/
sign /saɪn/
god /gɒd/
learn (learnt, learnt)
  /lɜːn (lɜːnt)/

invent /ɪnˈvent/
difficult /ˈdɪfɪkʊlt/
perfectly /ˈpɜːfɪktli/
correctly /kəˈrektli/
in your opinion
  /ɪn ˈjɔːr əˈpɪnjən/
according to /əˈkɔːdɪŋ tə/

Learn these words if you want to

aspect /ˈæspekt/
intonation /ɪntəˈneɪʃn/

Unit 11: Lesson B

Words and expressions to learn

Nouns
accent /ˈæksənt/
meaning /ˈmiːnɪŋ/
mother tongue /ˈmʌðə ˈtʌŋ/
style /staɪl/
adjective /ˈædʒɪktɪv/

Other words and expressions
change the subject /ˌtʃeɪndʒ ðə ˈsʌbdʒɪkt/
imitate /ˈɪmɪteɪt/
accept /əkˈsept/
formal /ˈfɔːml/

(See also list of formal and informal
expressions in Lesson 11B, Exercise 4.)

Revision: do you know these words?

rise (rose, risen) /raɪz (rəʊz, ˈrɪzn)/
fall (fell, fallen) /fɔːl (fel, ˈfɔːlən)/
divide /dɪˈvaɪd/
apologise /əˈpɒlədʒaɪz/
invite /ɪnˈvaɪt/
offer /ˈɒfə(r)/

Unit 12: Lesson A

Grammar and structures

Present perfect for news
There **has been** flooding in the south of the country.
News **has just come in** of a plane crash . . .

Simple past for past details
First reports say that two aircraft **were** involved, and that several people **were** killed.

Present perfect with expressions of 'time up to now'
Average earnings **have gone up** by 60% **over the last six months.**
Industrial output **has risen** by 43% **during the last year.**
I **have lived** here **since 1982.**

Simple past with expressions of finished time
About 5,000 people **took** part in **yesterday's** demonstration.
Dr Joseph Brodsk **died yesterday.**

Contrastive stress
Can you pronounce these correctly?
Democratic Fantasian Radio has a different political position from **Free** Fantasian Radio.
Free Fantasian Television has a similar political position to Free Fantasian **Radio.**
He's not forty-seven, he's forty-**eight.**
He's not forty-seven, he's **thirty**-seven.

Words and expressions to learn

Nouns
democracy /dɪ'mɒkrəsi/
action /'ækʃən/
damage /'dæmɪdʒ/
bomb /bɒm/
sympathy /'sɪmpəθi/
sunshine /'sʌnʃaɪn/
limit /'lɪmɪt/

Adjectives
democratic /demə'krætɪk/
latest /'leɪtɪst/
official /ə'fɪʃl/
economic /iːkə'nɒmɪk/
efficient /ɪ'fɪʃnt/
prompt /prɒmpt/
available /ə'veɪləbl/
continuous /kən'tɪnjuəs/

Other words and expressions
approximately /ə'prɒksɪmətli/
in spite of /ɪn 'spaɪt əv/
due to /'djuː tə/
per cent (%) /pə 'sent/

Revision: do you know these words?

voice /vɔɪs/
figures /'fɪgəz/
exports /'ekspɔːts/
stone /stəʊn/
building /'bɪldɪŋ/
army /'ɑːmi/
message /'mesɪdʒ/

crash /kræʃ/
detail /'diːteɪl/
temperature /'temprɪtʃə(r)/
hurt (hurt, hurt) /hɜːt/
average /'ævrɪdʒ/
industrial /ɪn'dʌstrɪʊl/
similar /'sɪmələ(r)/

Learn these words if you want to

management /'mænɪdʒmənt/
productivity /prɒdʌk'tɪvəti/
inflation /ɪn'fleɪʃn/
demonstration /demən'streɪʃn/
speech /spiːtʃ/
opposition /ɒpə'zɪʃn/
forecast /'fɔːkɑːst/

Unit 12: Lesson B

Words and expressions to learn

Nouns
equipment /ɪ'kwɪpmənt/
flame /fleɪm/
gap /gæp/
concrete /'kɒŋkriːt/

Verbs
vote /vəʊt/
mix up /'mɪks 'ʌp/
smash /smæʃ/
injure /'ɪndʒə(r)/
miss /mɪs/
rescue /'reskjuː/

Other words and expressions
bright /braɪt/
Celsius /'selsɪəs/
Fahrenheit /'færənhaɪt/

Revision: do you know these words?

subject /'sʌbdʒɪkt/
antiques /æn'tiːks/
emergency /ɪ'mɜːdʒənsi/

vehicle /'viːɪkl/
shoot (shot, shot) /ʃuːt (ʃɒt)/
cloudy /'klaʊdi/

Learn these words if you want to

collision /kə'lɪʒn/
pop star /'pɒp ˌstɑː(r)/
album /'ælbəm/
funeral /'fjuːnərʊl/
painting /'peɪntɪŋ/

dustbin /'dʌstbɪn/
investigate /ɪn'vestɪgeɪt/
tunnel /'tʌnl/
crawl /krɔːl/

Unit 13: Lesson A

Grammar and structures

Modal verbs + infinitive without *to*
We shouldn't go.
He **might follow** us.
He **can't be** around.

-*ing* form as subject
Thinking about him terrified her.

Preposition + -*ing* form
She laughed at her friend **for being** afraid.
She couldn't get home **without crossing** the ravine.

Somebody, something etc. + infinitive
something to drink
She didn't have **anything to eat.**
There was **no one to walk** her home.

Want, tell, ask + object + infinitive
She **wanted her friend to spend** the night.
She **told her not to be** silly.
They **asked him to close** early.

Hear, see + object + infinitive or -*ing* form
Complete actions: infinitive
She **heard a dog bark.**
He **saw her open** her purse.
Actions continuing: -*ing form*
She **heard someone walking** behind her.
She **saw a man leaning** against a wall.

Words and expressions to learn

Nouns
drugstore (US) /'drʌgstɔ:(r)/
movement /'mu:vmənt/
purse (US, = GB handbag) /pɜ:s/
author /'ɔ:θə(r)/

Verbs
terrify /'terɪfaɪ/
bark /bɑ:k/
lean (leant, leant) /li:n (lent)/
cross /krɒs/
compare /kəm'peə(r)/

Other words and expressions
single /'sɪŋgl/
around /ə'raʊnd/
maybe /'meɪbi/
over (= finished) /'əʊvə(r)/
My God! /,maɪ 'gɒd/

Revision: do you know these words?

map /mæp/
bridge /brɪdʒ/
stranger /'streɪndʒə(r)/
find out (found, found) /'faɪnd 'aʊt (faʊnd)/
waste /weɪst/
spend (spend, spent) /spend (spent)/
promise /'prɒmɪs/
check /tʃek/
lonely /'ləʊnli/
afraid /ə'freɪd/
against /ə'genst/

Unit 13: Lesson B

Words and expressions to learn

Nouns
the dark /ðə 'dɑ:k/
exit /'eksɪt/
lift /lɪft/

Verbs
bother /'bɒðə(r)/
can't bear /'kɑ:nt 'beə(r)/
admit /əd'mɪt/
be sick /bi: 'sɪk/
burst into tears (burst, burst)
  /'bɜ:st ɪntə 'tɪəz/

Adjectives
common /'kɒmən/
terrified /'terɪfaɪd/
damp /dæmp/
scared /skeəd/

Other expressions
at the front /ət ðə 'frʌnt/
at the back /ət ðə 'bæk/
in my late twenties

Revision: do you know these words?

height /haɪt/
mouse (*plural* mice) /maʊs (maɪs)/
ground /graʊnd/
feel (felt, felt) /fi:l (felt)/
show (showed, shown) /ʃəʊ (ʃəʊd, ʃəʊn)/
shake (shook, shaken) /ʃeɪk (ʃʊk, 'ʃeɪkn)/
breathe /bri:ð/
hate /heɪt/
frightened /'fraɪtənd/
properly /'prɒpəli/

Learn these words if you want to

snake /sneɪk/
spider /'spaɪdə(r)/
tiger /'taɪgə(r)/
lion /'laɪən/
panic /'pænɪk/
clutch /klʌtʃ/

Unit 14: Lesson A

Words and expressions to learn

Nouns
Member of Parliament
/ˌmembər əv ˈpɑːlɪmənt/
candidate /ˈkændɪdət/
civil service /ˌsɪvl ˈsɜːvɪs/
civil servant /ˌsɪvl ˈsɜːvənt/
House of Commons
/ˌhaʊs əv ˈkɒmənz/
lawyer /ˈlɔːjə(r)/

Verbs
achieve /əˈtʃiːv/
represent /reprɪˈzent/
depend on /dɪˈpend ɒn/

Adjectives
Labour /ˈleɪbə(r)/
Conservative /kənˈsɜːvətɪv/
present /ˈpreznt/
neutral /ˈnjuːtrʊl/
worthwhile /ˈwɜːθˈwaɪl/
physical /ˈfɪzɪkl/

Revision: do you know these words?

Parliament /ˈpɑːlɪmənt/
politics /ˈpɒlətɪks/
politician /pɒləˈtɪʃn/
job /dʒɒb/
quality /ˈkwɒləti/
ability /əˈbɪləti/
decision /dɪˈsɪʒn/
intelligence /ɪnˈtelɪdʒəns/

relationship /rɪˈleɪʃənʃɪp/
party /ˈpɑːti/
get rid of /ˈget ˈrɪd əv/
organise /ˈɔːgənaɪz/
elect /ɪˈlekt/
vote /vəʊt/
successful /səkˈsesfʊl/

Learn these words if you want to

constituency /kənˈstɪtjuənsi/
issue /ˈɪʃuː/
strain /streɪn/
clarity /ˈklærəti/
energy /ˈenədʒi/
attractiveness /əˈtræktɪvnəs/
sensitivity /sensəˈtɪvəti/
sympathy /ˈsɪmpəθi/
enjoyable /ɪnˈdʒɔɪəbl/
satisfactory /sætɪsˈfæktri/

Unit 14: Lesson B

Grammar and structures

Will used for promises
If you elect us, we **will** change your lives.
Your children **will** be safe.

They, them, their with singular reference
The individual can make **their** own choices about **their** own environment.

Words and expressions to learn

Nouns
environment /ɪnˈvaɪrənmənt/
philosophy /fɪˈlɒsəfi/
values /ˈvæljuːz/
individual /ɪndɪˈvɪdʒuʊl/
left-winger /left ˈwɪŋə(r)/
right-winger /raɪt ˈwɪŋə(r)/
weapon /ˈwepn/

Other words and expressions
administer /ədˈmɪnɪstə(r)/
rely on /rɪˈlaɪ ɒn/
traditional /trəˈdɪʃənl/
extreme /ɪkˈstriːm/

Revision: do you know these words?

economics /iːkəˈnɒmɪks/
economy /ɪˈkɒnəmi/
choice /tʃɔɪs/
political /pəˈlɪtɪkl/
responsible /rɪˈspɒnsəbl/
world /wɜːld/

Unit 15: Lesson A

Words and expressions to learn

Nouns
activity /æk'tɪvəti/
teenager /'ti:neɪdʒə(r)/
kid /kɪd/
committee /kə'mɪti/
reform /rɪ'fɔ:m/
size /saɪz/
class /klɑ:s/
aim /eɪm/

Adjectives
constructive
  /kən'strʌktɪv/
co-operative
  /kəʊ'ɒpərətɪv/
critical /'krɪtɪkl/
enthusiastic
  /ɪnθju:zi'æstɪk/
sensitive /'sensətɪv/
teenage /'ti:neɪdʒ/

Other expressions
all the time
  /'ɔ:l ðə 'taɪm/
on strike /ɒn 'straɪk/
there's no point (in)
  /ðəz 'nəʊ 'pɔɪnt/

Learn these words if you want to

schooldays /'sku:ldeɪz/
dump /dʌmp/
homework /'həʊmwɜ:k/

private lessons /,praɪvɪt 'lesənz/
blow up (blew, blown) /'bləʊ 'ʌp (blu:, bləʊn)/

disciplined /'dɪsɪplɪnd/
respectful /rɪ'spektfʊl/

Revision: do you know these words?

primary school /'praɪməri sku:l/
secondary school /'sekəndri sku:l/
opposite /'ɒpəzɪt/
education /edju'keɪʃn/
examination /ɪgzæmɪ'neɪʃn/
dislike /dɪs'laɪk/   typical /'tɪpɪkl/
explain /ɪks'pleɪn/   fair /feə(r)/
careful /'keəfl/   useful /'ju:sfʊl/
happy /'hæpi/   useless /'ju:sləs/
patient /'peɪʃənt/   outside /'aʊt'saɪd/

Unit 15: Lesson B

Grammar and structures

Present perfect progressive
I've been going to school for eight years.
  (NOT ~~I'm going . . .~~ OR ~~I go . . .~~)
'How long **have you been working** here?'
  'Since January.'

Let/*make* + object + infinitive
  without *to*
She **lets us do** anything we like.
My parents never **made me help** with
  the housework.

Words and expressions to learn

Nouns
method /'meθəd/
cartoon /kɑ:'tu:n/
upbringing /'ʌpbrɪŋɪŋ/

Verbs
tend /tend/
protest /prə'test/
prepare /prɪ'peə(r)/
bring up /'brɪŋ 'ʌp/

(See also list of expressions
for discussion in Lesson 15B,
Exercise 5.)

Revision: do you know these words?

problem /'prɒbləm/
chance /tʃɑ:ns/
parents /'peərənts/
housework /'haʊswɜ:k/
maths /mæθs/
freedom /'fri:dəm/
sex /seks/
drugs /drʌgz/
solve /sɒlv/
study /'stʌdi/
practical /'præktɪkl/
free /fri:/

Unit 16: Lesson A

Words and expressions to learn

Nouns
desert /'dezət/
interior /ɪn'tɪərɪə(r)/
space /speɪs/
climate /'klaɪmət/
vegetation /vedʒə'teɪʃn/
gold /gəʊld/
mine /maɪn/
landscape /'lændskeɪp/

Other words and expressions
bother /'bɒðə(r)/
mention /'menʃən/
moderately /'mɒdrətli/

Revision: do you know these words?

fact /fækt/
discussion /dɪs'kʌʃn/
idea /aɪ'dɪə/
coast /kəʊst/
culture /'kʌltʃə(r)/
environment /ɪn'vaɪrənmənt/
snow /snəʊ/

close /kləʊs/
complete /kəm'pli:t/
main /meɪn/
direct /dɪ'rekt/
physical /'fɪzɪkl/
depressing /dɪ'presɪŋ/
exactly /ɪg'zæktli/

Unit 16: Lesson B

Grammar and structures

Past perfect and simple past

He **told** me that I **had passed** my exams.
I **found** a plant that I **had never seen** before.

As soon as I **had found** somewhere to leave the space ship, I started to explore.
When I was a child I wanted to be an explorer.
(NOT ~~I had wanted . . .~~)

Words and expressions to learn

Nouns	Adjectives	Other words and expressions
variety /vəˈraɪəti/	soft /sɒft/	shine (shone, shone)
rock /rɒk/	level /ˈlevl/	/ʃaɪn (ʃɒn)/
atmosphere	vertical /ˈvɜːtɪkl/	gently /ˈdʒentli/
/ˈætməsfɪə(r)/	horizontal /hɒrɪˈzɒntl/	below /bɪˈləʊ/
opening /ˈəʊpənɪŋ/	rectangular	in(to) the distance
	/rekˈtæŋgjələ/	/ɪn(tə) ðə ˈdɪstəns/
	oval /ˈəʊvl/	

Learn these words if you want to

extract /ˈekstrækt/
section /ˈsekʃən/
explorer /ɪkˈsplɔːrə(r)/
planet /ˈplænɪt/
radioactivity /ˌreɪdɪəʊækˈtɪvəti/
horizon /həˈraɪzn/
describe /dɪsˈkraɪb/
detect /dɪˈtekt/
impressive /ɪmˈpresɪv/
monotonous /məˈnɒtənəs/

Revision: do you know these words?

ground /graʊnd/	wonder /ˈwʌndə(r)/	round /raʊnd/
kind /kaɪnd/	rise (rose, risen)	behind /bɪˈhaɪnd/
hill /hɪl/	/raɪz (rəʊz, ˈrɪzn)/	above /əˈbʌv/
distance /ˈdɪstəns/	natural /ˈnætʃərʊl/	away /əˈweɪ/
star /stɑː(r)/	low /ləʊ/	not far (away)
part /pɑːt/	high /haɪ/	/ˈnɒt ˈfɑː(r)/
area /ˈeərɪə/	deep /diːp/	a long way (away)
valley /ˈvæli/	square /skweə(r)/	/ə ˈlɒŋ ˈweɪ/

Unit 17: Lesson A

Grammar and structures

Passive tenses

Simple present:
The liquid **is boiled.**
Strips of wood **are sent** through a machine.
Present progressive:
Coffee **is being made.**
Vegetables **are being prepared.**
Simple past:
The library **was burnt** down.
Most of the houses **were damaged.**

Past progressive:
I arrived just as lunch **was being served.**
My trousers were damaged while they **were being cleaned.**
Present perfect:
The town **has been restored.**
Roads **have been cleared.**
Past perfect:
I heard that he **had been arrested.**
Future:
Your watch **will be repaired** by Tuesday.
Structures with passive infinitive:
A coin **can be used** as a screwdriver.
She **must be told** as soon as possible.
Nurses **should be paid** more.

Words and expressions to learn

Nouns		Verbs
pencil /ˈpensl/	Town Hall /ˈtaʊn ˈhɔːl/	boil /bɔɪl/
pump /pʌmp/	gas /gæs/	pour /pɔː(r)/
sugar /ˈʃʊgə(r)/	ton /tʌn/	dry /draɪ/
process /ˈprəʊses/	coin /kɔɪn/	break up (broke, broken)
heat /hiːt/	screwdriver	/ˈbreɪk ˈʌp (brəʊk, ˈbrəʊkn)/
stripe /straɪp/	/ˈskruːdraɪvə(r)/	glue /gluː/
pipe /paɪp/	bra /brɑː/	remove /rɪˈmuːv/
staff /stɑːf/		damage /ˈdæmɪdʒ/

Adjective
single /ˈsɪŋgl/

Revision: do you know these words?

coffee /'kɒfi/
toothpaste /'tu:θpeɪst/
factory /'fæktri/
liquid /'lɪkwɪd/
tube /tju:b/
chemical /'kemɪkl/
powder /'paʊdə(r)/
secret /'si:krɪt/

loss /lɒs/
add /æd/
push /pʊʃ/
destroy /dɪs'trɔɪ/
burn (burnt, burnt)
/bɜ:n (bɜ:nt)/
public /'pʌblɪk/
separately /'seprətli/
completely /kəm'pli:tli/

Learn these words if you want to

instant coffee /,ɪnstənt 'kɒfi/
pressure /'preʃə(r)/
jar /dʒɑ:(r)/
manufacturer
/,mænjə'fæktʃərə(r)/
vacuum /'vækjuəm/
strip /strɪp/
ruin /'ru:ɪn/

ash /æʃ/
roast /rəʊst/
grind /graɪnd/
evaporate /ɪ'væpəreɪt/
hollow /'hɒləʊ/
rapidly /'ræpɪdli/
repeatedly /rɪ'pi:tɪdli/

Unit 17: Lesson B

Grammar and structures

Position of adverbs of manner

Stir the soup **carefully**.
(NOT ~~Stir carefully the soup.~~)

She speaks English **well**.
(NOT ~~She speaks well English.~~)
I wrote my name **quickly**.
(NOT ~~I wrote quickly my name.~~)

Words and expressions to learn

toy /tɔɪ/
make a bed
/,meɪk ə 'bed/

stir /stɜ:(r)/
wooden /'wʊdn/
thoroughly /'θʌrəli/

Revision: do you know these words?

food /fu:d/
onion /'ʌnjən/
tomato
/tə'mɑ:təʊ/
salt /sɔ:lt/

pepper /'pepə(r)/
butter /'bʌtə(r)/
oil /ɔɪl/
plan /plæn/

crash /kræʃ/
wheel /wi:l/
cook /kʊk/
check /tʃek/

pick up /'pɪk 'ʌp/
clean /kli:n/
stupid /'stju:pɪd/
gently /'dʒentli/

Learn these words if you want to

garlic /'gɑ:lɪk/
herb /hɜ:b/

margarine /mɑ:dʒə'ri:n/
bacon /'beɪkn/

vegetable soup /,vedʒtəbl 'su:p/
fuse /fju:z/

Unit 18: Lesson A

Words and expressions to learn

Nouns
situation
/sɪtju'eɪʃn/
cause /kɔ:z/
poverty /'pɒvəti/
hunger /'hʌngə(r)/
Third World
/,θɜ:d 'wɜ:ld/
debt /det/
charity /'tʃærəti/
capital /'kæpɪtl/
interest /'ɪntrəst/
policy /'pɒləsi/
employee /ɪm'plɔɪi:/

Other words and expressions
repay (repaid, repaid)
/rɪ'peɪ (rɪ'peɪd)/
set up (set, set) /'set 'ʌp/
poor /pɔ:(r)/
certain /'sɜ:tn/
individual /ɪndɪ'vɪdjuəl/
directly /dɪ'rektli/
compared to /kəm'peəd tə/

Revision: do you know these words?

country /'kʌntri/
flood /flʌd/
million /'mɪljən/
percentage /pə'sentɪdʒ/
lend (lent, lent)
/lend (lent)/
concentrate on
/'kɒnsəntreɪt ɒn/
support /sə'pɔ:t/
main /meɪn/
local /ləʊkl/
rich /rɪtʃ/
regularly /'regjələli/

Learn these words if you want to

drought /draʊt/
administration
/ədmɪnɪ'streɪʃn/
consumption /kən'sʌmpʃən/
head office /'hed 'ɒfɪs/
surplus /'sɜ:pləs/
raise money /reɪz 'mʌni/
small-scale /smɔ:l 'skeɪl/
long-term /'lɒŋ 'tɜ:m/

Unit 18: Lesson B

Grammar and structures

Clauses with *before*
Before I lend them to you I'd like to ring her.
Before you cross the road, always look both ways.
I'll write to you before I come and see you.

Missing
There are two glasses **missing**.
Two glasses are **missing**.
Have you seen the **missing** glasses?

Lack
I need . . .
I'm short of . . .
I've run out of . . .
I'm right out of . . .
I haven't got any . . . left.

Asking to borrow things
Could I borrow a/some . . . (from you)?
I wondered if I could borrow . . . ?
Could you lend me a/some . . . ?
Have you got a/some . . . you could lend me?
You haven't got a/some . . . you could lend me, have you?
. . . if you've got one/any.
. . . by any chance.

Replying
Sure, glad to.
Glad to help.
When do you need it/them by?
Thanks a lot.
Is there anything else you need?
I'm all right otherwise, thanks.
I have got some, but the thing is . . .

Words and expressions to learn

Nouns
lack /læk/
set /set/
champagne /ʃæm'peɪn/
fiancée /fi'ɑ:nseɪ/

Other words and expressions
forgive (forgave, forgiven)
   /fə'gɪv (fə'geɪv, fə'gɪvn)/
precious /'preʃəs/
someone else /'sʌmwʌn 'els/
heaps of /'hi:ps əv/
out of /'aʊt əv/
I wouldn't dream of it.
   /aɪ 'wʊdnt 'dri:m əv ɪt/
See you in a bit. /'si: ju ɪn ə 'bɪt/

Revision: do you know these words?

box /bɒks/
fridge /frɪdʒ/
pepper /'pepə(r)/
cold /kəʊld/
need /ni:d/

recognise /'rekəgnaɪz/
borrow /'bɒrəʊ/
missing /'mɪsɪŋ/
enough /ɪ'nʌf/
otherwise /'ʌðəwaɪz/

Unit 19: Lesson A

Grammar and structures

Have got
1. Have got *means the same as* have. Have got *is more common in informal speech and writing.*
   We **have got** a good relationship.
   We **have** a good relationship.

2. Got *is mostly used with the present of* have. *It is not usually used with the past, infinitive or -ing form of* have.
   I'd like to **have** a sister. (NOT . . . to have got a sister.)

3. *When* have *is used to talk about an action,* got *is not used.*
   to **have** a bath (NOT to have got a bath)

Words and expressions to learn

Nouns
partner /'pɑ:tnə(r)/
point of view
   /,pɔɪnt əv 'vju:/

Verbs
argue /'ɑ:gju:/
communicate
   /kə'mju:nɪkeɪt/

Adjectives
bright /braɪt/
dull /dʌl/
tolerant /'tɒlərənt/
faithful /'feɪθful/
moody /'mu:di/
terrific /tə'rɪfɪk/
homosexual /həʊmə'sekʃuʊl/

Other
have something in common with

Revision: do you know these words?

relationship /rɪ'leɪʃənʃɪp/
decision /dɪ'sɪʒn/
marriage /'mærɪdʒ/
sense of humour
   /,sens əv 'hju:mə(r)/
couple /'kʌpl/
argument /'ɑ:gjumənt/

personality /pɜ:sə'næləti/
trust /trʌst/
quality /'kwɒləti/
friendship /'frendʃɪp/
society /sə'saɪəti/
stranger /'streɪndʒə(r)/
waste /weɪst/

Unit 19: Lesson B

Grammar and structures

Position of frequency adverbs

1. *Before one-part verbs:*
   I **often ask** my wife for advice.
   I **never ask** my father for advice.

2. *But after am/are/is/was/were:*
   Her advice **is often** useful.
   His advice **was never** any good.

3. *After the first part of longer verbs:*
   I **have often asked** friends for advice.
   I **would never have asked** her if I had known her better.

Words and expressions to learn

Verbs	Adjectives	Other words and expressions
make friends /ˌmeɪk ˈfrendz/	sensible /ˈsensəbl/	peace /piːs/
ignore /ɪgˈnɔː(r)/	imaginary /ɪˈmædʒənri/	totally /ˈtəʊtəli/
flirt /flɜːt/	considerate /kənˈsɪdərət/	in my twenties /ɪn maɪ ˈtwentɪz/
imagine /ɪˈmædʒən/	aggressive /əˈgresɪv/	
tempt /tempt/	thankful /ˈθæŋkfʊl/	(See also expressions for giving advice in Lesson 19B, Exercise 2.)

Revision: do you know these words?

advice /ədˈvaɪs/
happiness /ˈhæpɪnəs/
security /sɪˈkjʊərəti/
get married /ˈget ˈmærɪd/
go out with somebody
  /ˈgəʊ ˈaʊt wɪð ˈsʌmbədi/

improve /ɪmˈpruːv/
worry /ˈwʌri/
shy /ʃaɪ/
serious /ˈsɪərɪəs/
silly /ˈsɪli/
real /ˈrɪəl/

kind /kaɪnd/
bad-tempered /ˈbæd ˈtempəd/
lovely /ˈlʌvli/
usually /ˈjuːʒəli/
occasionally /əˈkeɪʒənli/
hardly ever /ˈhɑːdli ˈevə(r)/

Learn these words if you want to

beast /biːst/
dread /dred/
make excuses
  /meɪk ɪksˈkjuːsɪz/
snap /snæp/
beg /beg/
miserable /ˈmɪzrəbl/
peculiar /pəˈkjuːlɪə(r)/

Unit 20: Lesson A

Grammar and structures

Tenses in reported speech

She said the sky **was** grey,
  but actually it **is** blue.
She's sixteen, but I **thought**
  she **was** older.

Words and expressions to learn

Nouns	Verbs	Other words and expressions
description /dɪsˈkrɪpʃən/	confuse /kənˈfjuːz/	ready /ˈredi/
file /faɪl/	keep (kept, kept)	slightly /ˈslaɪtli/
cassette player	/kiːp (kept)/	shortly /ˈʃɔːtli/
/kəˈset pleɪə(r)/	remind /rɪˈmaɪnd/	along /əˈlɒŋ/
fun /fʌn/		at the moment
		/ət ðə ˈməʊmənt/

Revision: do you know these words?

mistake /mɪsˈteɪk/
journey /ˈdʒɜːni/
travel /ˈtrævl/
drive (drove, driven)
  /draɪv (drəʊv, ˈdrɪvn)/
explain /ɪkˈspleɪn/
leave (left, left) /liːv (left)/

turn up /ˈtɜːn ˈʌp/
introduce /ɪntrəˈdjuːs/
apologise /əˈpɒlədʒaɪz/
interrupt /ɪntəˈrʌpt/
realise /ˈrɪəlaɪz/
promise /ˈprɒmɪs/
grey /greɪ/

loud /laʊd/
enthusiastically
  /ɪnθjuːziˈæstɪkli/
actually /ˈæktʃəli/
downstairs
  /ˈdaʊnˈsteəz/
I don't mind
  /aɪ ˈdəʊnt ˈmaɪnd/

Unit 20: Lesson B

Revision: do you know these words?

crash /kræʃ/
size /saɪz/
kilometre /ˈkɪləmiːtə(r)/

litre /ˈliːtə(r)/
wait /weɪt/
save (money) /seɪv/

order /ˈɔːdə(r)/
repair /rɪˈpeə(r)/
funny /ˈfʌni/

stupid /ˈstjuːpɪd/
double /ˈdʌbl/

Unit 21: Lesson A

Grammar and structures

Need . . .ing (passive meaning)
A lot **needs doing** to it. (= needs to be done to it.)
Some bricks **need replacing**. (= . . . need to be replaced.)

Have something done
When the new owners moved in, they **had** a lot of things
   done.
They **had** some new ceilings **put in**.
I must **have** my watch **repaired**.

Words and expressions to learn

Nouns
outside /'aʊt'saɪd/
inside /'ɪn'saɪd/
roof /ru:f/
step /step/
aerial /'eərɪəl/
frame /freɪm/
owner /'əʊnə(r)/
ceiling /'si:lɪŋ/
fire escape
   /'faɪər ɪs,keɪp/
emergency exit
   /ɪ,mɜ:dʒənsi 'eksɪt/
ladies (toilet) /'leɪdɪz/
gents (toilet) /dʒents/

Verbs
paint /peɪnt/
arrange /ə'reɪndʒ/
lower /'ləʊə(r)/
raise /reɪz/
clean up /'kli:n 'ʌp/
put in /'pʊt 'ɪn/
take down /'teɪk 'daʊn/
change . . . into
   /'tʃeɪndʒ ɪntə/
turn . . . into /'tɜ:n ɪntə/

Adjective
handicapped
   /'hændɪkæpt/

Revision: do you know these words?

gate /geɪt/
path /pɑ:θ/
floor /flɔ:(r)/
ground floor /'graʊnd 'flɔ:(r)/
first floor /'fɜ:st 'flɔ:(r)/
plan /plæn/
cupboard /'kʌbəd/
repair /rɪ'peə(r)/
replace /rɪ'pleɪs/
divide /dɪ'vaɪd/
improve /ɪm'pru:v/
increase /ɪŋ'kri:s/
main /meɪn/

Learn these words if you want to

brick /brɪk/
hedge /hedʒ/
mess /mes/
rebuild /ri:'bɪld/
(re)decorate /ri:'dekəreɪt/
straighten /'streɪtn/
strengthen /'streŋθən/
widen /'waɪdn/
show somebody round
   /'ʃəʊ 'sʌmbədi 'raʊnd/
move in /'mu:v 'ɪn/
convert /kən'vɜ:t/
store /stɔ:(r)/

Unit 21: Lesson B

Grammar and structures

Should, ought to +
passive infinitive
More housing **should be owned**
   by the government.
Tenants **ought to be allowed** to
   make improvements to
   their accommodation.

Words and expressions to learn

Nouns
divorce /dɪ'vɔ:s/
student /'stju:dənt/
improvement
   /ɪm'pru:vmənt/
landlord /'lændlɔ:d/
tenant /'tenənt/
accommodation
   /əkɒmə'deɪʃn/
structure /'strʌktʃə(r)/

Verbs
entertain /entə'teɪn/
allow /ə'laʊ/

Adjectives
actual /'æktʃʊəl/
possible /'pɒsəbl/
particular /pə'tɪkjələ(r)/
illegal /ɪ'li:gl/

Other words and expressions
because of /bɪ'kɒz əv/
whose /hu:z/

Revision: do you know these words?

design /dɪ'zaɪn/
poverty /'pɒvəti/
budget /'bʌdʒɪt/

result /rɪ'zʌlt/
income /'ɪŋkʌm/
rent /rent/

increase /ɪŋ'kri:s/
afford /ə'fɔ:d/

Learn these words if you want to

mortgage /'mɔ:gɪdʒ/
host /həʊst/
bedsit /'bed'sɪt/

recession /rɪ'seʃn/
self-employed /'self ɪm'plɔɪd/

Unit 22: Lesson A

Grammar and structures

Descriptions

She has (She's got) blue eyes.
a woman **who has** (who's got)
    blue eyes
a woman **with** blue eyes
a **blue-eyed** woman

Prepositions

a man **with** a beard
a boy **with** glasses
a girl **in** a blue dress
a man **in** a grey jacket

Compound adjectives

a **blue-eyed** woman
a **brown-haired** man
a **thin-faced** girl
right-handed   **left-handed**
    long-legged

Words and expressions to learn

Nouns
chin /tʃɪn/
forehead /'fɔːhed/ or /'fɒrɪd/
eyebrow /'aɪbraʊ/
lip /lɪp/
cheek /tʃiːk/
businesswoman /'bɪznɪs,wʊmən/

Verb
describe /dɪs'kraɪb/

Adjectives
wide /waɪd/
generous /'dʒenərəs/
firm /fɜːm/
weak /wiːk/
overweight /'əʊvə'weɪt/
middle-aged /'mɪdl 'eɪdʒd/
elderly /'eldəli/
serious /'sɪərɪəs/
plain /pleɪn/
well dressed /'wel 'drest/

Revision: do you know these words?

height /haɪt/
expression /ɪks'preʃn/
appearance /ə'pɪərəns/
beard /bɪəd/
moustache /mə'stɑːʃ/
straight /streɪt/
bald /bɔːld/

thin /θɪn/
pointed /'pɔɪntɪd/
oval /'əʊvl/
round /raʊnd/
low /ləʊ/
broad /brɔːd/
narrow /'nærəʊ/

cheerful /'tʃɪəfl/
worried /'wʌrɪd/
friendly /'frendli/
good-looking /'gʊd 'lʊkɪŋ/
pretty /'prɪti/
beautiful /'bjuːtɪfl/
attractive /ə'træktɪv/

Learn these words if you want to

build /bɪld/
cheekbones /'tʃiːkbəʊnz/
scar /skɑː(r)/
curly /'kɜːli/

wavy /'weɪvi/
blond(e) /blɒnd/
slender /'slendə(r)/
muscular /'mʌskjələ(r)/

heavily-built /'hevəli 'bɪlt/
plump /plʌmp/
casually dressed /'kæʒəli 'drest/

Unit 22: Lesson B

Grammar and structures

Questions about frequency

How often do you . . . ?
Do you ever . . . ?
Have you ever . . . ?

Proportions:
singular and plural verbs

Nearly everybody **does**.
Most people **do**.
The majority **do**.
Some people **do**.
Several people **do**.
A few people **do**.
Hardly anybody **does**.
One person **does**.
Nobody **does**.
Two **out of** nine people **do**.

Words and expressions to learn

Adjectives
calm /kɑːm/
cold /kəʊld/
emotional /ɪ'məʊʃənl/
honest /'ɒnɪst/

mean /miːn/
pessimistic /pesɪ'mɪstɪk/
reserved /rɪ'zɜːvd/
self-confident /'self 'kɒnfɪdənt/
sensitive /'sensətɪv/

Revision: do you know these words?

the majority /ðə mə'dʒɒrəti/
aggressive /ə'gresɪv/
bad-tempered /'bæd 'tempəd/
easy-going /'iːzi 'gəʊɪŋ/
moody /'muːdi/
nervy /'nɜːvi/

optimistic /ɒptɪ'mɪstɪk/
polite /pə'laɪt/
practical /'præktɪkl/
rude /ruːd/
shy /ʃaɪ/
sociable /'səʊʃəbl/

Unit 23: Lesson A

Words and expressions to learn

Nouns
right (to) /raɪt (tə)/
goal /gəʊl/
body /'bɒdi/
faith (in) /feɪθ (ɪn)/

Other words and expressions
negotiate /nɪ'gəʊʃieɪt/
generalise /'dʒenrəlaɪz/
underpaid /'ʌndə'peɪd/
social /'səʊʃl/

obviously /'ɒbvɪəsli/
a great deal of /ə 'greɪt 'di:l əv/
as a whole /æz ə 'həʊl/
do the best they can

Revision: do you know these words?

opinion /ə'pɪnjən/
patient /'peɪʃənt/
nurse /nɜ:s/

hospital /'hɒspɪtl/
uniform /'ju:nɪfɔ:m/
staff /stɑ:f/

pain /peɪn/
accident /'æksɪdənt/
entertain /entə'teɪn/

organise /'ɔ:gənaɪz/
interested in /'ɪntrəstɪd ɪn/
actually /'æktʃəli/

Unit 23: Lesson B

Grammar and structures

Passive structures with modal verbs

Parents worry that a bone **may be broken.**
Severe bruising **can be treated** by rest.
The limb **should be raised.**

Negative imperatives

Do not cover the graze.
Do not apply a bandage.

Words and expressions to learn

Nouns
bandage /'bændɪdʒ/
human being /'hju:mən 'bi:ɪŋ/
supply /sə'plaɪ/
joint /dʒɔɪnt/
effort /'efət/
bruise /bru:z/
dirt /dɜ:t/

Verbs
get over /'get 'əʊvə(r)/
drown /draʊn/
reckon /'rekn/
dive /daɪv/

Other words and expressions
powerful /'paʊəfl/
stiff /stɪf/
apparently /ə'pærəntli/

Learn these words if you want to

antiseptic /'æntɪ'septɪk/
germ /dʒɜ:m/
heal /hi:l/
infected /ɪn'fektɪd/

Revision: do you know these words?

damage /'dæmɪdʒ/
lack /læk/
level /'levl/
rise (rose, risen) /raɪz (rəʊz, 'rɪzn)/
material /mə'tɪərɪəl/
bone /bəʊn/
accident /'æksɪdənt/
brain /breɪn/
power /'paʊə(r)/
illness /'ɪlnɪs/
blood /blʌd/
heart attack /'hɑ:t ə'tæk/
operation /ɒpə'reɪʃn/
bleed (bled, bled) /bli:d (bled)/
injure /'ɪndʒə(r)/
weak /wi:k/

Unit 24: Lesson A

Grammar and structures

Adverbs of degree

too expensive
extremely expensive
very expensive
rather expensive
quite expensive
fairly expensive
neither expensive nor cheap
not very expensive
not at all expensive

Structures used in comparisons

about the size of a fridge
a bit bigger than a TV
not quite as heavy as a telephone
small enough to hold in your hand

Words and expressions to learn

Nouns
dictionary /'dɪkʃənri/
key /ki:/
string /strɪŋ/
zip /zɪp/
wing /wɪŋ/

Verbs
look up /'lʊk 'ʌp/
hold (held, held) /həʊld (held)/

Adjectives
extra /'ekstrə/
blunt /blʌnt/
flexible /'fleksəbl/
fragile /'frædʒaɪl/
rigid /'rɪdʒɪd/
rough /rʌf/
shiny /'ʃaɪni/
smooth /smu:ð/
transparent /træns'pærənt/
unbreakable /ʌn'breɪkəbl/
waterproof /'wɔ:təpru:f/

Revision: do you know these words?

stripe /straɪp/
size /saɪz/
add /æd/
cheap /tʃi:p/
expensive /ɪks'pensɪv/

fast /fɑ:st/
flat /flæt/
narrow /'nærəʊ/
sharp /ʃɑ:p/
slow /sləʊ/

soft /sɒft/
wide /waɪd/
extremely /ɪk'stri:mli/
anything else /,eniθɪŋ 'els/
dull /dʌl/

Learn these words if you want to

butterfly /'bʌtəflaɪ/
background /'bækgraʊnd/
pattern /'pætən/

dot /dɒt/
medium-sized
  /'miːdɪəm 'saɪzd/

brownish /'braʊnɪʃ/
orangey-red
  /'ɒrɪndʒi 'red/

Unit 24: Lesson B

Grammar and structures

Structures used for comparison
See list in Lesson 24B, Exercise 3.

Words and expressions to learn

Nouns
mile /maɪl/
top speed /tɒp 'spiːd/
amount /ə'maʊnt/
gallon /'gælən/
passenger /'pæsɪndʒə(r)/

Revision: do you know these words?

the rest /ðə 'rest/
guarantee /gærən'tiː/
bargain /'baːgɪn/
fog /fɒg/
engine /'endʒən/

petrol /'petrʊl/
seat /siːt/
space /speɪs/
cost (cost, cost) /kɒst/
park /paːk/

economical /iːkə'nɒmɪkl/
similar /'sɪmələ(r)/
comfortable /'kʌmftəbl/
noisy /'nɔɪzi/

Learn these words if you want to

accessory /ək'sesəri/
mileage /'maɪlɪdʒ/
fog lamp /'fɒg læmp/
air conditioning /'eə kən'dɪʃənɪŋ/
petrol consumption
  /'petrʊl kən'sʌmpʃən/

engine capacity /'endʒən kə'pæsəti/
gear /'gɪə(r)/
acceleration /əkselə'reɪʃn/
bonnet /'bɒnɪt/
headlamp /'hedlæmp/

Unit 25: Lesson A

Words and expressions to learn

Nouns
exception /ɪk'sepʃən/
state /steɪt/
the public /ðə 'pʌblɪk/
document /'dɒkjəmənt/
data /'deɪtə/

Verbs
obtain /əb'teɪn/
copy /'kɒpi/
apply (to) /ə'plaɪ (tə)/
correct /kə'rekt/
protect /prə'tekt/

Other words and expressions
various /'veərɪəs/
general /'dʒenrl/
national /'næʃənl/
in general /ɪn 'dʒenrl/

Revision: do you know these words?

freedom /'friːdəm/
information /ɪnfə'meɪʃn/
right /raɪt/
record /'rekɔːd/
department /dɪ'paːtmənt/
policy /'pɒləsi/

the majority /ðə mə'dʒɒrəti/
law /lɔː/
individual /ɪndɪ'vɪdjuʊl/
meeting /'miːtɪŋ/
authority /ɔː'θɒrəti/
committee /kə'mɪtiː/

file /faɪl/
allow /ə'laʊ/
check /tʃek/
foreign /'fɒrən/
secret /'siːkrɪt/

private /'praɪvɪt/
similar /'sɪmələ(r)/
personal /'pɜːsənl/
official /ə'fɪʃl/
valuable /'væljəbl/

Learn these words if you want to

federal /'fedərʊl/
act /ækt/
citizen /'sɪtɪzn/
defence (US defense)
  /dɪ'fens/

contract /'kɒntrækt/
hire purchase /haɪə 'pɜːtʃəs/
credit /'kredɪt/
inspect /ɪn'spekt/
base /beɪs/

consult /kən'sʌlt/
reduce /rɪ'djuːs/
medical /'medɪkl/
mental /'mentl/

Unit 25: Lesson B

Grammar and structures

'Unreal' past tenses
Past tenses are often used with a present meaning, to talk about a situation that is imaginary or unreal.

You might say that it **was** not in the loft.
If somebody **gave** me a present for the baby, I would say how pretty it **was**.
You wouldn't tell somebody that they **were** dying.

Words and expressions to learn

Nouns	Verbs	Other words and expressions	
piece of clothing /ˌpiːs əv ˈkləʊðɪŋ/	lie /laɪ/	certain /ˈsɜːtn/	sufficiently /səˈfɪʃəntli/
dinner /ˈdɪnə(r)/	lack /læk/	clever /ˈklevə(r)/	in addition /ɪn əˈdɪʃn/
note (money) /nəʊt/	consider /kənˈsɪdə(r)/	by mistake /baɪ mɪsˈteɪk/	even if /ˈiːvn ɪf/
level /ˈlevl/	regret /rɪˈgret/	therefore /ˈðeəfɔː(r)/	have something wrong with you
purpose /ˈpɜːpəs/	require /rɪˈkwaɪə(r)/		

Revision: do you know these words?

interview /ˈɪntəvjuː/	possible /ˈpɒsəbl/
qualification /kwɒlɪfɪˈkeɪʃn/	nervous /ˈnɜːvəs/
standard /ˈstændəd/	silly /ˈsɪli/
firm /fɜːm/	(un)attractive /ʌnəˈtræktɪv/
poem /ˈpəʊɪm/	physical(ly) /ˈfɪzɪkl (ˈfɪzɪkli)/
deal with (dealt, dealt) /ˈdiːl wɪð (delt)/	routine /ruːˈtiːn/
involve /ɪnˈvɒlv/	typical /ˈtɪpɪkl/
pretty /ˈprɪti/	Ms /mɪz/ or /məz/

Learn these words if you want to

Christmas present /ˈkrɪsməs ˌpreznt/	spot /spɒt/
Christmas Day /ˌkrɪsməs ˈdeɪ/	stutter /ˈstʌtə(r)/
sin /sɪn/	skill /skɪl/
attitude /ˈætɪtjuːd/	handicap /ˈhændɪkæp/
bank clerk /ˈbæŋk ˈklɑːk/	bilingual /baɪˈlɪŋgwʊl/
applicant /ˈæplɪkənt/	publish /ˈpʌblɪʃ/
receptionist /rɪˈsepʃənɪst/	unconfident /ʌnˈkɒnfɪdənt/
	for instance /fər ˈɪnstəns/

Unit 26: Lesson A

Grammar and structures

Prepositions at the end of relative clauses
the most extraordinary runners (that) we'd ever heard **of**
for reasons (that) we're still not sure **of**
the clothes (that) you're running **in**

Keep + object + adjective
They'll **keep you comfortable**.
The suit **kept him warm**.

Words and expressions to learn

Nouns	Other words and expressions
opportunity /ɒpəˈtjuːnəti/	refuse /rɪˈfjuːz/
translator /trɑːnsˈleɪtə(r)/	make contact /meɪk ˈkɒntækt/
border /ˈbɔːdə(r)/	average /ˈævrɪdʒ/
clothing /ˈkləʊðɪŋ/	incredible /ɪŋˈkredəbl/
tyre (US tire) /ˈtaɪə(r)/	unbelievable /ʌnbɪˈliːvəbl/
	extraordinary /ɪksˈtrɔːdənri/
	chilly /ˈtʃɪli/
	unlucky /ʌnˈlʌki/
	for some time /fə ˌsʌm ˈtaɪm/
	continuously /kənˈtɪnjuəsli/
	ten miles per hour /ˈten ˈmaɪlz pər ˈaʊə(r)/
	over (= more than) /ˈəʊvə(r)/

Revision: do you know these words?

sport /spɔːt/	accommodation /əkɒməˈdeɪʃn/	wear (wore, worn) /weə(r) (wɔː(r), wɔːn)/
distance /ˈdɪstəns/	prove /pruːv/	gentle /ˈdʒentl/
trip /trɪp/	last /lɑːst/	confident /ˈkɒnfɪdənt/
reason /ˈriːzn/	seem /siːm/	approximately /əˈprɒksɪmətli/
suit /suːt/	breathe /briːð/	valley /ˈvæli/
match /mætʃ/	win (won, won) /wɪn (wʌn)/	

Unit 26: Lesson B

Words and expressions to learn

Nouns
footballer /'fʊtbɔːlə(r)/
season /'siːzn/
club /klʌb/
performance /pə'fɔːməns/
cup final /'kʌp faɪnl/
apprentice /ə'prentɪs/
sportsman /'spɔːtsmən/
sportswoman
　/'spɔːtswʊmən/
pressure /'preʃə(r)/

Adjectives
first-class /'fɜːst 'klɑːs/
talented /'tæləntɪd/
agreeable /ə'griːəbl/
disagreeable /dɪsə'griːəbl/

Adverbs
specially /'speʃəli/
next /nekst/

Revision: do you know these words?

career /kə'rɪə(r)/
advice /əd'vaɪs/
free time /'friː 'taɪm/
advantage /əd'vɑːntɪdʒ/
disadvantage
　/dɪsəd'vɑːntɪdʒ/
retire /rɪ'taɪə(r)/

accept /ək'sept/
win (won, won)
　/wɪn (wʌn)/
complete /kəm'pliːt/
plan /plæn/
professional /prə'feʃənl/
besides /bɪ'saɪdz/

Unit 27: Lesson A

Grammar and structures

Future perfect tense
By next July **I'll have been here** for eight months.
In a few weeks the ice **will have melted**.

Future progressive tense
At half past eight tomorrow **I'll be driving** to work.
This time next Saturday **I'll be lying** on a beach in
　Morocco.

Words and expressions to learn

Nouns
shock /ʃɒk/
wedding anniversary
　/'wedɪŋ æni,vɜːsəri/
builder /'bɪldə(r)/
actress /'æktrɪs/
tennis court /'tenɪs ,kɔːt/

Verbs
receive /rɪ'siːv/
tear up (tore, torn)
　/'teər 'ʌp (tɔːr, tɔːn)/
settle down /'setl 'daʊn/
pass an exam /,pɑːs ən ɪg'zæm/
melt /melt/
fetch /fetʃ/

Adjectives
qualified /'kwɒlɪfaɪd/
European /jʊərə'pɪən/
excellent /'eksələnt/

Other expressions
if possible /ɪf 'pɒsəbl/
in bed /ɪn 'bed/
in time /ɪn 'taɪm/
the day before yesterday
(by) this time next year

Revision: do you know these words?

a couple /ə 'kʌpl/
swimming pool /'swɪmɪŋ ,puːl/
zoo /zuː/
manage /'mænɪdʒ/
get married /get 'mærɪd/
retire /rɪ'taɪə(r)/

become (became, become)
　/bɪ'kʌm (bɪ'keɪm, bɪ'kʌm)/
brush one's teeth
　/,brʌʃ wʌnz 'tiːθ/
promise /'prɒmɪs/
upset /ʌp'set/

famous /'feɪməs/
mad /mæd/
as soon as possible
　/əz ,suːn əz 'pɒsəbl/
I look forward to hearing from you.

Unit 27: Lesson B

Words and expressions to learn

Nouns
meal /miːl/
rise /raɪz/
reorganisation
　/riːɔːgənaɪ'zeɪʃn/

Other words and expressions
ask out (= invite out) /'ɑːsk 'aʊt/
give somebody a ring /'gɪv 'sʌmbədi ə 'rɪŋ/
short of time /'ʃɔːt əv 'taɪm/
away (= not at home) /ə'weɪ/
the day after tomorrow /ðə 'deɪ 'ɑːftə tə'mɒrəʊ/

even /'iːvn/
in fact /ɪn 'fækt/
for ages /fər 'eɪdʒɪz/
some time /'sʌm taɪm/
unless /ən'les/
a whole lot of /ə 'həʊl 'lɒt əv/

(See also list of expressions in
Lesson 27B, Exercise 5.)

➡

Revision: do you know these words?

headache /'hedeɪk/
accept /ək'sept/
continue /kən'tɪnju:/
refuse /rɪ'fju:z/
busy /'bɪzi/

until /ən'tɪl/
because of /bɪ'kɒz əv/
it depends /ɪt dɪ'pendz/
maybe /'meɪbi/

just a minute /'dʒʌst ə 'mɪnɪt/
one of these days /'wʌn əv ðɪ:z 'deɪz/
come round /'kʌm 'raʊnd/
to your place /tə 'jɔ: 'pleɪs/

Unit 28: Lesson A

Words and expressions to learn

Nouns	Verbs	Adjectives
root /ru:t/	miss /mɪs/	bilingual /baɪ'lɪŋgʊl/
attitude /'ætɪtju:d/	preserve /prɪ'zɜ:v/	positive /'pɒzətɪv/
relation /rɪ'leɪʃn/	pass on /'pɑ:s 'ɒn/	keen /ki:n/
refugee /refju'dʒi:/	settle /'setl/	stubborn /'stʌbən/
community /kə'mju:nəti/	take part in (took, taken)	
way of life /,weɪ əv 'laɪf/	/,teɪk 'pɑ:t ɪn (tʊk, 'teɪkn)/	**Adverbs**
generation /'dʒenə'reɪʃn/	vary /'veəri/	fluently /'flu:əntli/
the UK /ðə ,ju:'keɪ/	react /ri:'ækt/	as well /əz 'wel/
choir /'kwaɪə(r)/		

Revision: do you know these words?

religion /rɪ'lɪdʒən/
culture /'kʌltʃə(r)/
contact /'kɒntækt/
church /tʃɜ:tʃ/
club /klʌb/
organisation /ɔ:gənaɪ'zeɪʃn/
kid /kɪd/
history /'hɪstri/
can't wait /kɑ:nt 'weɪt/
set up (set, set) /'set 'ʌp/
local /'ləʊkl/
various /'veərɪəs/
fairly /'feəli/
abroad /ə'brɔ:d/

Unit 28: Lesson B

Grammar and structures

Prepositions at the end of questions
Where do you come **from**?
Who does she live **with**?

Prepositions at the end of relative clauses
I didn't like the people (that) I was at school **with**.
I've never been back to the place (that) I was born **in**.

Words and expressions to learn

Nouns	Other words and expressions	
dozen /'dʌzn/	occupy /'ɒkjəpaɪ/	increasingly /ɪŋ'kri:sɪŋli/
phrase /freɪz/	scattered /'skætəd/	continually /kən'tɪnjəli/
birthplace /'bɜ:θpleɪs/	recent /'ri:sənt/	within /wɪ'ðɪn/
immediate family /ɪ'mi:djət 'fæməli/	rootless /'ru:tləs/	a number of /ə 'nʌmbər əv/
extended family /ɪk'stendɪd 'fæməli/		
isolation /aɪsə'leɪʃn/		

Revision: do you know these words?

stranger /'streɪndʒə(r)/
knowledge /'nɒlɪdʒ/
farm /fɑ:m/
relative /'relətɪv/
death /deθ/
neighbour (US neighbor) /'neɪbə(r)/

yard /jɑ:d/
environment /ɪn'vaɪrənmənt/
village /'vɪlɪdʒ/
town /taʊn/
city /'sɪti/
recognise /'rekəgnaɪz/

grow up (grew, grown)
/'grəʊ 'ʌp (gru:, grəʊn)/
personal /'pɜ:sənl/
social /'səʊʃl/
related to /rɪ'leɪtɪd tə/
almost /'ɔ:lməʊst/

Unit 29: Lesson A

Grammar and structures

Shall and will
I shall/will (I'll)
you will (you'll)
he/she/etc. will (he'll etc.)
we shall/will (we'll)
they will (they'll)

I shall/will be a star one day.
He will be rich one day.

Offering: asking for information
Compare:
Shall I carry your bag?
When **will I** get the papers?

Tenses
When I **am** an old woman I **shall wear** purple.

Warnings and promises
When I am old, I will (I'll) . . .
I will . . .
I will not . . .
I will (not) be able to . . .
I will (not) have to . . .
I (don't) suppose I will . . .
I doubt if I will . . .
I am sure I will (not) . . .
I might . . .

Predictions
I don't think . . . will . . .
I don't suppose . . . will . . .
I'm sure/certain that . . . will (not) . . .
There will be . . .
There won't be . . .
It's likely | that . . . will . . .
    not very likely
    unlikely
    very probable
    quite probable
    possible

Words and expressions to learn

Nouns
beauty /'bjuːti/
waist /weɪst/
glove /glʌv/
sandal /'sændl/
member /'membə(r)/
game /geɪm/
bell /bel/
earth /ɜːθ/

Other words and expressions
spit (spat, spat) /spɪt (spæt)/
exist /ɪg'zɪst/
overcrowded /'əʊvə'kraʊdɪd/
limited /'lɪmɪtɪd/
forward /'fɔːwəd/
no longer /neʊ 'lɒŋgə(r)/
no such thing as
a quarter of an hour
in 50 years
in 50 years' time
50 years from now

Revision: do you know these words?
religion /rɪ'lɪdʒən/
climate /'klaɪmət/
planet /'plænɪt/
problem /'prɒbləm/
hunger /'hʌŋgə(r)/
situation /sɪtju'eɪʃn/
education /edju'keɪʃn/

solve /sɒlv/
private /'praɪvɪt/
democratic /demə'krætɪk/
likely /'laɪkli/
unlikely /ʌn'laɪkli/
seriously /'sɪərɪəsli/
instead /ɪn'sted/

Learn these words if you want to
shadow /'ʃædəʊ/
soul /səʊl/
youth /juːθ/
alarm /ə'lɑːm/
stick /stɪk/

railing /'reɪlɪŋ/
slippers /'slɪpəz/
murmur /'mɜːmə(r)/
pick flowers /'pɪk 'flaʊəz/
uninhabitable /ʌnɪn'hæbɪtəbl/

Unit 29: Lesson B

Grammar and structures

Regrets: I wish and if only
I wish I **had listened** to my mother's advice.
If only I **had listened** to my mother's advice.

Regrets: *ought to have* . . .
I **ought to have listened** to my mother's advice.

Wishes for the present and future: *I wish*
I wish it **was** warmer.
I wish I **spoke** better English.
I wish somebody **would write** me a letter.

Words and expressions to learn

Nouns
memory /'meməri/   edge /edʒ/
hope /həʊp/   cliff /klɪf/
safety /'seɪfti/   wish /wɪʃ/

Other words and expressions
flood /flʌd/
get into trouble /,get ɪntə 'trʌbl/
leave school (left, left) /,liːv 'skuːl (left)/
surprising /sə'praɪzɪŋ/
anybody /'enibɒdi/
I can't wait /aɪ 'kɑːnt 'weɪt/

Revision: do you know these words?
thought /θɔːt/
luck /lʌk/
brain /breɪn/
stone /stəʊn/
pleasure /'pleʒə(r)/
advice /əd'vaɪs/
unemployment /ʌnɪm'plɔɪmənt/
receive /rɪ'siːv/
meet (met, met) /miːt (met)/
shoot (shot, shot) /ʃuːt (ʃɒt)/
pull /pʊl/
throw (threw, thrown)
  /θrəʊ (θruː, θrəʊn)/

kiss /kɪs/
laugh /lɑːf/
cry /kraɪ/
be born /bi 'bɔːn/
look after /'lʊk 'ɑːftə(r)/
divide /dɪ'vaɪd/
wonderful /'wʌndəfʊl/
cool /kuːl/
honest /'ɒnɪst/
common /'kɒmən/
darling /'dɑːlɪŋ/

Unit 30: Lesson A

Grammar and structures

Should have + past participle
Clive **should have gone** to see Annette.
Annette **shouldn't have gone** to see Clive.

Words and expressions to learn

Nouns
queue /kju:/
passport control /'pɑ:spɔ:t kən,trəʊl/
terrorist /'terərɪst/
representative /reprɪ'zentətɪv/
picnic /'pɪknɪk/
centimetre /'sentɪmi:tə(r)/
haircut /'heəkʌt/

menu /'menju:/
purse /pɜ:s/
rock /rɒk/
second /'sekənd/
towel /taʊl/
zero /'zɪərəʊ/

Other words and expressions
work out /'wɜ:k 'aʊt/
crazy /'kreɪzi/
asleep /ə'sli:p/
quick /kwɪk/
taste /teɪst/
tie /taɪ/
on time /ɒn 'taɪm/

Revision: do you know these words?

relationship /rɪ'leɪʃənʃɪp/
fare /feə(r)/
bomb /bɒm/
handbag /'hændbæg/
hand-baggage /'hænd ,bægɪdʒ/
security check /sɪ'kju:rəti ,tʃek/
coach /kəʊtʃ/

catch (train etc.) (caught, caught) /kætʃ (kɔ:t)/
go wrong /gəʊ 'rɒŋ/
can't stand /kɑ:nt 'stænd/
can't afford /kɑ:nt ə'fɔ:d/
in time /ɪn 'taɪm/
on business /ɒn 'bɪznɪs/

Unit 30: Lesson B

Words and expressions to learn

Nouns
joke /dʒəʊk/
prize /praɪz/
iron /'aɪən/
steel /sti:l/
means of transport
  /,mi:nz əv 'trɑ:nspɔ:t/

lighter /'laɪtə(r)/
wire /'waɪə(r)/
the Middle East /ðə ,mɪdl 'i:st/
the Far East /ðə ,fɑ:r 'i:st/
the Atlantic /ði: ət'læntɪk/
the Pacific /ðə pə'sɪfɪk/

Revision: do you know these words?

coast /kəʊst/
chess /tʃes/
game /geɪm/
price /praɪs/
metal /'metl/
office /'ɒfɪs/

manufacture
  /mænju'fæktʃə(r)/
point /pɔɪnt/
string /strɪŋ/
sensible /'sensəbl/
sensitive /'sensətɪv/

Additional material

Lesson 5B, Exercise 1

LITTLE OLD LADY IN KNIFE RAID

A little grey-haired woman armed with a knife robbed an Oxfordshire shop after threatening the assistant.

The untidily dressed woman walked into The Sandwich Man shop in Parsons Street, Banbury at 9.30 at night and pulled out the bread knife from beneath her coat.

She threatened the young girl assistant and forced her to open the till before grabbing the entire day's takings.

The robbery happened on Saturday night, and police at Banbury are appealing for witnesses.

The shop owner, Mr Ken Woodd of Deddington, who also runs George's Café and Georgina's in the Covered Market, Oxford, said: "It is unbelievable. It has never happened before in the 38 years I have been in business."

Police took the assistant around pubs in the town after the robbery to try to find the woman, but with no luck.

Mr Woodd said the day's takings were snatched. He said it might have been as much as £180.

(The Oxford Mail, 25 March 1986)

Lesson 10A, Exercise 9

WHEN

When we're all alone or talking on the phone,
You're romantic.
When we walk in the night, you always hold me tight.
You're romantic.
When we're far apart, you always send me flowers,
And when I'm sad you talk to me for hours.
You're generous and kind, and I've got you on my mind.
You're romantic.

But when we're on the town, and your friends are all around,
Oh you're jealous – oh so jealous.
Someone asks me for a dance, no you never let me dance.
You're jealous – oh so jealous.
When it comes to pay the bill, you never find your wallet.
I can play it mean my friend if that's the way you want it.
You're mean and you're so tough, I think I've had enough.
(Be)cause you're jealous.

When you come home late at night, when you're fussing and you fight,
You're sorry – oh so sorry.
When you're selfish and you're mean, and you're out to cause a scene,
You're sorry – oh so sorry.
Many times you let me down, I've tried so hard to leave you.
Sorry is an empty word, so how can I believe you?
But then I change from being mad to being oh so sad,
(Be)cause you're sorry.

You've been out with someone new, I can smell her sweet perfume.
You're a liar, such a liar.
You say she's just a friend, but this has got to end.
You're a liar, such a liar.
Oh but when I passed your house, I saw shadows on your curtain.
I saw you with someone else, and now I feel so certain
That I'll be moving on, I've just got to stand up strong,
(Be)cause you're a liar.

Many times you let me down . . .

(Steve Hall)

153

Lesson 5B, Exercise 2

MUGGER MEETS LITTLE OLD LADY

Jose Ramos is an experienced mugger, but he didn't know about little old English ladies. Now he does.

87-year-old Lady Vera Tucker was walking down New York's East 66th Street. She looked like an easy prey – small, grey-haired and expensively dressed, carrying a handbag over her shoulder.

Ramos came up on his bicycle and grabbed the handbag. Lady Tucker hit him on the head with her umbrella, knocking him off his bicycle, and started screaming at the top of her voice.

The unfortunate mugger tried to get back onto his bicycle and escape, but Lady Tucker kept hitting him. A lorry driver, hearing her screams, came and joined in the fight.

Holding his head, Ramos pushed the handbag at the driver and said 'Here it is. It's over, it's over.' 'The hell it's over,' said the driver. They went on fighting, and Lady Tucker went on screaming, until a policeman arrived and took Ramos prisoner.

Lady Tucker refused medical help, saying that she felt fine. But she did allow the policeman to take her arm and escort her home.

(The South-Western Herald, 28 May 1986)

Lesson 13A, Exercise 7

THE LONELY ONE (*continued*)

Lavinia ran across the bridge.

Oh God, God, please please let me get up the hill! Now up the path, now between the hills, oh God, it's dark, and everything so far away. If I screamed now it wouldn't help; I can't scream anyway. Here's the top of the path, here's the street, oh, God, please let me be safe, if I get home safe I'll never go out alone; I was a fool, let me admit it, I was a fool, I didn't know what terror was, but if you let me get home from this I'll never go without Helen or Francine again! Here's the street. Across the street!

She crossed the street and rushed up the sidewalk.

Oh God, the porch! My house! Oh God, please give me time to get inside and lock the door and I'll be safe!

And there – silly thing to notice – why did she notice, instantly, no time, no time – but there it was anyway, flashing by – there on the porch rail, the half-filled glass of lemonade she had abandoned a long time, a year, half an evening ago! The lemonade glass sitting calmly, imperturbably there on the rail . . . and . . .

She heard her clumsy feet on the porch and listened and felt her hands scrabbling and ripping at the lock with the key. She heard her heart. She heard her inner voice screaming.

The key fit.

Unlock the door, quick, quick!

The door opened.

Now, inside. Slam it!

She slammed the door.

'Now lock it, bar it, lock it!' she gasped wretchedly.

'Lock it, tight, *tight*!'

The door was locked and bolted tight.

Behind her in the living room, someone cleared his throat.

(from Dandelion Wine by Ray Bradbury)

Lesson 16B, Exercise 6

I WILL TAKE YOU THERE

I lie awake at night and I go sailing,
When the worry of the day won't let me be.
I dream of a place where the sky is crystal blue,
And the sand reaches miles into the sea.
From my head down to my toes the sun it warms
    me,
And the pine spreads a sweetness in the air.
Should I sleep in the shade with a cool lemonade,
Or go running through the waves without a care?

I go sailing, yes I'm sailing; from the four walls of
    my room on a rainy afternoon.
I go sailing, yes I'm sailing; if you dream awhile
    then I will take you there.

I lie awake at night and I go skiing,
When the worry of the day won't let me go.
I dream of a place where the sky is cold and clear.
I go flying like an eagle down the slope.
I can hear the sound of laughter in the mountains.
I can hear the rush of wood upon the snow.
Should I sit by the fire, or take a cable ride?
I can watch the tiny people down below.

I go sailing, yes I'm sailing; . . .

I lie awake at night and I go flying,
When the worry of the day won't let me be.
I dream of a place where the earth is small and
    round,
And the stars reach as far as you can see.
I can float above the world and it's so peaceful.
I'm a long long way from home and I don't care.
A million miles away from the heat of the day.
A million miles but I can take you there.

Let's go sailing, we'll go sailing; . . .

(Steve Hall)

Lesson 18B, Exercise 2, Dialogue A

**Pairs of students should work to invent lines
for Duncan. Each student should write ONLY
Duncan's lines on a separate sheet of paper.**

MARILYN: 342235.
DUNCAN: ....
MARILYN: Oh, hello, Duncan. How are you?
DUNCAN: ....
MARILYN: Well, I have got some, but the thing is,
they're rather precious. They were my
mother's.
DUNCAN: ....
MARILYN: Well, OK, but do get back to me if you
can't find any. Is there anything else you
need?
DUNCAN: ....
MARILYN: Sure, heaps of it. Can you come round
now and get it? I'll be going out later.
DUNCAN: ....
MARILYN: Not at all. See you in a minute. Bye,
Duncan.
DUNCAN: ....

Lesson 20B, Exercise 7

FIDDLING ACROSS THE USA

I left my home when I was ten.
Haven't seen my folks since then.
They sent me home from school one day,
So I took my fiddle and I ran away.

I had no money but I had some luck.
Got a ride in a pickup truck.
Driver bought me some rice and beans,
And took me all the way down to New Orleans.

Well, I've been to the East Coast, been to the West
    Coast,
Down on the border with Mexico.
Played my fiddle in the wind and rain
And storms and deserts and ice and snow. (*twice*)

Well, I've travelled round on boats and trains,
Buses, bikes, cars and planes.
Played in restaurants, clubs and bars,
Played in the street to the passing cars.

I learned how to fiddle as I went along.
Guess I know a thousand songs.
One of these days I'll settle down,
But for now I'll just keep moving around.

Well, I've been to the East Coast, . . .

(Jonathan Dykes and Robert Campbell)

Lesson 22A, Exercise 1

GOLD DIGGER

He was the kind of guy that made you check your
    purse,
Pulled his hat down low as he kicked the dirt.
His teeth were shiny and his eyes were cold,
Shot left to right as he dug for gold.
His tie was tight and his cuffs were clean.
He was the sharpest guy that I'd ever seen.

Chorus
Gold digger – he was a gold digger – digging it up.
    (*twice*)

She was the kind of girl that turned every eye,
Strutting like a cat (be)cause her heels were high.
Her jewellery rattled as she sat at the bar,
Waiting for a man with a big fast car.
Her skin was tanned from the southern sun.
She was digging for gold so you'd better run.

He was the kind of guy that made you cross the
    street,
A scar on his face, he had two big feet.
His suit hung loose, he was big, he was mean,
A gun in his pocket and a blade in his sleeve.
Looking for action – a time and a place.
You'd better watch out, don't get in his way.

She was the kind of lady made you straighten your
    tie,
Dressed in black with a cool clear eye.
Her diamond rings they were so discreet,
With short black hair that was combed so neat.
In her bag is a telephone
To see how stocks and shares have grown.

(Steve Hall)

Lesson 28B, Exercise 7

NO USE FOR HIM

Now my father was a big strong man
Who worked hard all his life.
He was always in a whisky glass
And never out of strife.
For he called no man his master
And very few his friend.
A proud and stiff-necked man he was
Who would never bow nor bend.
But they broke him in the end
When they'd no use for him.

For they took away his job
When they'd no use for him any more.
After nearly 30 years,
They kicked him out the door.
But they let him keep his railway jacket,
Overcoat and cap,
And a pension of nine bob a week
– he was lucky to get that.
And they nearly broke his heart
When they'd no use for him.

Now I spent much of my childhood days
Up in the signal box,
High in my father's castle
Twenty feet above the tracks.
And crash would go the signals
As he flipped them with his hand,
And the mighty cars of steam and steel
Would stop at his command.
And oh, but it was grand.
And they'd a use for him.

But they took away his job . . .

When you're 55 years old
And you're looking for some work,
Nobody wants to know your face,
No-one gives you a start.
So I watched him growing older
And more bitter every day
As his pride and self-respect,
Well, they slowly drained away.
There was nothing I could say.
They had no use for him.

For they took away his job . . .

Yes, I know they broke his heart
When they'd no use for him.

(Eric Bogle)

Lesson 18B, Exercise 2, Dialogue B

Pairs of students should work to invent lines for Marilyn. Each student should write ONLY Marilyn's lines on a separate sheet of paper.

MARILYN: ....

DUNCAN: Hello, Marilyn? Duncan here.

MARILYN: ....

DUNCAN: Fine, thanks. Well, in a bit of a panic, actually. You haven't got six champagne glasses you can lend me, have you?

MARILYN: ....

DUNCAN: Oh, no, I wouldn't dream of it, then. I'd never forgive myself if I broke one. I'll try someone else.

MARILYN: ....

DUNCAN: Well, yes, icing sugar, if you've got any.

MARILYN: ....

DUNCAN: Yeah, of course. I'll be over in a few minutes. Leave it on the doorstep if you want to go out before I get there. Thanks a lot, Marilyn.

MARILYN: ....

DUNCAN: Bye.

Acknowledgements

The authors and publishers would like to thank the following institutions for their help in testing the material and for the invaluable feedback which they provided:

Regent School of English, London; ESIEE, Paris, France; Teach-in Language and Training Workshop, Rome, Italy; London School of English, London; Newnham Language Centre, Cambridge; The British School, Rome, Italy; Eurocentre, Lee Green, London; International House, Terrassa, Spain; Bell School, Cambridge; International House, Coimbra, Portugal; Eurocentre, Brighton; Cambridge School of English, Granollers, Spain; The British Institute, Madrid, Spain; Britannia Cultural e Comercial, Rio de Janeiro, Brazil; Central School of English, London; Centre d'Etude des Langues, INFOP, Dijon, France; The British Institute, Barcelona, Spain; London Study Centre, London; The British Council, Thessaloniki, Greece; The British Institute, Bilbao, Spain; International House, Valencia, Spain; Speakers' Corner School of English, Sabadell, Spain; Klubschule Migros, Berne, Switzerland; Swan School of English, Oxford; Godmer House School of English, Oxford; Audiovisuelles Sprachinstitut, Zürich, Switzerland; International Language Institute, Heliopolis, Egypt; Ecole Supérieure de Commerce, Geneva, Switzerland; International House, Barcelona, Spain; The British Council, Amman, Jordan; The British Institute, Rome, Italy; University of Berne, Berne, Switzerland; University of Santiago de Compostela, Spain; College de Candolle, Geneva, Switzerland.

The authors and publishers are grateful to the following copyright owners for permission to reproduce photographs, illustrations, texts and music. Every endeavour has been made to contact copyright owners and apologies are expressed for any omissions.

page 13: 'Meditatio', taken from *Collected Shorter Poems* by Ezra Pound, published by Faber & Faber Ltd; and from *Personae*, copyright 1926 by Ezra Pound. Reprinted by permission of New Directions Publishing Corporation. *bl* and *br* Reproduced by permission of *Punch*.   page 19: Texts of radio commercials used by kind permission of GWR Radio.   page 25: *br* Reproduced by permission of Syndication International (1986) Ltd.   page 29: 'Mini-sagas' reproduced by permission of *The Telegraph Sunday Magazine*.   page 36: Dialogues adapted from *People – Book 2*, by permission of Françoise Houdart, Michael Swan and Librairie Hatier.   page 37: *bl* Reproduced by permission of *Punch*.   page 41: 'The worst musical trio', taken from *The Book of Heroic Failures* by Stephen Pile, published by Routledge & Kegan Paul, Ltd.   page 43: *br* Reproduced by permission of *Punch*.   page 45: *bl* Reproduced by permission of *Punch*.   page 47: Line drawings from 'The Earliest Precursor of Writing' by Denise Schmandt-Besserat. Copyright June 1978 by *Scientific American*, Inc. All rights reserved. Photographs (previously published in *Scientific American*) courtesy of the Musée du Louvre, Paris, France.   page 48: *tr* Reproduced by permission of *Punch*.   page 57: *bl* and *br* Reproduced by permission of *Punch*.   page 60: *br* Reproduced by permission of *Punch*.   page 61: *bl* Reproduced by permission of *Weekend Extra*.   page 64: *tl* Reproduced by permission of *Punch*. *tr* © Ronald Searle, 1948.   page 80: 'For the ten years . . .', 'I am married . . .' and 'I've been going . . .' reproduced by permission of Syndication International (1986) Ltd. 'I don't remember . . .' and 'When I was a teenager . . .' reproduced by permission of *The Sun*. 'Dear Cathy & Claire' reproduced by permission of D.C. Thomson & Co. Ltd.   page 81: *bl*, *tr*, *cr* and *br* reproduced by permission of *Punch*.   page 82: 'Pfeifer und Trommler' by Albrecht Dürer reproduced by permission of the Wallraf-Richartz-Museum, Cologne, West Germany.   page 84: *tl*, *bl*, *bc* and *br* Reproduced by permission of *Punch*. *cl* and *cr* Reproduced by permission of Syndication International (1986) Ltd.   page 96: '"Drowned" people . . .' adapted by permission of Anthony Tucker and *The Guardian*. 'ZZZZZZ . . .' adapted by permission of Gyles Brandreth. 'Bed rest . . .' adapted by permission of *Living Magazine*.   page 107: Advertisement reproduced by permission of Bill Rodgers & Company.   page 109: *br* Reproduced by permission of D.C. Thomson & Co. Ltd.   page 116: Abridged from *A Nation of Strangers* by Vance Packard, © David McKay Books (Random House, Inc.).   page 118: 'When you are old and grey' © 1953 Tom Lehrer. Copyright renewed. Used by permission. 'Warning' © Jenny Joseph, from *Rose in the Afternoon*, Dent, 1974.   page 124: *cl* and *br* Reproduced by permission of *Punch*. *cr* Reproduced by permission of Mail Newspapers p.l.c. *bl* Reproduced by permission of Syndication International (1986) Ltd.   page 153: 'Little Old Lady . . .' reproduced by permission of *The Oxford Mail.*   page 154 (and recording for 13A): Reprinted from *Dandelion Wine* by Ray Bradbury by permission of Don Congdon Associates, Inc. Copyright © 1953 by Gourmet Inc.; Renewed 1981 by Ray Bradbury.   page 156: Song *No Use For Him* by Eric Bogle, courtesy of Larrikin Records (Australia) and Sonet Records (London).

The following songs were specially written for *The Cambridge English Course* Book 3: *When* (Lesson 10A, page 153), *I Will Take You There* (Lesson 16A, page 154), *Gold Digger* (Lesson 22A, page 155) and *High Pressure* (Lesson 26B, page 109) by Steve Hall (lyrics and music); *Fiddling Across The USA* (Lesson 20B, page 155) by Jonathan Dykes (lyrics) and Robert Campbell (music). The song *Boogey Woogey Man* (Lesson 9A, Exercise 1) was performed by George Melly with John Chilton's Feetwarmers, courtesy of John Chilton and the Mechanical Copyright Protection Society Ltd. The folk song *Lamorna* (Lesson 9A, Exercise 5) was performed by Len and Barbara Berry. The recorded material for Lesson 4A, Exercise 4 (page 19) and Lesson 12B, Exercise 2 (page 52) is used by kind permission of GWR Radio.

Andrew Campbell: page 16 *cl.*   Mark Foxwell: page 6 *r*, 35 *b*, 62 *l*, 63 *b*, 88.   Robert Harding Picture Library: page 6 *l, cl, cr.*   Magnum/Capa and John Hillelson Agency: page 22.   Monitor Press Features: page 58.   Oxford United Football Club: page 108.   Procolour Studios: page 14.

John Craddock: Malcolm Barter, pages 20 *l*, 23 *br*, 120;   Roberta Colegate-Stone, pages 54 *t*, 78 *l*; Dennis Curran, pages 66–68, 116 *t*;   Mike Mosedale, pages 45 *br*, 49 *tl*, 52 *t*, 92–93;   Alexa Rutherford, pages 24, 32 *t*, 51 *bl*, 94–95;   Jacqui Figgis: Peter Bowman, page 86;   The Organisation: David Eaton, pages 40, 72, 76;   Sue Hellard, page 29 *r*.

Nancy Anderson, page 12 *tr*;   Anita Bryon, page 62 *tr*;   Nigel Hawtin, pages 10, 11 *tl*;   Sue Hitchens, pages 11 *cl, bl, tr*, 98;   Andrew Kennedy, page 34;   Joe McEwan, pages 8, 19, 26–27, 30–31, 36, 38–39, 70–71, 74–75, 97 *bl*, 99, 112, 122;   Maria Richer, pages 90, 114.

(Abbreviations: t = top b = bottom c = centre r = right l = left)

Phonetic symbols

Vowels

symbol	example	symbol	example
/iː/	eat /iːt/	/eɪ/	day /deɪ/
/i/	happy /'hæpi/	/aɪ/	my /maɪ/
/ɪ/	it /ɪt/	/ɔɪ/	boy /bɔɪ/
/e/	when /wen/	/aʊ/	now /naʊ/
/æ/	cat /kæt/	/əʊ/	go /gəʊ/
/ɑː/	hard /hɑːd/	/ɪə/	here /hɪə(r)/
/ɒ/	not /nɒt/	/eə/	chair /tʃeə(r)/
/ɔː/	sort /sɔːt/; all /ɔːl/	/ʊə/	tour /tʊə(r)/
/ʊ/	look /lʊk/		
/uː/	too /tuː/		
/ʌ/	up /ʌp/		
/ɜː/	bird /bɜːd/; turn /tɜːn/		
/ə/	about /ə'baʊt/; mother /'mʌðə(r)/		

Consonants

symbol	example	symbol	example
/p/	pen /pen/	/h/	who /huː/; how /haʊ/
/b/	big /bɪg/	/m/	meet /miːt/
/t/	two /tuː/	/n/	no /nəʊ/
/d/	do /duː/	/ŋ/	sing /sɪŋ/
/k/	look /lʊk/; cup /kʌp/	/l/	long /lɒŋ/
/g/	get /get/	/r/	right /raɪt/
/tʃ/	China /'tʃaɪnə/	/j/	yet /jet/
/dʒ/	Japan /dʒə'pæn/	/w/	will /wɪl/
/f/	fall /fɔːl/		
/v/	very /'veri/		
/θ/	think /θɪŋk/		
/ð/	then /ðen/		
/s/	see /siː/		
/z/	zoo /zuː/; is /ɪz/		
/ʃ/	shoe /ʃuː/		
/ʒ/	pleasure /'pleʒə(r)/; decision /dɪ'sɪʒn/		

Main stress and secondary stress are shown by marks in front of the stressed syllables.

mother /'mʌðə(r)/
about /ə'baʊt/
China /'tʃaɪnə/
Japan /dʒə'pæn/
entertainment /ˌentə'teɪnmənt/
kidnapper /'kɪdˌnæpə(r)/

Irregular verbs

Infinitive	Simple Past	Past Participle
be /biː/	was /wəz, wɒz/ were /wə, wɜː(r)/	been /bɪn, biːn/
beat /biːt/	beat /biːt/	beaten /'biːtn/
become /bɪ'kʌm/	became /bɪ'keɪm/	become /bɪ'kʌm/
begin /bɪ'gɪn/	began /bɪ'gæn/	begun /bɪ'gʌn/
bend /bend/	bent /bent/	bent /bent/
bet /bet/	bet /bet/	bet /bet/
bite /baɪt/	bit /bɪt/	bitten /bɪtn/
bleed /bliːd/	bled /bled/	bled /bled/
break /breɪk/	broke /brəʊk/	broken /'brəʊkn/
bring /brɪŋ/	brought /brɔːt/	brought /brɔːt/
build /bɪld/	built /bɪlt/	built /bɪlt/
burn /bɜːn/	burnt /bɜːnt/	burnt /bɜːnt/
burst /bɜːst/	burst /bɜːst/	burst /bɜːst/
buy /baɪ/	bought /bɔːt/	bought /bɔːt/
catch /kætʃ/	caught /kɔːt/	caught /kɔːt/
choose /tʃuːz/	chose /tʃəʊz/	chosen /'tʃəʊzn/
come /kʌm/	came /keɪm/	come /kʌm/
cost /kɒst/	cost /kɒst/	cost /kɒst/
cut /kʌt/	cut /kʌt/	cut /kʌt/
deal /diːl/	dealt /delt/	dealt /delt/
do /dʊ, də, duː/	did /dɪd/	done /dʌn/
draw /drɔː/	drew /druː/	drawn /drɔːn/
dream /driːm/	dreamt /dremt/	dreamt /dremt/
drink /drɪŋk/	drank /dræŋk/	drunk /drʌŋk/
drive /draɪv/	drove /drəʊv/	driven /'drɪvn/
eat /iːt/	ate /et/	eaten /'iːtn/
fall /fɔːl/	fell /fel/	fallen /'fɔːlən/
feel /fiːl/	felt /felt/	felt /felt/
find /faɪnd/	found /faʊnd/	found /faʊnd/
fly /flaɪ/	flew /fluː/	flown /fləʊn/
forget /fə'get/	forgot /fə'gɒt/	forgotten /fə'gɒtn/
forgive /fə'gɪv/	forgave /fə'geɪv/	forgiven /fə'gɪvn/
get /get/	got /gɒt/	got /gɒt/
give /gɪv/	gave /geɪv/	given /'gɪvn/
go /gəʊ/	went /went/	gone /gɒn/ been /bɪn, biːn/
grow /grəʊ/	grew /gruː/	grown /grəʊn/
have /həv, hæv/	had /(h)əd, hæd/	had /hæd/
hear /hɪə(r)/	heard /hɜːd/	heard /hɜːd/
hide /haɪd/	hid /hɪd/	hidden /'hɪdn/
hit /hɪt/	hit /hɪt/	hit /hɪt/
hold /həʊld/	held /held/	held /held/
hurt /hɜːt/	hurt /hɜːt/	hurt /hɜːt/
keep /kiːp/	kept /kept/	kept /kept/
know /nəʊ/	knew /njuː/	known /nəʊn/
lead /liːd/	led /led/	led /led/
lean /liːn/	leant /lent/	leant /lent/
learn /lɜːn/	learnt /lɜːnt/	learnt /lɜːnt/
leave /liːv/	left /left/	left /left/
lend /lend/	lent /lent/	lent /lent/

Infinitive	Simple Past	Past Participle
let /let/	let /let/	let /let/
lie /laɪ/	lay /leɪ/	lain /leɪn/
lose /luːz/	lost /lɒst/	lost /lɒst/
make /meɪk/	made /meɪd/	made /meɪd/
mean /miːn/	meant /ment/	meant /ment/
meet /miːt/	met /met/	met /met/
pay /peɪ/	paid /peɪd/	paid /peɪd/
put /pʊt/	put /pʊt/	put /pʊt/
read /riːd/	read /red/	read /red/
rewind /riː'waɪnd/	rewound /riː'waʊnd/	rewound /riː'waʊnd/
ride /raɪd/	rode /rəʊd/	ridden /'rɪdn/
ring /rɪŋ/	rang /ræŋ/	rung /rʌŋ/
rise /raɪz/	rose /rəʊz/	risen /'rɪzn/
run /rʌn/	ran /ræn/	run /rʌn/
say /seɪ/	said /sed/	said /sed/
see /siː/	saw /sɔː/	seen /siːn/
sell /sel/	sold /səʊld/	sold /səʊld/
send /send/	sent /sent/	sent /sent/
set /set/	set /set/	set /set/
shake /ʃeɪk/	shook /ʃʊk/	shaken /'ʃeɪkn/
shine /ʃaɪn/	shone /ʃɒn/	shone /ʃɒn/
shoot /ʃuːt/	shot /ʃɒt/	shot /ʃɒt/
show /ʃəʊ/	showed /ʃəʊd/	shown /ʃəʊn/
shrink /ʃrɪŋk/	shrank /ʃræŋk/	shrunk /ʃrʌŋk/
shut /ʃʌt/	shut /ʃʌt/	shut /ʃʌt/
sing /sɪŋ/	sang /sæŋ/	sung /sʌŋ/
sit /sɪt/	sat /sæt/	sat /sæt/
sleep /sliːp/	slept /slept/	slept /slept/
smell /smel/	smelt /smelt/	smelt /smelt/
speak /spiːk/	spoke /spəʊk/	spoken /'spəʊkn/
spell /spel/	spelt /spelt/	spelt /spelt/
spend /spend/	spent /spent/	spent /spent/
spill /spɪl/	spilt /spɪlt/	spilt /spɪlt/
spit /spɪt/	spat /spæt/	spat /spæt/
stand /stænd/	stood /stʊd/	stood /stʊd/
steal /stiːl/	stole /stəʊl/	stolen /'stəʊlən/
stick /stɪk/	stuck /stʌk/	stuck /stʌk/
swim /swɪm/	swam /swæm/	swum /swʌm/
take /teɪk/	took /tʊk/	taken /'teɪkn/
teach /tiːtʃ/	taught /tɔːt/	taught /tɔːt/
tear /teə(r)/	tore /tɔː(r)/	torn /tɔːn/
tell /tel/	told /təʊld/	told /təʊld/
think /θɪŋk/	thought /θɔːt/	thought /θɔːt/
throw /θrəʊ/	threw /θruː/	thrown /θrəʊn/
understand /ˌʌndə'stænd/	understood /ˌʌndə'stʊd/	understood /ˌʌndə'stʊd/
wake up /'weɪk ʌp/	woke up /'wəʊk ʌp/	woken up /'wəʊkn ʌp/
wear /weə(r)/	wore /wɔː(r)/	worn /wɔːn/
win /wɪn/	won /wʌn/	won /wʌn/
wind /waɪnd/	wound /waʊnd/	wound /waʊnd/
write /raɪt/	wrote /rəʊt/	written /'rɪtn/